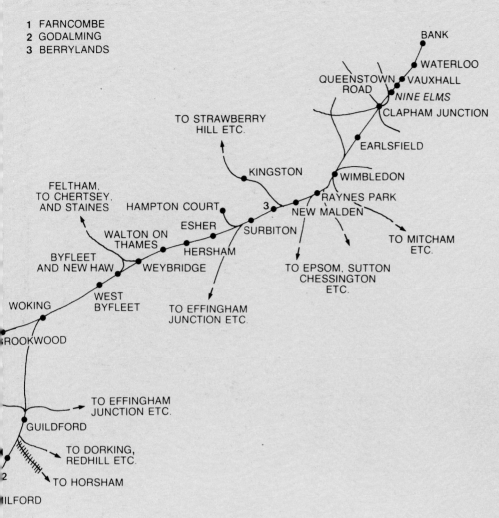

1 FARNCOMBE
2 GODALMING
3 BERRYLANDS

BANK
WATERLOO
QUEENSTOWN ROAD
VAUXHALL
NINE ELMS
CLAPHAM JUNCTION
EARLSFIELD
TO STRAWBERRY HILL ETC.
KINGSTON
WIMBLEDON
RAYNES PARK
FELTHAM, TO CHERTSEY, AND STAINES
HAMPTON COURT
3
NEW MALDEN
ESHER
SURBITON
TO MITCHAM ETC.
WALTON ON THAMES
HERSHAM
BYFLEET AND NEW HAW
WEYBRIDGE
TO EPSOM, SUTTON CHESSINGTON ETC.
WOKING
WEST BYFLEET
TO EFFINGHAM JUNCTION ETC.
ROOKWOOD
TO EFFINGHAM JUNCTION ETC.
GUILDFORD
TO DORKING, REDHILL ETC.
2
TO HORSHAM
ILFORD
LEY

The Waterloo to Weymouth Line
Waterloo-Winchester

Brand new 'Britannia' Class Pacific No 70009 Alfred the Great *on the 'Bournemouth Belle' at Clapham Junction on 23 June 1951* (Brian Morrison).

The
Waterloo to Weymouth
Line

Michael Baker

Patrick Stephens
Wellingborough, Northamptonshire

For Tony, Bob and Paddy

First published in 1987

British Library Cataloguing in Publication Data

Baker, Michael H.C.
   The Waterloo to Weymouth line.
   1. London & South Western Railway—History
   History 2. British Rail, *Southern Region*—History
   I. Title
   385'.09422   HE3020.L66

ISBN 0-85059-835-4

Patrick Stephens Limited is part of the
Thorsons Publishing Group

Printed in Great Britain by Butler & Tanner Limited, Frome, Somerset

10 9 8 7 6 5 4 3 2 1

Contents

Preface

There is a certain amount of truth in the notion that the closer one is to one's subject the less clearly one sees it. It is quite certain that this account of the line on which I have lived and travelled for many years is neither totally objective nor unbiased. Perhaps if I had written it in Kathmandu, as I did one piece on the Southern twenty years ago, I might have seen the overall picture more clearly. But books and pieces of original research on the line between Waterloo and Weymouth are relatively scarce in Nepal and the reader is probably better served by the author working from Wareham! The truth is that the first completely bias free piece of writing does not yet exist — I, like everyone else, have my prejudices but I hope that they have been kept in check and that a recognizable overall picture of a line which had its origins over 150 years ago and which was completed twenty years later will be seen to have emerged by the final chapter.

I have greatly enjoyed my task although inevitably there have been frustrations. One was an inability to uncover anything other than bare facts regarding J. R. Scott, the architect of the Victory Arch at Waterloo and of Surbiton station. The contrast between the styles of the two is so great that I would have loved to learned more about the man who was able to encompass both. At one point I thought I had found him when I discovered J. R. Scott, an architect, was living in retirement at Hindhead. Alas the charming letter which came back told me that the writer 'had nothing to do with railways' although he did 'remember Waterloo Station being rebuilt'. I consulted various architect friends and architectural bodies and journals but drew a complete blank. Was he related to the great Scott family, Gilbert of St Pancras and Giles of Liverpool Cathedral? I do not know.

Another frustration was the minute books of the London and Southampton and the early London and South Western Railway companies. At some time they had become soaking wet and although now kept in perfect conditions at the Record Library, Kew, the writing is so faded in places as to be impossible to decipher.

Which brings me to libraries. I have become quite an expert on the libraries along the line from London down to Weymouth. Without exception the librarians were helpful, polite, patient — and underpaid. If I had to be stranded on a desert island or in a lift and could choose the occupation of those with me I think I would go for librarians, but I should think very hard about allowing those who allocate them their funds and design their buildings to join us. I should have perfect confidence in anyone from Hampshire; Basingstoke has a splendid, modern, sunlit library in the heart of the shopping complex and Southampton is all that a big city library should be, whilst Winchester is without equal. It has more books on the subject of railways alone than many libraries have on everything, its local history section is superbly comprehensive and efficiently run, and as for historic photographs it produces the most excellent copies remarkably quickly at a price which is competitive to say the least. And if all this wasn't enough it has a staff which is knowledgeable, patient and unfailingly polite. Winchester really should add its library service to the long list which makes the city such a tourist attraction.

Surrey and Dorset were patchy. Kingston-on-Thames seemingly had only four books on local history, although one was worth fifty of most others, an absolute gem, a piece of High Victorian floridly over-the-top prose, the work of the superbly named F. Somner Merryweather. Dorchester, although excellent in many ways, was taken aback by my request for copies of a couple of pictures in their collection and eventually came up with a price so enormous that this tome would have had to outsell *Hollywood Wives* to justify it. Weymouth has been struggling on in premises which should have been condemned around VE day; Poole, like Basingstoke, has excellent facilities in the middle of a modern shopping complex, whilst Chris and his staff in Wareham are all that good librarians should be. But I cannot over-emphasize that whatever the shortcomings of the facilities the librarians themselves were universally excellent. Our free public libraries are amongst the most precious assets we possess and we should fight like anything to preserve them and see that they are decently financed.

I owe thanks to lots of other people. Local papers, particularly the *Bournemouth Echo* and the *Southampton Southern Evening Echo,* were an invaluable historical source and a present-day help. Then there were the railwaymen and women, from those friends employed locally to all the others with whom I came into contact during the course of my researches and travels. Some I shared footplate rides with and was regaled with the sorts of tales all railwaymen who care about their job tell so well but are often best not recorded in print, others were officials, Gloria Pearson and Graham Boyes in particular, at Waterloo. There are the friends and acquaintances who supplied me with photographs, so many in the end that deciding what to leave out became agonizing. The preservationists must not be forgotten, they who have done so much to recreate many aspects of the way things used to be.

Although this is a history containing, here and there, references to things which have gone which perhaps should not have done, I hope that the impression which emerges at the end is of a vigorous, modern railway, one of which the people who work on it look optimistically to the future and those who travel on it regard it as a safe, efficient, indispensible means of travel, something which has always been there and always will be.

Two rebuilt Bulleid Pacifics, No 34098 Templecombe *in the foreground, at Waterloo in 1965.*

Chapter 1
The beginning

The hero, or maybe it is heroine, of our story began life as the Southampton, London and Branch Railway and Dock Company. As a title is was both accurate and inelegant; no matter, like most railways and some of the Hollywood film stars it was to become intimate with a century later it was to change its name several times. Its character was fixed early on and whilst no-one would have expected this to have remained unaltered in a period stretching from pre-Victorian days to the present time, it is recognizably the same railway it was 150 years ago. Note the 'dock' in its title; very important this, for apart from the lines from London to Dover and Folkestone no other railway route in England has been so closely bound up with ships and the sea. Southampton will loom large in the tale we have to tell, but we shall make sure we do not neglect Portsmouth, Gosport, Fawley, Lymington, Poole, Swanage, Weymouth and Portland. Neither will we neglect the Basingstoke Canal nor rivers such as the Thames, the Itchen, the Hamble, the Test, the Bourne, the Piddle and the Wey.

Southampton is about as old a port as one could find anywhere. It goes back at least as far as the Romans, who called it Clausentum. When the Saxons invaded from the east, filling the vacuum left by the departing Romans, two of their chiefs, Cedric and Cynric, established a bridgehead on the site of Southampton opening the way for the conquest of Wessex. By the Middle Ages Southampton ranked immediately behind London and Bristol in importance. Henry V sailed from it to Agincourt and glory, and in 1554 King Philip II of Spain landed at Southampton on his way to marry Mary Tudor one July day in Winchester Cathedral. Mary, it would seem, loved her Philip, but for him it was very much a political marriage. He was nominally King of England, equal to Mary, but he was never crowned. They lived together for eighteen months but there were no children, the hope of which was one of the chief reasons for Mary's advisers allowing the marriage. Philip returned to Spain, four years later Mary was dead and her sister, Elizabeth, queen. Philip courted her too, but in the end resorted to force to try to secure the English throne. Although Drake's fleet

which harrassed and finally dispersed the Armada in 1588 was based in Plymouth, some of the ships came from Southampton. The rivalry between the two ports was to continue down to modern times.

Southampton did great trade with Italy and sent out wool to many parts of the world, but in the 17th century things went into decline. Southampton played no part in the slave trade which made the fortunes of Bristol and Liverpool merchant venturers. In the mid 18th century the fashionable set discovered Southampton and some of the elegant terraces dating from that period can be seen to the north of the city centre, in various states of preservation and decay. The threat of invasion by Napoleon saw works of protection put in hand and the enormous upsurge in trade throughout the country which the Industrial Revolution brought about spread to Southampton even though it was remote from the smoke-blackened Midlands, South Wales, Lancashire, Yorkshire and the North-East. In 1803 an Act of Parliament enabled the building of the first docks at Southampton and it was inevitable that once the Liverpool and Manchester Railway had shown the way, Southampton, like all towns with aspirations towards prosperity, should want rail facilities. Thus the promotion of the Southampton, London and Branch Railway and Dock Company in 1831.

It was fast work, for the Liverpool and Manchester had opened scarcely a year earlier, on 15 September 1830. Perhaps it was a bit too fast for nothing much happened for three years. Despite its early entry into the field, it preceded the Great Western for example, it was a company of little ambition and the directors suggested that five locomotives would serve all its needs, two for passenger traffic and three for goods. Ludicrous as this may seem we have to remind ourselves that not everyone at this time was convinced railways were anything more than a passing fancy. The Duke of Wellington, Prime Minister at the time of the opening of the Liverpool and Manchester, declared 'I see no reason to suppose that these machines will ever force themselves into general use'. We may therefore perhaps better understand the timidity of the proposers of Southampton's first railway.

However bolder spirits soon prevailed. The original company became the London and Southampton Railway, and Northern financiers injected capital, more than doubling the total. In May 1834 Frank Giles, the Engineer in Charge, estimated that the total cost of building the line would be £1 million and that construction would take three years. After a fierce struggle through Parliament the railway was incorporated on 25 July 1834. On 11 September 1834 the Minute book of the Court of Directors records, in the beautiful copperplate writing of the time but now so faded as to be barely legible, 'Colonel Henderson be appointed Superintendent of the Undertaking with a salary of £1,000 pa'. A letter was read at that meeting from Mr Richard Heathfield agreeing to be Secretary for £600 pa. Three assistants were to be placed near Kingston, Frimley and Basingstoke whose task would be to inspect the construction work. One would receive £400 pa, and two £300 each. 'Four to six foremen will be required between London and Popham, whose joint salaries should be about £400 a year.' The navvies who built the line earned around three shillings a day.

The work continued, but not very effectively. Giles, the Engineer, seems to have been rather a liability and the Board persuaded him to step down. His replacement was none other than Joseph Locke. Giles must have already realized which way the wind was blowing for some time earlier on 20 December 1836 the Minute Book has it thus: 'It was resolved that the Court deem it essential to have Mr Giles's new estimate of the line and the cost of constructing the same examined by another Engineer of eminence, in order to give satisfaction to the Proprietors and to give evidence in Parliament in regard to the Capital to be realized and the actual expenses to be incurred — That for such purposes the assistance of Mr Locke be sought'. Joseph Locke had been with George Stephenson on the Liverpool and Manchester and had gone from there to take charge of the Grand Junction, the Link between the Liverpool and Manchester and the London and Birmingham Railways. The Grand Junction was a fine line and Locke had kept within his budget, which was something indeed; the London and Southampton would not achieve this. Locke's reputation was considerable and the London and Southampton Railway is essentially his rather than poor Giles's. In the words of Michael Robbins in his book *The Railway Age*: 'The long swing over the Hampshire chalk between Basingstoke and Winchester bears the mark of classic railway building'. It is the section least changed today.

There is, as there has always been, but one station, Micheldever, in the 18½ miles of this section. Four tunnels, none of any great length, cut through the chalk. The summit is at Litchfield Tunnel, eight miles from Basingstoke. Either side the ruling gradient is around 1 in 250, which is clear evidence of Locke's concern for the limited locomotive power of the day. On either side of the line, where no tunnels or cuttings obscure the view, rolling fields, chalky-brown in winter, green in summer, undulate away to Salisbury Plain to the north-west, and to the South Downs to the south-east. The furrows of today are ploughed in autumn by tractor power, whereas in Locke's time a team of oxen might well have plodded its way across the chalk uplands just as it had done since King Alfred's day and would continue to do until spiralling meat prices during the First World War persuaded the farmers to send their oxen to the slaughter house. The heavy, sure-footed ox was long favoured on the chalk downs of Southern England and there are those still alive who can remember the teams at work. Elsewhere along the lineside there are many trees, part of Micheldever Forest, the remnants of the great forest which once almost totally covered the Weald, stretching from here, across Hampshire, Surrey, Sussex and Kent to within sight of the French coast. The demands of the charcoal and iron industries, and of shipbuilding, had so drastically reduced it that by the reign of Henry VIII restrictions were placed upon tree felling and thus we still have so many of the oak, ash and beech, although not alas the elm, trees today.

Locke, his assistants, and his navvies, would certainly have no trouble finding their bearings today, although the occasional explosive roar of a military jet hurtling low across the landscape would certainly disconcert them. Locke went on to build in much wilder country, for the Caledonian Railway across the border from Carlisle, in France between Paris and Le Havre and Nantes and Cherbourg (both routes over which boat trains would work in connection with London and South Western steamers) and in Holland and Spain. He died in 1860, the year after Brunel and Robert Stephenson, like them in his mid-50s, like them worn out through superhuman efforts, working long hours out in all weathers.

The first section of the line opened officially on 21 May 1838, Queen Victoria's 19th birthday. This was the 23 mile stretch from Nine Elms to Woking Common. It was never intended that the former should be the permanent London terminus, being out in an unfashionable part of the suburbs, but it would suffice for the present. Nevertheless a grand Georgian stuccoed building was provided by the company's architect, Tite. Wyld's Guide, a contemporary publication, actually stated that despite being three miles and nine chains from the Royal Exchange Nine Elms was 'nearer to the Heart of London' than any other section of railway, but how this can be squared with

Vauxhall in 1961, beside which Nine Elms terminus originally stood. 'King Arthur' No 30798, Sir Hectimere, with the 2.54 pm Waterloo to Basingstoke and 4-SUB electric multiple unit No 4375 on a Hounslow Loop working.

the claims of Euston, London Bridge and the Minories, which were already in existence, I cannot fathom. It all depends what you mean by the heart of London I suppose. Certainly the description which Wyld goes on to give us hardly squares with that of a district close to the centre of what was the greatest city in the world, with a population of around three million. It was, we are told, 'partly occupied by villas and partly by garden ground and wharfs. Here are perhaps some of the nearest cornfields in the metropolitan district. A large brook passes through it from under the rail-road and on falling into the Thames turns a mill.'

Most passengers arrived at Nine Elms either by horsebus or on the river. Traffic congestion on the roads was already chronic and the Thames steamer business was flourishing. It was not without its dangers, there being twelve serious accidents between May 1835 and November 1838. Nevertheless a trip down the river was and still is a favourite outing, the difference being that nowadays it is one mostly indulged in by visitors whereas in the 19th century Londoners used the river both for business and pleasure. With the coming of the London and Southampton Railway the Iron Steam Boat Company started a half-hourly service from London Bridge to Nine Elms. The single fare was 4d. Railway expansion in the next decade forced successive fare

reductions until by 1847 one could go as far as Chelsea for 2d.

Nine days before the official opening of the line on 12 May 1838 the first passenger train set out carrying directors and their guests. Three accounts of the event have survived. One puts the departure time from Nine Elms as 'just before 2 pm' and gives an overall running time for the '23½ miles' as a very creditable 45 minutes. But in *Woking and District, A Dictionary of Local History* compiled by G.B. Greenwood in 1938 it is asserted that the 'journey took rather more than an hour each way, hampered by a strong headwind and a leaking stream [sic] cylinder'. A third writer, Arthur Locke in his *A Short History of Woking*, goes into the greatest detail. From Nine Elms, he tells us 'the train proceeded at a rapid way to Ditton Marsh. From that place to Woking Common progress was much slower, owing to a leakage of the steam-engine boiler. This, however, caused no chagrin, being attributable to one of those accidents which must sometimes occur when extensive and complicated machinery is employed, especially before a fair trial.' The first writer asserts that the return journey was made in 43 minutes and adds that a light engine following the directors' party 'reached almost 60mph', but the third eye-witness says the return took 1 hour, 1 minute precisely.

Whatever the precise details of the run out and back the directors were obviously well satisfied, for a week later and two days before the public opening two celebratory trains with nearly 400 ladies and gentlemen aboard set off for Woking Common. Tents had been set up on the common for the traditional feast and both outward and return journeys were cheered by thousands lining the route.

Chapter 2
The line opens

The London and Southampton Railway opened to the public on 21 May 1838. There were six intermediate stations. These were Wandsworth (now Clapham Junction), Wimbledon, Kingston (now Surbiton), Ditton Marsh (now Esher), Walton and Weybridge.

F. Somner Merryweather in his *Half a Century of Kingston History* published in 1887, recorded his impressions. 'Crowds came to Surbiton from all parts of the neighbourhood to see the train of steam coaches pass, filled inside with passengers and with more venturesome travellers on the roof holding their hats, and flying merrily along at the perilous rate of 20 mph.' The first class carriages were 'low and narrow inside', the second had 'bare seats with open unsashed windows which made umbrellas requisite in rainy weather'. Third class, of which there was only one train a day, were purposefully made as uncomfortable as possible and were attached to a heavy goods train which shunted at almost every station; they were open trucks with the rudest of benches. The guard sat on the roof and worked his brake by way of a rod connected to the blocks on the wheels. He might have to suffer terrible conditions and sometimes was frozen virtually solid and had to be lifted off his perch at the end of the journey!

It is as well to note just how much of a pioneer the London and Southampton was. It was less than a year since trains had started running in and out of Euston and not much more than that since London Bridge, the very first central London terminus, had opened.

There were five trains in each direction during the week and four on Sundays, the latter a generous number for a Victorian sabbath when on many lines there were none at all. The first class fare from Nine Elms to Woking Common was five shillings, second class three shillings and sixpence.

Joseph Woods was the Locomotive Engineer. The very first engine was *The Lark*, a Bury four-wheeler similar to those found on the London and Birmingham Railway. *The Lark* had 5 ft 6 in driving wheels and was built in 1835 which, of course, makes it older than the first section of the railway. The explanation is that it was used by Locke's contractors, Thomas Brassey, for ballasting work and was bought by the London and Southampton from them. Three similar Nasmyth

engines, *Hawk, Raven* and *Falcon* arrived in 1838. But, like all Bury engines, they were underpowered and 2-2-2s for passenger work and 0-4-2s for goods soon became the order of the day. Locke obviously had a say in the motive power for the Minutes of the Locomotive Power Committee of 24 April 1846 note: 'Letter received from Bury re costs of loco powers on London and Birmingham and Grand Junction Railways. No action pending resolution of objections of Mr Locke.' Sharp Roberts supplied both 2-2-2s and 0-4-2s, Rothwells built only the passengers engines, whilst others came from J. & G. Rennie.

The patrons were still pretty excited by all this, for it was truly without comparison, and in the second week of operations the company found itself utterly flummoxed when 5,000 prospective passengers turned up hoping to board trains to take them to the Derby. The directors had been quite pleased with the 1,000 who travelled on the line in the first week, now there were five times that number in one morning. They stormed in, crammed themselves into every available inch of rolling stock, whether the items concerned had any intention of heading for the Kingston-Ewell road crossing, the nearest point to the racecourse, or not. The confusion was tremendous and total. Eventually the constabulary managed to evict them, but not before a fair amount of damage was done. Eight trains in all were marshalled to convey the punters and the receipts for the second week in the career of the London and Southampton Railway increased tenfold over the first. This was the way to make money. The Chairman, Sir John Easthope, was a racing man and no doubt rejoiced in this particular class of business. Later that summer excursions were advertised to the Ascot races, which were a good seven miles from the nearest point to the railway which was Woking, but then people in those days were used to walking long distances, and of course if you managed to beat the bookie then you could hire a post-chaise back. The reputation of the London and Southampton as a line which had a particular liking for racegoers was established.

Woking, that is Old Woking, was a village of something less than 600 inhabitants and was 1½ miles from its station. But this was nothing and its star began to ascend, and like so many hitherto inward looking rural communities the railway was to transform it. Some ceremony attached to the departure of each train, a bell in the station roof being chimed five minutes before it was due out. When Woking Common ceased to be a terminus a handbell sufficed. A small locomotive shed was built and at its peak around 60 men were employed there. Guildford, a much more ancient and important place, had to swallow its pride and for seven years until the railway reached it a coach left the White Lion Inn for the 6½ mile journey to Woking to connect with the London trains.

Construction of the line between Woking and Southampton was going ahead at various sites and the next section to open was the 15½ miles from Woking Common to Shapley Heath, Winchfield on 24 September 1838. There was one intermediate station, Farnborough. It is recorded that this was the regular royal station for Windsor until the GWR opened a station in Windsor itself beneath the walls of the castle in October 1849. The LSW opened its own a little later on 1 December that year. Queen Adelaide, the widow of William IV, first used the Great Western route in August 1840, followed by Frederick IV of Prussia in January 1842 who went to Windsor via Slough for the Prince of Wales's christening. Queen Victoria herself made her first Great Western journey in June 1842 and was a regular traveller from then on. She did not travel on the Southampton line until 1843, and then it was to visit the Duke of Wellington at his home at Stratfield Saye, given to him by a grateful nation. This was seven miles west of Basingstoke and would later find itself

more handily served by the Didcot, Newbury and Southampton Railway, but not until May 1885, by which time the Iron Duke had finally met his Waterloo and had been conveyed by means more ethereal than a steam train to the World beyond. He did, however, apparently unbend sufficiently to commend the Southampton Railway's Chairman on the general arrangements when the Queen visited him at Stratfield Saye.

The aforementioned Didcot, Newbury and Southampton line was to fall into the hands of its mighty neighbour the Great Western. For nearly nine decades the rivalry between the London and South Western (as the London and Southampton was shortly to become) and the Great Western would be ferocious. It continued for another 25 years between the Southern and the Great Western and even into British Railways days there would be snappings and snarlings, bruisings and blood spilling between the Western and Southern interests. Peace would seem to have broken out of late, although there are those in Weymouth for example who to my certain knowledge claim not to have heard the cease fire; very likely there are protagonists still squaring up to each other in other parts too.

The very last item in the minutes of the final meeting of the Court of Directors of the London and Southampton Railway, on 14 June 1839, reads: 'That the Secretary be instructed to provide a seal of the Railway having been altered from the London and Southampton to that of the London and South Western Railway'. Two weeks later the new company met, although of course all that was changed was the name for the same minute book is used, the directors and Secretary are unchanged and the company servants went about their duties as before.

The down branch line platform at Raynes Park, c1910 (Lens of Sutton).

Left Victoria, *a Beattie 2-2-2 with 6 ft 6 in driving wheels and 16 in by 21 in cylinders, built in 1859. It survived until 1885, the very last single on the LSW. It is shown in its final condition* (LPC).

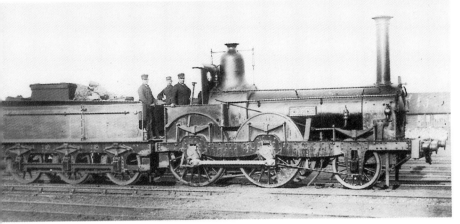

Left Leeds, *a Beattie 2-4-0 in original condition* (LPC).

Below *The Basingstoke Canal near Woking in 1986.*

The reason for the change of name was that Portsmouth was now on the agenda. There was no way the proud citizens of that venerable port would put up with a branch from a railway called the London and Southampton, and so when the company received the Act of Parliament authorizing it to build a branch from Bishopstoke (Eastleigh) to Gosport on 4 June 1839 its name was changed at the same time. In actual fact the branch was not all that it might have been for it was rather indirect and when it finally got to its terminus passengers were faced with a trip across the water to Portsmouth proper. No wonder that both the LSW and the London, Brighton and South Coast companies would be prevailed upon to, and eventually did, provide more convenient, shorter routes.

June 1839 was a particularly busy month for in addition to changing its names, obtaining permission for the Gosport branch and ordering a new seal, the Directors presided over the opening of two more sections of their main line. These were the twelve miles from Winchester to Southampton and the seven and three-quarter miles from Shapley Heath to Basingstoke.

Basingstoke is one of those places about which some people like to make smart remarks — first prize one week in Basingstoke, second prize two weeks... Ho Ho Ho! *Hutchinson's Beautiful Britain,* a 1920s publication scheduled to appear in 49 parts but which actually spread itself over 52, so it hadn't anything to be cocky about, put it this way: 'It requires an effort of imagination to find such country towns as Basingstoke or Andover picturesque in the ordinary sense, though each has memorable features, of which more anon.' A real damning with faint praise, particularly as we never do get more anon! The modern Basingstoke actually has a lot to commend it. The one bit of Basingstoke *Beautiful Britain* does go into detail about is Basing House, which, if it were still standing could be seen from the railway, but as it isn't it can't. It is nevertheless an impressive ruin which began as a Roman villa, and was rebuilt by the Normans. Queen Elizabeth I, of course, stayed there. It was demolished during the Civil War but excavations since 1962 have revealed much of interest.

Basing House is approached by a bridge over the Basingstoke Canal. Canals are not a significant feature of the transport scene in Southern England and that makes this one all the more interesting, particularly as much of it is still navigable, or rather has once again become so following the dedicated work of a group of enthusiasts. There were originally plans for the canal to form part of a through route from London to the Hampshire coast, but these foundered and it never got beyond Basingstoke. However it was a useful link between North-East Hampshire and, by way of the Woking and Wey Navigation, the capital. Work on its

construction began in 1788, the first section from the Wey to Horsell opened in 1791, and it was fully opened in 1794. Its subsequent history was similar to so many waterways which found themselves in competition with the railway. Between Woking and Basingstoke canal and railway ran close together and there are several places where the canal can be seen from the train. In the years 1838-39 the canal was busier than it had ever been, or would be again, carrying some 39,000 tons, chiefly building materials for the railway. But of course it was living on borrowed time, for once the railway opened traffic on the canal dwindled away until it reached a nadir in 1885 when a mere 301 tons was carried. However this was not the end, for those with time to so indulge themselves were discovering the delights of boating and pleasure traffic was beginning to build up; it would play a significant part in the subsequent story of the Basingstoke Canal.

The population of Basingstoke when the railway arrived was 4,000. It was to increase steadily in the subsequent decades, boosted by the arrival of the GWR in 1848 and the opening of the Salisbury line in 1857. By 1871 Basingstoke's population was 5,500 but the great expansion would not come for another eighty years. One local inhabitant who took an intimate interest in the coming of the railway was a farmer, William Whistler. He received compensation from the London and Southampton Company of £905 for the disruption of the access to his mill. Basingstoke station, a small two platform affair, was situated to the north of the town, but close to the centre and immediately below the ruins of Basingstoke's second oldest building. This was the Chapel of the Holy Ghost, built by William Sands and Bishop Richard Fox of Winchester in 1218, and unlike Basing Castle ruins, these can be seen from the railway.

The first train out of the station 'took people for a joy-ride to Woking'. It apparently had no seats, but in compensation perhaps the locals were impressed by the opulence of the guards uniform which consisted of a frock-coat with brass buttons, a patent leather belt worn across the shoulder with a pouch containing a regulation watch, and a cap resembling that worn by present-day French soldiers, with a large badge.

The excitement was too much for some of the locals, as the *Hampshire Chronicle and Southampton Courier* recorded: 'An individual who had been refractory' was being taken to the police station at the end of the day when the police 'were attacked by a party of the railway labourers in order to effect a rescue but after a sharp contest the police secured their prisoner'. Next day he was fined £1 with costs or one month's hard labour. The Mayor 'took the opportunity of declaring his determination in order to preserve good order at the railway station that the full penalty of the law should be enforced'.

Chapter 3
Southampton is reached

The attainment of Southampton was the original object of the London and Southampton Railway but although the first public train pulled out of Southampton station on Monday 10 June 1839 it proceeded no further than Winchester, for the most difficult section of the route, between there and Basingstoke with its four tunnels, had yet to be completed. However this did not put a damper on the rejoicing as this report from the *Southern Daily Echo* testifies.

Pulled by a 'powerful engine, appropriately named *Pegasus*, the first train left at 7.45 am' amid the cheers of an immense concourse of spectators. It was speedily found that the regular time of starting, previously announced, would not accommodate the number applying for places; and it was consequently resolved not only to place additional carriages on the road, but to run the trains from either end as fast as they could be got ready.' In this manner some 1,200 passengers were carried between Southampton and Winchester on the first day. Presumably *Pegasus* had sole charge; hard work for a small 2-2-2, trundling up and down the 13 miles with its consignments of excited passengers. We do know that shortly afterwards 'another (engine), called after the principal engineer, *Locke*, has since been placed on the Railroad'. Both were brought to Southampton by sea from London.

Initially there were no intermediate stations between Southampton and Winchester. The first Southampton station was a temporary one at Northern Road, now Northam, but in May 1840 trains began to use the imposing terminus built by Tite. Its classical facade was almost identical to the same architect's Nine Elms and I imagine it would have been quite possible to totally confuse an inebriated tar as to which end of the line he was at.

The original Northam terminus was on the edge of the town which in 1840 had a population of 28,000. Northam farmhouse still exists today, converted to a public house. Another large residence in the vicinity was the now vanished Portswood House, whilst St Denys was out in the country and would not have a station for another twenty years; when it was built it was originally called Portswood.

The golden years of Southampton were about to begin. On 8 July 1833, four years before her accession to the throne, Princess Victoria opened the pier named after her, which became the principal arrival and departure point for the Isle of Wight and Channel Island services. The Southampton Dock Company was formed in 1836, and on 12 October 1838, eight months before the railway started operations, a truly magnificent occasion attended by upwards of 20,000 people saw the laying of the first stone of the docks proper, close to what is now gate number 1. The stone itself is now a monument set up beside Central Road close to the town end of what used to be the Ocean Terminal. The first ocean liners to use the new, as yet uncompleted, dock were the P&O's *Tagus* and *Liverpool* on 29 August 1842. *Tagus* was a Greenock-built paddle steamer of 738 tons. She carried 86 passengers and after her career as a P&O mail steamer she was chartered to Hills of Southampton; she was broken up in 1864. The 450 ton, Greenock-built *Liverpool* had begun her career as a barque, being fitted with engines in 1835. She was broken up at Southampton in 1845.

Railway tracks extended along the quayside and passengers and cargo passed directly into the trains. Ironically P&O were to move their headquarters to London in 1874, although they would return.

And how did the cathedral city of Winchester feel about the incursion of the steam railway? No doubt very pleased on the whole, but not so the Reverend C.J. Hoare, Archdeacon and Prebendary of the cathedral; at least not on Sundays. He wrote to the Directors of the London and Southampton Railway on behalf of 'the undersigned Clergy of Winchester and Southampton and their vicinities' pointing out that running trains on Sunday was 'a direct infringement of a Divine command'. God had clearly kept up with all aspects of the Industrial Revolution, at least in the view of the good Archdeacon, although it was significant that when one of the directors asked whether the Bishop had added his signature to the letter the answer was 'no'. The letter went on to deplore Sunday working as 'tending to corrupt public morals' and asked the Directors to 'reconsider the propriety of allowing the practice... to continue'. It is easy to mock the pompous phraseology of a Victorian cleric but the sentiments expressed were no doubt sincerely felt and, of course, Sunday opening remains a contentious issue to this day. Perhaps today's preservationists have the answer — Sunday is the busiest day on restored steam

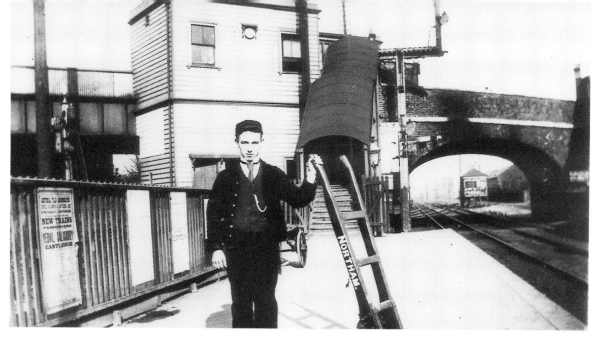

Above *Northam station, Southampton, c1900* (Southampton University Industrial Archaeology Group).

Below *The Royal Pier, Southampton, c1895* (Hampshire Libraries).

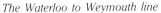

Left *The London Hotel, opposite Southampton Terminus station.*

Below left *The approach to Winchester station (Hampshire Libraries).*

railways and practically all the operators are unpaid volunteers. The Chairman of the London and Southampton Railway gave the Archdeacon a full and spirited answer ending in a manner which must surely stand as the last word on the subject, then and now. 'Religion would best be advanced by means of charity, and love, and kindness, which were taught without giving unnecessary offence.'

The last section of the London and Southampton Railway, between Basingstoke and Winchester, was formally opened on 11 May 1840. The ceremonial train, complete with directors and brass band, left Nine Elms at 8.00 am and reached Southampton in three hours, to a 21 gun salute. It then retraced its route as far as Micheldever, then known as Andover Road, where the contractor Thomas Brassey had laid on lunch.

Brassey could feel well pleased with the line he and Locke had built. Although faced with no great geographical or geological obstacles it was nevertheless beautifully engineered. The confidence the Directors had in Brassey is exemplified in his being awarded the contract to maintain the line for the next ten years. Not that this would have been his sole occupation. As Asa Briggs remarks in *Iron Bridge to Crystal Palace* 'Brassey — outstanding among the great railway contractors of the 19th century — sometimes employed 80,000 men in five continents'.

Expresses between London and Southampton took three hours. The fare was £1 first class single. On slow trains, which stopped at all twelve intermediate stations, the first class single fare was 18 shillings, second class 12 shillings and third class 7 shillings. The latter mode of travel was said to be 'equal in all respects to the outside of a stagecoach' which can hardly have been true for the rail journey would have been infinitely faster, if a good deal dirtier and colder.

The twelve original intermediate stations were Wandsworth, Wimbledon, Kingston, Ditton Marsh, Walton, Weybridge, Woking Common, Farnborough, Shapley Heath, Basingstoke, Micheldever and Winchester. Today there are 29, not counting Wimbledon Staff Halt. Although there have been renamings and alterations and Southampton area closures, the only stations on the 79¼ miles of route traversed by Waterloo to Southampton trains today to have been closed are Clapham Common and Bramshott Golfers Halt. There can be few, possibly no stretches of line which have escaped the ravages of the motor vehicle and Dr Beeching so lightly.

Chapter 4
Expansion to the east and west

The completion of the Southampton line, far from being the end of the story, merely marked the end of the beginning. Even before the first excavations had begun the company had expressed a desire for further conquests, and as we have seen it was now actively preparing for these. The linking of London and Southampton at so early a stage in the history of railway development in this country was perfectly logical. West of Southampton it was a different story, from here on through Hampshire and Dorset was a deeply rural England. The combined populations of the next seven largest towns hardly equalled that of Southampton. The LSW was much more interested in Portsmouth and Salisbury.

The 15¾ mile long Eastleigh to Gosport line opened the year following the completion of the main line, on 29 November 1841, but it didn't stay open very long on

Port Brockhurst, junction for the Gosport and Lee-on-Solent branches, c1910. The 0-6-0ST has charge of the Lee-on-Solent branch train (LPC).

account of the collapse of part of Fareham No 2 tunnel three days later. It took two months to effect repairs and then the line opened for good. But the Portsmouth citizens would not be content with a branch off someone else's main line. The 1840s were the railway mania years and three different routes to Portsmouth were given the assent of the House of Commons in 1845, although only one, that of the Brighton and Chichester, got through the Lords. A line via Brighton was no more direct than the Eastleigh and Gosport one and for this reason the London and South Western raised no objection.

Chichester was linked to Brighton on 6 June 1846 and a year later, on 14 June 1847, Portsmouth was reached and thus LBSC rather than LSW trains inaugurated direct through travel between London and Portsmouth. The LSW could not let their rivals establish a monopoly and on 1 October 1848 the 6¾ mile long link from Fareham to the junction with the Brighton line at Portcreek, immediately east of Cosham was opened and LSW through trains now ran between

Above *LSW Drummond 'T9' 4-4-0 No 115 passing Dean with a Salisbury to Portsmouth train in 1935* (Dr Ian C. Allen).

Left *The Gosport to Portsmouth ferry passing the Sealink Isle of Wight ferry* Brading *off the Pierhead, Portsmouth, September 1986.*

Below *The junction at Havant in September 1986. On the left is the 16:00 Portsmouth Harbour to Manchester Piccadilly which will swing left just beyond the footbridge; partly hidden by the train on the right, the 14:17 Victoria to Portsmouth Harbour, is the former LBSC signalbox.*

London and Portsmouth. The section from Cosham to Portsmouth was joint property and receipts were pooled. It was all very civilized, but it wasn't to last.

Both routes were indirect and although this didn't much bother the companies operating them, as long as the pooling agreement existed, it did not please the citizens of Portsmouth. A third force was what was needed and one was found in the shape of Thomas Brassey. Michael Robbins in his *The Railway Age* calls him 'The greatest of the race of railway engineering contractors' and we might indeed best remember Brassey above all other of the railway pioneers for whereas the works of the mechanical engineers were inevitably soon outmoded and swept away the great works of Brassey, his cuttings, embankments, bridges, tunnels, viaducts, the very track beds, still exist and are serving their original purpose.

Following the opening of the Eastleigh to Gosport line, the second branch off the main London to Southampton line was that from Woking Common to Guildford, opened on 5 May 1845. It was the occasion for free beer for all the navvies who built it. This may sound like a licence for mayhem but in fact the men who constructed the main line, under Brassey's watchful eye, were remarkably well behaved, giving the locals little to fear when the shanty towns which sprang up as the work advanced, appeared amidst the peaceful Surrey and Hampshire countryside. On 15 October 1849 the line was extended to Godalming and four years later Brassey received the Royal Assent to build the 32 miles to link with the Brighton to Portsmouth main line at Havant; the new line would shorten the distance from London to Portsmouth by 20 miles. Portsmouth was delighted, the LBSC and the LSW were aghast.

Brassey's line was a speculation, to be built on the assumption that one of the Portsmouth rivals would buy it to prevent it falling into the hands of the other, and if neither took the bait then there was always the possibility of a third party stepping in, perhaps the South Eastern which had cut right across Brighton and South Western territory with its Redhill to Reading line in 1849. Brassey's shrewd move worked. The LSW, which owned the line north of Godalming, leased the new line and obtained running powers over LBSC tracks from Havant.

Not surprisingly the Brighton company turned nasty and for over a year the tracks grew rusty whilst the two parties haggled. Eventually the LSW lost patience and on 28 December 1858 sent a goods train down the line towards Havant and Portsmouth. The LBSC was ready. The points had been uprooted and an engine plonked four-square on the crossing. The LSW train reached Havant early in the morning and the Brighton desperadoes, no doubt satisfied that their night's evil deeds, had retired to a hearty breakfast. The LSW

removed the Brighton engine and reinstated the points. When the Brighton gang returned, wiping the scrambled egg and cow pie from their stubbly chins, they breathed fire and brimstone and regained the initiative by uprooting a piece of rail behind the LSW engine, immobilizing it. Both parties were now really enjoying themselves, hurling insults at each other and offering to take on all comers. This went on for two hours, to the vast entertainment of the locals. No-one gave a thought to any poor prospective passengers, both sides had far better things to do. Eventually, after this novel way of spending a Tuesday morning, the LSW retired and the Battle of Havant was over.

LSW passenger trains started working over the direct line as far as Havant on 1 January 1859, whence connections were made with a horse bus. Meanwhile the legal department had been busy and had got a restraint order slapped upon the LBSC, and on 24 January that year the first LSW train ran right through from London via Woking to Guildford, Godalming, Havant and Portsmouth. The Portsmouth Direct was at last a reality, the citizens rejoiced, and were even more pleased when the fares came tumbling down as the LBSC and the LSW fought for their custom. Eventually a new pooling arrangement was agreed, the LSW getting two-thirds, the LBSC one.

As well as expanding eastwards the LSW had its eye on Salisbury and the West of England. On reaching Basingstoke the LSW had secured a contract from the Post Office to carry the Exeter mails which went thence by stage coach. It would dearly have loved to provide the principal rail route from London right through to the West Country. This ambition at once brought it into competition with the Great Western. The inevitable confrontation came when the LSW's 23 mile long line from Eastleigh to Salisbury, opened on 7 June 1847, met the Great Western's broad gauge one from Warminster which reached Salisbury in 1856. By this time the LSW's line west of Southampton was in existence and very much involved in the struggle for the West of England, and it is to this we will now turn.

There may have been no great centres of population west of Southampton but this did not mean that the inhabitants of such towns as Dorchester, Poole and Weymouth felt themselves unworthy of rail communication. Indeed one of the driving forces behind the growth of the railway system was civic pride. Weymouth and Poole were hardly likely to benefit from the general increase in trade if they remained remote from the rail network, particularly as Southampton was so obviously prospering from it. Poole, having lost the Newfoundland trade which had made so many of its merchants rich, had fallen on hard times, and Weymouth was in competition with Southampton for the Channel Islands business.

It was Charles Castleman, a solicitor of Wimborne

Minster, who in 1844 put forward proposals for a railway from Southampton to Dorchester by way of Brockenhurst, Ringwood, Wimborne, Poole and Wareham. Weymouth was left out at this stage on account of the expense of tunnelling through the downs which separated it from Dorchester. It was not pleased.

In May 1844 William Moorson, who had worked on the London and Birmingham and the Birmingham and Gloucester Railways, was appointed Engineer. He suggested that Weymouth might be placated with an atmospheric railway which would allow steeper gradients. The atmospheric principle was still considered to have great possibilities at this time. In theory it did, but as Brunel discovered on the South Devon Railway and between Kingstown and Dalkey in Ireland, existing technology was insufficiently advanced to make it practicable. Nothing further was heard of the Weymouth atmospheric proposal.

Like the Portsmouth Direct line Castleman's railway would have to link up with, and hopefully be taken over by, an already established company. Commonsense dictated that this should be the LSW and in order to make the proposition more attractive Castleman suggested that the line be extended westwards from Dorchester on to Exeter. The LSW badly wanted to get a share of the West of England traffic which the GW presently monopolized. But the LSW preferred the option of extending its Salisbury line and so Castleman approached Paddington. The Great Western saw its chance of discomforting the London and South Western and signed a provisional agreement in the autumn of 1844. The GW had by this time reached Exeter by way of Bristol. The Paddington agreement was that the Southampton to Dorchester line should be broad gauge and would connect with the Wilts, Somerset and Weymouth Railway which was to come down from the Paddington to Bristol main line through Frome.

There were other schemes during this railway mania period planned for Dorset but there would not have been the least chance of anyone making anything other than a substantial loss if any more than the two which the Railway Board recommended had come into existence. W. E. Gladstone, when President of the Board of Trade, had been instrumental in setting up this Board whose task it was to sift through the huge number of schemes and put its stamp of approval only on those which it felt would best serve the public. The favoured two were the Wilts, Somerset and Weymouth, and the Southampton and Dorchester. This latter was also endorsed by the Duke of Wellington who, late in the day, had come to see the strategic value of railways. But the Railway Board suggested that it would be best if this line came within the LSW's empire and was standard, rather than broad gauge.

The GW might have been expected to oppose such a notion. But it didn't because there was a wider understanding defining GW and LSW territory which suited both companies well enough. So it was agreed that the LSW should work the line between Southampton and Dorchester and the GW from Dorchester to Weymouth, when built.

The Southampton and Dorchester Railway received the Royal Assent on 21 July 1845, Castleman's achievement being celebrated with a dinner in his honour held at Ringwood a couple of week earlier. Quite the oddest clause in the bill was that eight miles of the route east of Dorchester should be of mixed gauge, equal to the eight miles from Dorchester to Weymouth. This eight miles came to an end in the wilds of Winfrith Heath where the only possible customers could have been adders, deer and Thomas Hardy.

The famous engineer Samuel Peto was contracted to build the line and he began work in August 1845. As at Southampton and on many other lines which approached the sea, the rails and other materials were shipped in. Poole was the handiest port and soon the earthworks were being constructed and rail laid to the east and west of that town.

A glance at the map on the endpapers will show instantly that the route chosen by Castleman was far from direct. Nevertheless it was logical in that it took in

most of the settlements of any size between Southampton and Dorchester. Its winding course earned it the title Castleman's Corkscrew, and over the years cut-offs would be constructed to shorten the distance covered by through trains.

One place the line ignored was Bournemouth. What is now said to be the largest resort in Britain simply did not exist before the 19th century and in 1840 its population was only 200. So there was little profit in putting it on the railway map. Many resorts grew enormously with the coming of the railway but none can surely equal the stupendous rise of Bournemouth. As we shall see this was despite the fact that it wasn't at all sure the railway was a good thing and did little to encourage it; quite the opposite on more occasions than not.

The first section of Castleman's Corkscrew to be finished was that between Ringwood and Dorchester. Being totally isolated from the rest there was little point in operating trains on it and the first did not run until much of the section through the New Forest — where the heavy clay and a wet winter had caused considerable problems for Peto and his navvies — was open. A special worked from Lyndhurst to Dorchester on 1 May 1847.

Moorson, the Southampton and Dorchester's engineer, had to modify his route through Southampton to link up with the London line several times. Originally it had been agreed that it should run from Millbrook on the western outskirts of the town across reclaimed land to a station at the Royal Pier. From there a connecting line would continue to the LSW's terminus, but the Pier Commissioners insisted that horses, not locomotives, should be the motive power on the connecting line. Not surprisingly the Railway would have nothing to do with such a crackpot notion and instead opted for an inland route over which the harbour authorities could exercise no authority. This would pass immediately to the north of the town centre, above the ancient Bargate, and through an intended public park. Many Southampton residents,

and their elected representatives, objected and so it was agreed that the tunnel would be much longer, 528 yards instead of 160.

The tunnel was built almost entirely on the cut and cover system, although one short section was tunnelled. There were several earthslips, one involving the destruction of some almshouses, and further problems were caused by the proximity of an old abandoned canal tunnel. Perhaps the most embarassing mishap occured on 30 May 1847 after the Government Inspector had approved the work and the line was only two days away from opening. The old tunnel had been blocked and where it passed under the new one water had gathered and rendered the clay unstable, causing the rail tunnel wall to subside.

There was a station immediately to the west of the tunnel called Blechynden. Because the problems with the tunnel prevented the running of through trains on the appointed day of opening, 1 June 1847, locomotives and carriages had to be dragged through the streets of Southampton and put on the rails at Blechynden. Peto had some difficulty in persuading his men to work in the dangerous conditions of the tunnel slip and an initial offer of 15 shillings a day was refused. However the work was eventually done and the tunnel opened. The tunnel has always been regularly and carefully inspected and from time to time heavy repair works have had to be carried out.

Two trains ran from Blechynden to Dorchester and one in the return direction on 1 June. Unusually there were neither many passengers nor spectators at any point along the line. Their absence was particularly commented upon at Southampton. It was presumed that the tunnel had kept them away, both because it was generally disapproved of on account of its cutting right through the town, and also that if the town had to put up with it then it might have done its job properly and provide a connection between east and west. Nevertheless despite this unpromising start traffic built up quite satisfactorily and with the eventual opening of the tunnel in August 1847, first to goods then to passenger trains, the transformation of Western Hampshire and much of Dorset was under way.

Signalling was fairly primitive, as on all early lines, and there were several accidents, fortunately none fatal, including a collision between the mail train and a light engine in the curving cutting at Worgret, west of Wareham. Then, as now, the mail train featured large in the business and social lives of the local people. From October 1847 it became possible to receive a letter from London anywhere along the line between Southampton and Dorchester and send a reply back the same day. It was a revolution in communications and ended for ever the sense of remoteness in both time and distance which had seemed the natural order of things for the Dorset country folk. It was a world which Thomas Hardy was to capture in his novels, although the railway is not totally absent from his stories.

The electric telegraph was installed throughout the line by the end of 1847, enabling far better communication between stations and much reducing the chances of accidents, serious or otherwise.

A view from Wareham signal box. The 08:12 Newcastle to Weymouth stands in the station, July 1986.

There were originally 13 stations on the 60½ mile long line, plus Poole which was on a 1¾ mile branch and was really in Hamworthy (the station is now known as Hamworthy Quay), and Leonards Bridge between Ringwood and Wimborne which consisted of a passing loop and a porter but apparently no building. The stations proper were Blechynden, Redbridge, Lyndhurst, Beaulieu, Brockenhurst, Christchurch Road, Ringwood, Wimborne, Poole Junction (later Hamworthy Junction), Wareham, Wool, Moreton and Dorchester. Moorson commissioned Sancton Wood to produce one blueprint which could be used for the entire set. The result was not unattractive, being of brick in a style which was said to be Tudor.

Sancton Wood was a well known railway architect. Most of his designs, chiefly found in East Anglia, were unpretentious buildings, being commissioned by companies which had no money to spare on anything other than basics. He did get just one opportunity to show what he could do when given his head. This was Kingsbridge, the Dublin terminus of Ireland's largest railway, the Great Southern and Western, and is quite the finest piece of railway architecture in the country. Its striking, classical facade was, and is, a great contrast to the surviving Sancton Wood stations in Hampshire and Dorset.

Once the service had settled down there were five trains in each direction between Southampton and Dorchester on weekdays, four on Sundays, four of the former and two of the latter being either through London trains or connecting with London trains. The fastest took 5¼ hours overall. The mail train left Dorchester at 10.05 pm and arrived at Nine Elms at 4.25 next morning. Today it leaves at 11 pm and gets to Waterloo at 3.26 am. Thus in 140 years its average speed has increased from 22.5 mph to 31.6 mph, but then the only members of the public who ever travel on mail trains, then and now, are those who have missed the last sensibly-timed train, those who prefer not to be seen out and about in daylight, runaway lovers, and on this line in particular, soldiers and sailors returning off leave at the last possible moment.

At the fifteen stations between Southampton and Dorchester there was a total of 110 staff. Today, despite rationalization, there are 437. Each figure includes signalmen, although in 1847 many of these were primarily gatekeepers. In 1987 there remained one set of gates which were still hand worked. This is at East Burton, between Wareham and Wool, set between the River Frome and the hamlet from which it takes its name and, which consists of little more than a converted schoolhouse and a deserted church. Whilst a picturesque relic of days gone by it is an expensive one and will pretty certainly disappear with electrification.

Chapter 5
Waterloo

Our railway is now operating between Nine Elms and Dorchester, but it has not yet got to its furthest extremities and here we turn to the origins of what was to become London's largest terminus.

When a new nine arch bridge, designed by Sir John Rennie, linking the south bank of the Thames at Lambeth and the north in the vicinity of the Strand, was opened in 1817 it was natural that it should commemorate the great battle of two years earlier. Like Southwark Bridge a toll of one old penny was imposed. Westminster and Blackfriars bridges were free. No stage carriages or omnibuses used the new Waterloo Bridge at first. When the LSW announced plans for a new terminus at the southern end of the bridge it was logical that it should take its name. Indeed until 1886 the station was officially called Waterloo Bridge, although by this time the bridge suffix had been dropped in general usage; some also called it York Road for a time.

The LSW had always intended to have a terminus closer to the heart of the London than Nine Elms and the extension was sanctioned in 1844. Indeed not even this was meant to be the ultimate push north-eastwards and a year later Parliament passed an act permitting the LSW to extend to London Bridge. This was a period when promoters were scrambling with much haste to reach the heart of the City of London and the West End. In the year 1846 no less than nineteen such lines were proposed, each with its own terminus. If they had all been built there would have been precious little room for anything else. A Royal Commission was set up and took a wide ranging view over a London which was changing and growing faster than ever before.

A powerful argument against further expansion was put on behalf of the poor living on the fringes of the central business and fashionable districts. They would be displaced by the new lines, they would not benefit from them as they had insufficient money to travel by train, and they would be crowded even closer together in yet more insanitary conditions. Embankments such as those leading to London Bridge and that proposed for the Waterloo extension cut off one district from another. The suggestion of one central station for all the railways which wished

to reach the heart of London was given serious consideration. But congestion on the streets was already bad and a big new station would add greatly to it. As it was carriers often had to wait two hours at the present termini to unload and they might just as well spend the time driving to a station two miles further out; less distance between stations did not necesarily mean any saving in time.

One major omnibus operator who gave evidence to the Commission had done a survey and discovered that the average cab ride cost one shilling, and the average bus ride cost sixpence. Not surprisingly he pointed out that far more people could be accommodated in an omnibus and thus less road space would be used. It was one of the earliest recommendations for giving public transport precedence in the heart of London, but then, as now, too many vested interests thwarted what would in the main have been to the advantage of the great majority. Although the Traffic Superintendent of the Blackwall Railway reported that since the opening of the very short but vital 400 yard, £¼ million extension into the heart of the City at Fenchurch Street three years earlier traffic had increased by 50 per cent, the Commission doubted that overall the cost of extending lines into the city would be offset by increased income.

In general the Commission came out against more railways in the heart of London, and 140 years on we may look back and agree with it for they would have added both to the murderous pollution of Victorian London and to the traffic congestion. Two extensions south of the Thames were given conditional assent. One of these was that of the LSW to Waterloo.

The 1¾ miles was estimated at £800,000 and this sum was considered so enormous that the LBSC was invited to share it by way of running powers, perhaps by a connection over the ancient Surrey Iron Railway, which the LBSC had bought, at Earlsfield. The Brighton company declined, wisely, for there were to be only three platforms and it was not thought traffic would ever warrant any enlargement of this number. But sharing notions were not unknown; the Great Western had planned to run into Euston, which is why its line suddenly swings south

Left *'First Class—The Meeting, And at first meeting loved' a painting by Abraham Solomon (1824-1862) (Southampton City Art Gallery).*

Right *An up 'Ocean Liner Express' from Southampton Docks curves through Vauxhall behind 'Lord Nelson' Class 4-6-0 No 30853,* Sir Richard Grenville, *1 July 1961.*

Below right *Beattie 2-2-2 express engine* Sappho *at Waterloo, 1865.*

at Old Oak Common instead of continuing straight on to join the West Coast main line at Willesden Junction as had been intended, and Midland Railway trains actually used Kings Cross for ten years until St Pancras was opened.

A feature of the Waterloo extension is its sinuous nature, more curvaceous than the approach to any other London terminus. This was necessitated by the reluctance of the owners of the Vauxhall Gardens, Lambeth Gasworks and Lambeth Palace to have Southampton boat trains and the Exeter Mails steaming through their valuable properties, so they had to curve around them.

As it was 1,600 cottages, houses, commercial buildings and parcels of land were bought up. The line branched off at the approach to Nine Elms, which became a goods depot and was replaced by a passenger station at Vauxhall. This served the pleasure gardens, originally known as Fawkes Hall Gardens. These in their heyday were the most famous in Britain and Vauxhall became the universal title for such places of entertainment, both here and on the Continent. The Sydney Gardens in Bath, for instance, a fragment of which remains and through which the former Great Western main line passes, was one. The London Vauxhall Gardens opened in 1732 and evening entertainments were put on for the 'better classes of society'. And indeed the better classes, from royalty downwards, availed themselves of them. Haydn, on a visit in 1792, described the music as 'fairly good', and many famous musicians, actors, actresses and entertainers of all descriptions appeared. It cost half-a-crown to get in, and for this tea and coffee was served free of charge.

By the time the railway arrived the fashionable had

long since gone and Vauxhall was old, shabby, and like much of the area in which it found itself, not very respectable. It outlasted the other London pleasure gardens at Marylebone and Ranelagh but closed eleven years after the railway arrived. The trees were cut down and the builders moved in, quickly obliterating all physical traces of this once most splendid facility for enjoyment and enlightenment, although the memories of the setting for Thackeray's *Vanity Fair* and many other adventures and escapades in both fiction and fact lingered long. A ghost stirred for me one Fifth of November evening when, as I was idly looking out of the window of the 18:35 to Weymouth accelerating through Vauxhall, a rocket shot into the sky, a faint echo of the great firework displays which the gardens used to stage.

Waterloo itself was built on derelict pleasure gardens. The original estimate was handsomely exceeded and the final cost of the extension was £1¼ million. Even so it was generally considered that the LSWR had by no means been overcharged. But it was a vast sum for the company to pay out, a quarter of the entire capitation for 1849. Between Nine Elms and Waterloo there were 290 arches of London stock brick, and these were made waterproof so that they could be rented out and thus a little of their cost recouped. The railway arches leading to the great London terminii rapidly became the objects of fascination, disapproval and a distinctive life style, which continues to the present time. Flanagan and Allen did not specify under which railway their celebrated hit of the 1930's 'Underneath the Arches' was set, but certainly down and outs, the unemployed and all classes of drifting, abandoned humanity have long found shelter of a sort beneath the arches

approaching Waterloo, in between the garages, work-shops of various descriptions, warehouses, street traders stores and much else. Opposite the Great War memorial arch, beneath the approach from Waterloo Eastern to Hungerford Bridge a distinctly up-market store has opened fairly recently beside the Festival Hall, whilst on the other side of the river the Players Theatre has long had its home beneath Charing Cross station, but such glamorous establishments are very much the exception rather than the rule.

Waterloo station was due to open on 30 June 1848, but despite a heart-rending plea from the Directors to the Board of Trade that the shareholders would lose money if it did not, the Board was having none of it. An Inspector had walked the line and inspected it from below on 28 and 29 June and found the track 'roughly laid' and the bridge over Westminster Bridge Road 'slighter in construction than any I have yet seen in railway construction for such a wide span' (it was 90 ft). After frantic repair work and further pleas a senior inspector was summoned. He declared himself satisfied and the station opened on 11 July.

The first up train did not appear until early in the morning of 13 July. It was the night mail from Southampton and it pulled in at 4.30 in the charge Rothwell single driver *Hornet*.

There were four lines running over the arches from Nine Elms, two for the Windsor trains and two for the main line ones. The buildings were undistinguished in the extreme, rather in the manner of the original Heathrow Airport facilities, temporary shacks which were replaced by something more permanent, though hardly more imposing, in 1853. The station covered ⅓ acre, approximately where the present platforms 7 to 11 are, with four 600 ft long platforms. It was 280 ft wide with two extra middle roads for storage, an arrangement familiar in many early termini. All roofing was of timber. A turntable sufficed for the four-wheel carriages to reach their sidings west of the station buildings. Beyond them was the engine shed, another turntable and more carriage sidings. All trains stopped outside the station for tickets to be collected and were then hauled by rope into the platforms. This primitive arrangement didn't last long and ticket collecting was transferred further out to Vauxhall where it continued into the early twentieth century. A distinctive sound associated with the earliest days of Waterloo was the ringing of a gong near the platform ends when a train was approaching. It was operated by a lever situated close to Westminster Bridge Road and the number of beats indicated the number of the platform.

The early Waterloo, as we have indicated, was no architectural gem. Although it was to grow there was never the least chance that the ugly duckling would turn into a swan, certainly not during the 19th century, and this may well be accounted for by the

Adams 'A12' 'Jubilee' Class 0-4-2 No 645 at the old Waterloo, c1900 (National Railway Museum).

hankering the Directors harboured for many years of a yet more central terminus. It is quite possible that they did not see Waterloo as something permanent, and by the time circumstances had dictated that this was as far east as London and South Western expresses were ever going to get it was quite impossible to provide even a cosmetic facelift to the rambling rabbit warren of nooks, crannies, additions, extensions, arches, alleys and confused humanity which made up the old Waterloo. Jerome K. Jerome's description in his masterpiece *Three Men in a Boat* of the lottery involved in both clients and employees lighting upon the train they were seeking is justly famous.

Waterloo may have been the most spectacularly disastrous of the LSWR stations from a design (or lack of it) point of view, but it was by no means unique. Although the company had lots of quite acceptable buildings and some which even aspired to the rank of distinguished — Nine Elms and Southampton Terminus for example — it had some awful ones too. A mid-Victorian architectural writer commented that some of its suburban ones 'are the ugliest stations near the metropolis — that at Mortlake being an especially abominable "contraption" of iron, wood

and zinc. We ought to improve in railway architecture as we have done in other branches of the art. The South Western Railway are retrograding. Have they an official, salaried architect and is that the reason or is it mere parsimony and callousness? In any case it is deplorable.' The answer would seem to be that a number of architects were employed at different times. There was certainly no overall guiding hand and often those commissioned for a particular station or stations found themselves so hamstrung by lack of finance that the result was often something of which they were fully entitled to feel ashamed.

We are now in the third decade of Queen Victoria's reign. The fortunes of Great Britain and her Empire are at a high water mark. The Industrial Revolution is sucking in raw materials from the four corners of the Earth, and from beneath it, and is disgorging out great wealth, great misery, amazing innovations and inventions, and changing the face of Britain with a speed which is breath-taking, terrifying and thrilling. Before his death in 1852 the Duke of Wellington had been forced to admit that his doubts on the future of railways was not only ill-considered but positively ridiculous. The LSW's London terminus, which he graciously allowed to be named after his greatest triumph, had to be extended several times to cope with the ever-increasing number of trains using it.

The population of London more than doubled in the fifty years between 1801 and 1851, from around one million to over 2¼ million. The railways encouraged the growth of suburbs wherever they ran, but this did nothing to relieve the fearful overcrowding in and around the centre of London. The LSW, like other lines, cut a great swathe through tightly packed residential areas on its approach to its terminus, but the displaced inhabitants merely crowded ever closer together in the space left in order to remain within walking distance of their place of work, for it was only the relatively affluent who could afford to use public transport, whether train or horse bus. Something like 75 per cent of the population still lived in the inner suburbs and walked, and it was only from around six miles out and beyond that railways had much effect on the living and working habits of people. By the mid 1850s there were 27,000 railway commuters in London, compared with 244,000 who travelled by foot and bus.

The first bus ran in London in 1829, the invention of George Shillibeer, who was English by birth but had all sorts of French connections. His omnibus was one such which he imported from Nantes. Even London Transport's predecessor, the London General Omnibus Company, was originally the Compagnie Générale des Omnibus de Londres. Shillibeer made a great deal of money for a while, but the London and Greenwich Railway defeated him within weeks of its opening in 1836 and he went into the undertaking business at Walworth where he did well enough. Others took up Shillibeer's idea and during the Great Exhibition year of 1851 the celebrated London double-decker was invented by the simple method of sticking the extra passengers on the roof when there was no more room for them inside. Hence the time honoured 'full up inside' as a No 68 heads up Waterloo Road. The LGOC, which by the mid 1850s controlled 600 buses, two-thirds of all those operating in London, began on short routes close to the centre but then grew more ambitious and was eventually working deep into LSW suburban territory to Chertsey and Hampton Court.

Trams came to Britain rather later than buses. The first appeared in Birkenhead in 1861 and a year later they reached the capital. The first line in LSW territory was one of the pioneers, from Westminster to Kennington, although it lasted less than a year. In 1870 trams became properly established in London and that year an application was made to cross

Top *A London County Council 'E1' Class tram and a London United Tramways 'Diddler' trolleybus outside Wimbledon station, 1932* (Alan B. Cross).

Above *'330' Class 0-6-0STs and 'G6' Class 0-6-0Ts at Nine Elms shed, c1920* (LPC).

Vauxhall Bridge, the original, hump-backed, cast iron one. Although the application did not succeed trams did begin to run in Vauxhall Bridge Road and on the other side of the river from Vauxhall Station to Greenwich, and would continue to do so for eighty years, although not until electrification in the first decade of the twentieth century would the London tram system reach its full glory. As we shall see this would force the LSW to inaugurate electrification of its suburban network and thus would begin the vast and complex Southern Electric system of today.

We have seen how rapidly the population of London grew in the first fifty years of the nineteenth century. More births meant more deaths. The Victorians are sometimes depicted as having a morbid obsession with death, following the example set by their Queen after the death of Prince Albert in 1861. Perhaps they did, but if this was so then like many images we have of the Victorian period it is a middle and upper class one. The vastly more numerous working class had neither the time nor the opportunity for such indulgences. Premature death was an everyday occurrence from insanitary living and working conditions, and general neglect; it pounced regularly on the families living in the slums of London. Cremation was virtually unknown and in 1851 there was no more ground dedicated for burying the dead than there had been fifty years earlier. Corpses were piled upon corpses, and amongst the most horrific aspects of this indifference to human remains was the well established trade of shipping quantities of human bones to Northern England to be crushed for fertilizer.

One might have expected that the public authorities would have had their consciences sufficiently stirred to bring about reform. They did make half-hearted attempts but it was left, bizarrely for a matter of such universal concern, to private enterprise, which could see handsome profits looming, to take the initiative.

Passengers alighting at Woking who have time to spare may reflect that what appears to be the front entrance of the station is facing away from the town whilst the entrance which leads directly into its centre is little more than a hole in the up platform wall. This is due to the wheelings and dealings of one George Rastrick who from 1859 onwards bought up much land, including that between the station and Old Woking, thus for some years preventing any development in the intervening 1½ miles. Mr Rastrick bought the land from the London Necropolis and National Mausoleum Company. This concern came into existence on 30 June 1852 to provide burial places for London's dead on a scale which could cope with the problem for as far into the future as anyone could see.

The choice of Woking made sense on several counts. It was beyond any foreseeable expansion of London, the ground was heathland of little agricultural use and therefore could be had quite cheaply, and it was well served by the railway. The Necropolis Company purchased no less than 2,000 acres, extending five miles along the London and Southampton Railway from east of Woking station to Brookwood station. Southwards it extended either side of the Guildford line whilst to the north it stretched to the Basingstoke Canal. It was certainly a bold solution to the horrendous problem of dealing with London's dead, so bold that only a fraction of the 2,000 acres was ever needed.

Before any land was bought the company began discussions with the London and South Western Railway as to how the business might best be carried out, the reception of the mourners and the coffins at the London end of the line, their conveyance to and their disposal at the cemetery. Waterloo was the obvious site for the terminus and the arches on which it was built provided a perfect resting place for the coffins. William Tite was commissioned to design a Necropolis station on the east side of the LSW station. The Consulting Engineer was Sir William Cubitt. The entrance was in York Road, with a siding alongside the single platform two floors up. The train carrying the dead and the bereaved ran once a day every day. Special hearse vans and ordinary carriages were used, although a private saloon could be readily hired. The station and the vans belonged to the Necropolis Company, the carriages and the locomotive were provided by the LSW.

Great care was taken to ensure the customer got what he paid for, even the coffin vans being divided into three classes, whilst discretion was the key word in ensuring that different denominations and religions were segregated within the train. The journey from Waterloo to Brookwood took fifty minutes and on arrival at the Necropolis black horses were hitched to the rear of the train and they hauled it over a junction on to the siding which led into the cemetery grounds. It must have been an extraordinary sight when glimpsed from a passing express.

Inside the cemetery were two stations, one for the Established Church and one for everyone else. The train came to a halt at the appropriate one, the mourners and coffin alighted, a service was held in the chapel and interrment then took place.

In June 1864 the LSW opened the present station at Brookwood on the main line and at the same time a run round loop was provided so that the horses with the black plumes could be dispensed with and the funeral train propelled by its engine into the cemetery.

The coffin train, as it inevitably soon became known, ran until the Second World War when the Necropolis station at Waterloo was destroyed in an air raid. By then there were many alternative burial grounds for Londoners and the service never resumed. Long before this it had become evident that the Necropolis enterprise was vastly over ambitious. For a variety of reasons it attracted only a fraction of London burials. Highgate and other new cemeteries took much of its projected business and, as John M. Clarke in his authoritative history records, the average annual number of burials at the Necropolis between 1854 and 1874 was 3,200 whilst the average number of deaths in London was over 50,000. Of the 2,000 acres which the London Necropolis Company bought it used only 400, which has nevertheless resulted in an extensive cemetery. The rest, nearly a quarter of the parish of Woking, was sold off by Rastrick and his successors, largely for residential and golf course development.

Above *An Eastleigh built Pacific returns to the Southern. No 35028* Clan Line *pulls out of Salisbury with the 'Blackmore Vale Express', October 1986.*

Below *The up main line platform, Bournemouth (formerly Central) station, May 1979.*

Above *No 33008* Eastleigh, *named after the works from which it has just reappeared after overhaul and restoration to its original green livery, October 1986.*

Right *Waterloo, 22 November 1986; Class '405' 4SUB No 4732 and 2BIL No 2090 and, in the distance, a Class '455'.*

Below *The Royal train in the charge of a Class '47' stands in the carriage sidings, Weymouth, in June 1981.*

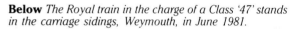

Above Class '47' Institute of Civil Engineers *at Wool with an electrification works engineers train, October 1986.*

Below *In the days when Class '03' diesel shunters worked the Weymouth Harbour tramway, No 2084 stands ready to depart with the boat train for Waterloo, August 1972.*

Chapter 6
Engines and carriages

What of the engines which the LSWR provided to haul its goods and passenger trains in the early days? We have noted some of the original ones produced by various outside contractors whilst Joseph Woods was in charge. In 1841 Woods was succeeded by a man with a famous name, John Viret Gooch was the older brother of Daniel, he who had been put in charge by Brunel of locomotive building at Swindon at the age of twenty. Born in the North-East, like so many of the pioneer railway engineers, J. V. Gooch came to the LSWR from the Manchester and Leeds Railway. Whilst not confronted with the chaotic situation his brother found on the Great Western there was nevertheless much to do in the direction of standardisation. But probably J. V.'s greatest achievement was in setting up the locomotive works at Nine Elms. This turned out its first engine, *Eagle* in 1843. *Eagle* was an express 2-2-2, one of a class of four with 6 ft 6 in drivers, which were the biggest used anywhere in Britain at that time, other than those of brother Daniel's broad gauge singles, although both brothers' efforts were soon to be put in the shade by Trevithick's LNWR *Cornwall* which was turned out from Crewe in 1847 with 8 ft 6 in drivers, a record which was never surpassed.

Cornwall and her enormous drivers still exist as part of the National Railway Museum's Collection, chiefly because in rebuilt form she lasted no less than eighty years, ending her working life in charge of inspection saloons on the LMS. The normal lifespan of a locomotive, particularly an express one, of this era was infinitely less. In 1868, for example, the average age of the company's stock of 265 engines was a mere 7.5 years, four years later the 282 engines averaged 8.9 years, and by 1880 the total of 390 averaged 11.5 years.

Woods and Gooch gave engines names, not numbers, although as early as 10 April 1839 there is a reference in the Company minutes to Engine No 2 (Locke) so there must have been some use of numbers for a time. The names given were a pretty catholic collection, generally associated with power or speed, often mythological. *Elk* despite its name, was a close relative of the pioneer Nine Elms-built *Eagle*, although actually constructed by Fairburn's in

Manchester, and was endowed with a fair turn of speed for in 1846 it ran the 78 miles from Southampton to Nine Elms in 93 minutes. Even though the load was a featherweight of three four-wheelers, an average speed of 50.3 mph was remarkable for the time and better than anything achieved anywhere else other than on the broad gauge.

No very precise details of the earliest LSWR engines have survived, although we know both inside and outside cylinders were employed on the singles, and they were painted Indian red. Photography was a cumbersome business much dependent upon perfect lighting conditions and was practised by only a few professionals and wealthy amateurs when they were in their prime, so we have to rely chiefly on artist's impressions for pictures of them, although one or two rebuilt examples lasted into more modern times. John Dawson, who was locomotive foreman at Northiam, made a model of an engine called *Comet* which is today in the Science Museum at South Kensington, and this is identical to a 2-2-2 *Southampton*, constructed by the Millbrook Foundry, which ended its days as No 176 in the Hamworthy area in 1865. *Etna* was a member of Gooch's final express class, the Vulcans, eight of which came out of Nine Elms in 1849-50. *Etna* survived until 1880, despite playing a leading part in the death of Queen Victoria's physician extraordinary, one Dr Baily. He was travelling in an express hauled by *Etna* when its tender derailed near Raynes Park, and ran down an embankment into the road below, carrying several carriages with it including that containing the unfortunate Dr Baily. His was the only fatality, although other passengers were injured.

Gooch went off to the Eastern Counties Railway in 1850 and was succeeded by an Irishman, Joseph Beattie. No problem identifying his engines for not only does ample photographic evidence exist but, remarkably, two of the locomotives themselves are still with us. These are the celebrated 2-4-0 well tanks, LSWR numbers 0298 and 0314. There were once 85 of them, built originally for the London suburban traffic which was increasing greatly when the first of them came out in 1863. Later they were to be found on practically all the country branches,

The model of a Gooch single built by John Dawson, shedmaster at Northiam, in 1846 (The Science Museum).

not just off the Southampton, Bournemouth and Weymouth lines, but deep in Devon and Cornwall. Three, much rebuilt, lasted on the Wenford Bridge line into the electric and diesel era, not being withdrawn until 1963. No 0314 is now at Quainton and No 0298 at Buckfastleigh. Whilst hardly the prototype to make a best selling model for Hornby or Lima, I did see a delightful scratchbuilt Beattie 2-4-0

speeding round the layout of the local model railway society set up on the down platform of Andover station during the two day rail event held in that town in March 1986.

However long lived Joseph Beattie's engines were, he himself takes us right back to the beginnings of railways for he had been Jospeh Locke's assistant when the latter was Engineer for the Grand Junction Railway. He had moved on with him to the London and Southampton and had been in charge of much of the civil engineering and, once the line was in operation, carriages, wagons and station buildings.

The pioneer railway engineers were nothing if not versatile. They had to be. They were operating in fields where they had no predecessors or precedents to follow and they discovered the rules by trial and error as they went along. That there were so few serious accidents, let alone disasters, says much for their innate skills and common sense and the speed with which they absorbed and rose to each new challenge.

Joseph Beattie had a long reign, 21 years. He died in office in 1871. His engines had little claim to elegance, indeed although to late twentieth century eyes their appearance is endearingly quaint, with something of the air of a traction engine, harsher judges might call them ugly. Their ill-assorted collection of buxom curves, box-like splashers and cab side-sheets, unashamed plethora of exposed pipes, rodding, valves and various additional pieces of apparatus which their ingenious designer had attached in order to improve their performance, produced locomotives which reminded one irresistably of an itinerant tinker and kettle mender, of French or German extraction at that. But they performed well enough, although Beattie quickly abandoned the single. He produced a batch of inside-cylinder 2-4-0s and then some outside cylinder 2-2-2s which he found rather prone to slip with the increasing weight of the rather more civilized carriages which were being provided for all classes. So he rebuilt one into a 2-4-0. *Victoria* was the very last single produced for the LSWR. She came out in 1859. It is interesting to reflect that the last Great Western single came out forty years later and that this company, along with the GER, the Midland, the Great Central and the Great Northern were still using 4-2-2s on expresses in the first decade of the twentieth century. By this time one had to be middle aged to have travelled behind a single on the LSWR.

The company got its money's worth out of Joseph Beattie's engines. The lifespan of No 1, *Sussex*, for example approximately paralleled the period its creator was in charge. It cost £2,992 when it came out in June 1852 and its replacement in December 1870 cost precisely the same, although *Sussex* actually lasted a bit longer, until June 1872. One always has to treat locomotive buildings and replacement costs with some scepticism for they are often figures dreamed up in the accounts department in order to provide a neat and orderly balance, but they do give us some idea of actual costs and comparisons. Certainly the replacement for No 5 *Gannymede* of June 1855 which had cost £1,849 was nearly double in June 1873 — £3,227. But No 20 *Princess* cost, so it is officially recorded £2,960 to build in June 1854 and, like *Sussex*, precisely the same amount to replace in December 1871.

At the end of Joseph Beattie's reign, in 1870, the 272 locomotives owned by the company covered a total of 3,386,089 miles, which worked out at an average of 12,449 for each one. As an aside we may note that an East Coast HST set covers around that distance each fortnight. The total expenditure on LSWR locomotive repairs in 1868 was £44,978 which worked out at 3.65 old pennies per locomotive mile, or 3.66d per train mile.

One of Gooch's inventions was a feed-water heater which ensured that his engines were just about the most economical around. Another was the double firebox which enabled the smoke from one section to be consumed by the fire in the other, thus greatly reducing the amount of black smoke emitted. There were strict government regulations about this, which was only right, for the atmosphere in the cities of Britain in mid-Victorian times was pretty poisonous, and most companies attempted to comply with them by using the more expensive coke.

To handle the company's goods traffic, which was nothing like as heavy as on those lines which served the great industrial heartlands of Britain, Beattie used at first 2-4-0s with 5 ft drivers, but by the mid-1860s switched, like so many companies, to the 0-6-0 and this wheel arrangement remained the standard for fifty years. Few South Western locomotives were exclusively employed on goods traffic and the 0-6-0s were expected to be able to handle such passenger work as race and troop specials and excursions when required.

Superficially the locomotive scene of the mid-Victorian London and South Western may have looked rather archaic but in fact it was in good shape, relatively standardized and able to cope competently with the demands made upon it; which was not something all of its contemporaries could claim with any honesty.

For the first twenty years the livery was Indian red with black bands. Around 1859 Beattie changed the red to a darker chocolate but added white lining, and vermilion in the case of some of the principal passenger engines. Carriages were basically brown. Some were painted chocolate like the engines, but others in Joseph Beattie's time had the teak or mahogany woodwork varnished rather than painted. Initially the company's coat of arms was carved on the middle doors. We have no carriages left from the early days of the Southampton line, but we do have three from Cornwall which were built for the Bodmin and Wadebridge Railway, later absorbed by the LSWR around 1840 and as Michael Harris in his *Preserved Railway Coaches* states: 'may be the oldest railway passenger coaches in existence in the world'. They were built locally and are very typical of what ran all over the LSWR, and elsewhere. The third is literally open with no windows or roof and resembles nothing more closely than something out of a fair ground and weighs no more than 3 tons. The other two are enclosed, a second, and a composite. A carriage which did work regularly on the Southampton line in the 1840s was Joseph Beattie's saloon for the use of Queen Victoria on her journeys between London and Gosport. It was, of course, infinitely more luxuriously appointed than the Bodmin and Wadebridge primitives. In later LSWR days it was numbered 7 and was sold out of service, after rebuilding, in 1908. A hundred years after its construction it was still around, on Colonel Stephens' Shropshire and Montgomeryshire Railway. Hamilton Ellis, in his *Railway Carriages in the British Isles 1830 to 1914*, quotes a soldier he knew 'who regularly slept in it'. This was during the Second World War when the military had taken over the line and it was sometime in the 1940s that No 7 finally gave up the ghost in the regions of the Welsh Border, a couple of hundred miles and a hundred years from its exalted beginnings.

All early LSW carriages were four-wheelers. They were said to be smoother riding than on many lines although the Parliamentary thirds, which all railways were forced to provide following Mr Gladstone's Act of 1844, had little to recommend them in any other respect. They were grudgingly given roofs, as the law demanded, and tarpaulin curtains where the higher classes had windows. These kept out some of the elements but also, of course, the light; the two roof skylights were hardly adequate substitutes. In the late 1860s six-wheelers began to come into service, but there was still plenty of work for the four-wheelers. A photograph of a Swanage branch train taken in the summer of 1885 shortly after its opening shows Beattie 2-4-0T No 209 in charge of five four-wheelers of various ages — the leading brake, with its massive birdcage affording the guard a fine view over the oil pots of the almost flat roofed carriages behind and of the Purbeck Hills, looks particularly ancient. However all had gone, apart from those in departmental service, by the grouping in 1923. This may not seem an achievement of massive proportions, but it was more than either of the other Southern constituents, the Brighton and the South Eastern, could boast, whilst the Great Western, for all its superb Dreadnoughts and Toplights, was still hauling Welsh miners around in four-wheelers when British Railways came into existence!

Chapter 7
On to Weymouth

We have now reached Waterloo in our story, but we have not yet got to Weymouth and it is in that direction we must now head. It will be recalled that much of the impetus for extending the railway west of Southampton was in order that this port might not gain too great an advantage over Poole and Weymouth. Well Poole was now rail connected, although truth to tell its decline, although slowed, was not halted. Dorchester had been reached and there everything had come to a halt.

The citizens of Weymouth fumed, but the Channel Islands packets kept faith with the Dorset port and the Great Western Railway inched its stately way south from Westbury. The latter town was reached from Thingley Junction on the Paddington to Bristol

GW/LSW notice in the yard at Weymouth.

main line on 5 September 1848. Two years later it had progressed another 5½ miles to Frome. Nearly six years more and it had covered another 26 miles to Yeovil and trains began running thus far on 1 September 1856.

Having got within sight of the Dorset border the Great Western summoned all its energies and courage and thenceforward positively dashed head-first, casting caution to the winds and on 20 January 1857 Weymouth was at last attained. Hamilton Ellis, looking back on the occasion, records that all was sweetness and light between the GW and LSW officials, Charles Saunders and Henry Lacy, who 'took wine together most amicably'. Down at local level there was surprisingly little enthusiasm. Well perhaps not so surprising when we consider how long it had taken the promised rail link to materialize. Ten days after the opening the *Western Gazette*, a paper which still flourishes, carried the following comment on the inaugural festivities which took place exactly a week after the frist train ran into Weymouth. 'It is usual to have such rejoicings on the day of opening, but the railway was so long about, so many rumours were raised that it was to be open next week — the week after for certain — positively on the 1st proximo etc, that it is excusable that Weymouth took a whole week to convince itself that the railway was really opened and in operation.'

The first train out of Weymouth was a Great Western broad gauge one, the 6.15 am to Yeovil, whilst the first LSW one left for Southampton five minutes before noon. The weather was no better than anyone had any right to expect for mid-January and this no doubt did little to fire enthusiasm. Nevertheless it wasn't at all a bad railway now that it had finally arrived. It cost £44,000 and for this the Great Western got a handsome Brunel designed station built of wood and iron, a goods shed, and an engine shed. These were built largely on marshy land reclaimed from the eastern shore beside the meandering River Wey.

Having been without its promised rail connection for so long Weymouth now rejoiced in two routes to London. The LSW's was the shorter, 147½ miles against the GW's 168½, but there was little difference

in timings and both routes did good, if not sensational business. Much of it was intermediate. The Eldridge Pope brewery at Dorchester, beside the South station, which had prospered under the energetic Sarah Eldridge, provided the LSW with plenty of trade, whilst on both routes, LSW and GW, milk and agricultural produce generally were the mainstay.

A joint station would have been the ideal in Dorchester, although both stations were pretty central and not much above five minutes walk apart. The LSW was the oldest by ten years but to bring GW trains into it would have involved either an expensive detour or reversal, neither solution being considered feasible. However through LSW trains had to reverse to get in and out of their station on account of it being built on a west/east line as Castleman still hoped when he opened it that it would form part of a through route to Exeter. The line to Weymouth curved sharply away to the south at the

Radipole Halt, the last station before Weymouth c1900, with its distinctive GWR designed pagoda huts which lasted into the mid-1970s (Author's collection).

approach to the station in order to avoid a Roman amphitheatre and to link up with the Great Western at Dorchester Junction on the southern edge of the town. By the time this opened the LSW had turned to the Salisbury line as a way through to Exeter and the West, but having saddled itself with a station built inconveniently on a stub end at Dorchester it was stuck with it. So for over 100 years every up train had to shoot past the station and then reverse into it, although down ones were provided with the luxury of a through platform on the curve from 5 May 1879. The two tracks in the terminus section had no less than three platforms and an allover roof, This latter and the island platform were removed in the 1930s. Although trains ceased to use the remaining main terminus platform following the introduction of the diesel-hauled push-pull service when the Waterloo-Bournemouth line was electrified in 1967 and an up platform was finally built on the through curve, it still existed until 1986.

The seven miles from Dorchester to Weymouth were, and are, the most spectacular in terms of gradients of the entire Waterloo to Weymouth railway. They are, perhaps, visually the most appealing, rivalled in their different ways by the approach to Waterloo with its panorama of some of the capital's most famous landmarks culminating in the Houses of Parliament, the run through the western approaches to Southampton along the docks, although now that ocean liners are such rare visitors this is not quite what it once was, and the stretch west of Poole alongside the harbour.

Looming up ahead as the train curves sharply southwards out of Dorchester are the Downs. Immediately to the west, forming the foothills, is Maiden Castle, the grandest of the many pre-Roman hill settlements found in Dorset. Maiden Castle is generally reckoned to be the most extensive Neolithic settlement in all Britain and the railway climbs at 1 in 91 a few hundred yards from its ramparts. Although it is the inevitable bloodier episodes in its long history which ended with the Roman invasion and its replacement by Dunovaria (Dorchester) which attract most attention, Maiden Castle was chiefly a hill town where the Britons lived and worked, grazed their sheep and cattle, practised their crafts, traded, and went peacefully about their lives.

As it climbs higher the line enters a deep, curving cutting. In it is Bincombe signal box, of GW design, derelict and out of use since the replacement of steam by diesel removed the necessity for bankers. Bincombe tunnel, 819 yards long, takes the line under Ridgeway Hill. It emerges into another cutting, passes under the Weymouth to Dorchester road which a hundred yards further on does a gear-crunching U-turn and twists back under the railway which has meanwhile passed the now closed Upwey Wishing Well Halt.

Directly ahead lies Weymouth Bay and the Isle of Portland. The view is splendid. From Napoleonic times onwards vast fortifications were built up and today, as when the railway arrived 130 years ago, naval ships are always exercising and manoeuvering in the Bay and beyond. Far to the west a tower stands on one of the highest points of the Downs, above the village of Portesham. It marks the spot where Admiral Hardy, he who had charge of the *Victory* at Trafalgar and whose name was on the dying Nelson's lips, used to sit in his old age and look over the warships he had once commanded.

Down through what is now Upwey and Broadwey

A Weymouth to Waterloo express in the deep cutting below Maiden Castle, October 1985.

station but which used to be the junction for the GW's Abbotsbury branch, and descending all the way through the outskirts of Weymouth, past the site of the recently demolished Radipole Halt, the line finally comes to Weymouth.

The engine shed at Weymouth was chiefly for the use of Great Western broad gauge locomotives; LSW ones lived at Dorchester in a two road brick shelter on the south side of the station. Ten years later, to cope with the increase in traffic consequent upon the opening of the Weymouth line, Dorchester shed was doubled in size, another two road shed being built, this time of wood — perhaps money was a bit tight or perhaps it was not intended to be permanent. However wooden engine sheds were common enough throughout the land and the wooden extension became a fixture.

Chapter 8

Bournemouth at last

To have completed seven chapters with scarcely a mention of Bournemouth, a resort which claims to be the largest in the country, may seem remarkable. When the nineteenth century opened Bournemouth simply did not exist and in 1838 it was scarcely large enough to claim the status of a village. Not even its name was fixed — some called it Bourne, after the stream around which it clustered between the pine trees and the sea, whilst the inhabitants of the long-established Poole, Christchurch, Mudeford and Holdenhurst referred to it as Coypond. It was thus no wonder that it did not feature in any of the railway schemes being put forward to serve Hampshire and Dorset in the 1830s and 40s.

Poole was vastly more important and a coach connection between its station and Bournemouth was considered perfectly adequate. And when, as hotels, guest houses, and homes for the elderly and infirm began to proliferate as the advantages of the mild climate became better known, and proposals were put forward for a station in the Bournemouth area, there were some citizens who wanted to know nothing about them.

Not to put too fine a point on it there was an element in the town which had a positively paranoic fear of contamination by the lower classes. Allied with illusions of good taste, which in reality resulted

in an excess of discreet vulgarity, it fought like billy-o to keep the railway at bay and as a consequence Bournemouth has one of the most inconveniently sited stations of any English resort. Just compare its brisk twenty minute walk from the town centre to the position of the stations at Torquay, Weymouth, Eastbourne, Hastings, Margate or any one of a dozen other South Coast resorts and you will see what I mean.

Christchurch, with its ancient priory dating back to Norman times and the pre-Roman settlement of Hengistbury Head at the opposite side of the harbour, had been a place of some importance for centuries and Castleman's original line between Southampton and Dorchester might well have taken it in had it not been for the fact that Castleman moved to the western edge of Ringwood in 1844 and decided to route his railway through that town instead. But Christchurch was not to be denied and moves were soon afoot to put it on the railway map, moves which involved the first concrete proposals for a station at Bournemouth.

The Ringwood, Christchurch and Bournemouth Company received its act in August 1859, but only for the 7½ miles between Christchurch and the junction with the Southampton and Dorchester line at Ringwood. Even so this took long enough to build.

Left *Hurn station on the line from Ringwood to Christchurch, as restored in 1986 with a 1960-built Pullman car alongside the platform.*

Right *Adams 4-4-2T No 56 on the Branksome triangle, c1902. This locomotive was built in 1882 and withdrawn in 1921 (National Railway Museum).*

Funds were short and in order to keep costs to a minimum the line twisted its way across heathland and through pine forest, avoiding all embankments and cuttings. Trains were restricted to a maximum speed of 25 mph over this line of such little ambition, and there was but one intermediate station, not very close to the village of Hurn, plus a private halt at Avon Lodge for Lord Egmont, this being provided in gratitude for the noble lord permitting the railway to cross his land. The line, which was independent but worked by the LSW, was opened on 13 November 1862.

The directors of the railway intended to pursue their ambition to get to Bournemouth, although Bournemouth itself was not so sure. Laurence Popplewell in his *Bournemouth Railway History* quotes the following which appeared in the *Bournemouth Visitor's Directory*:

'Tis well from far to hear the railway scream;
And watch the curling, lingering clouds of steam;
But let not Bournemouth-health's approved abode
Court the near presence of the Iron road.'

The Ringwood, Christchurch and Bournemouth Railway hardly proved a goldmine; but this perhaps made it all the keener to reach the now substantial resort beside the mouth of the Bourne and tap its traffic potential. Late in 1865 work began on the Bournemouth extension. As with the original Christchurch line the work was slow but the three mile, 52 chain line was eventually finished on 14 March 1870.

It was nothing to boast about. The station was on the very edge of the town. Local opposition had seen to that. It was small and shabby, the buildings being little better than huts, inadequate right from the start. Free rides were given on the opening day and traffic soon built up but the residents, for ever wanting the best of both worlds, soon began to complain about the state of the station.

The LSW did nothing to endear itself to them. Instead of making a bold drive for the town with a grand terminus building of which the citizens could be proud, as in so many Victorian resorts, it kept costs to the barest minimum, skulking through the pines as though aware that being in trade meant it had no right to attempt to rise above its allotted station in life. When the inhabitants to the east of Bournemouth, in the fast growing Pokesdown and Boscombe, quite reasonably asked that the trains might stop in their vicinity, the LSW refused.

The population of Bournemouth was now almost 6,000. It was increasing all the time, was clearly going to go on doing so, and if the London and South Western, which had now totally absorbed the Ringwood, Christchurch and Bournemouth Railway, was intent on pussyfooting around there were other concerns prepared to jump in and snatch all this potential revenue from it. The first to succeed in building another line to Bournemouth as opposed to proposing one, which was a very different thing, was the Salisbury and Dorset Junction Railway which on 20 December 1866 opened from Alderbury, a little to the east of Salisbury on the Salisbury to Eastleigh line, to West Moors on Castleman's Corkscrew. The LSW was quick to sense the threat to its monopoly and arranged from the outset to work the line. This meant there was now a direct railway route between Salisbury and its nearest stretch of coastline, though to Poole rather than Bournemouth.

Poole station was at this time still at the end of a branch line and not very convenient for the town centre. Through carriages to Waterloo had commenced running in May 1860 and the branch had been doubled, along with the main line, in 1863-64, but the inhabitants objected to the walk across Poole Harbour bridge, which involved paying a toll.

Meanwhile another line was approaching Poole.

Just to mention its title, the Somerset and Dorset, brings a sigh to many a noble breast and a tear to the eye. It had, and has, a veritable army of admirers but unfortunately never much more than a platoon of customers. Formed by an amalgamation of two companies, the Dorset Central and the Somerset Central in August 1862, the final section of its line from Highbridge on the Bristol Channel was opened on 10 September 1863, when trains began working through to Wimborne, where they reversed for the final run over LSW metals to Poole.

A new station was opened at Poole on 2 December 1872. It was slap in the middle of the town, a great contrast with the situation in Bournemouth, and was built on a new section of railway which left the main line at Broadstone. The station stood on a sharp bend adjoining the High Street. The railway encountered a second road at the western end of the station, and both were negotiated by level crossings, which was logical enough given the flat nature of the land and the shortage of space. But much congestion arose from the start and the crossings were a bone of contention throughout their existence. There were fears of horrendous happenings should a train ever come charging through at excessive speed and to allay these Poole Corporation and the LSW signed an agreement that all trains would be scheduled to stop in Poole station.

The new line to Poole was part of a greater enterprise, the Poole and Bournemouth Railway. Amongst its features was an extension from Poole to a station at the western end of Bournemouth, and a tramway serving the north side of Poole Quay; the original Poole station, which was in Hamworthy, served the south side. The Bournemouth extension began as an independent operation but in July 1871 the LSW obtained powers to take it over.

For those not familiar with the area we had best make clear the distinction between Poole Harbour and Poole Quay. The Quay is the commercial port at the end of the High Street, the Harbour is the natural harbour which extends almost as far west as Wareham and east to Sandbanks and encloses four islands, the largest of which, Brownsea, once featured a narrow gauge, hand propelled line serving the short-lived clay workings. After many vicissitudes, which included the very first Scout camp, Brownsea Island is now in the safe hands of the National Trust.

Trains began to use the new Poole station on 2 December 1872, although at first only Somerset and Dorset ones, the LSW continuing to work to and from the old Hamworthy station until the necessary legislation was obtained. Once this happened there was little demand for passenger trains on the old branch. A regular service lasted until 1896, since when the

line has essentially been goods only.

The new line from Poole to Bournemouth involved some of the heaviest engineering on any section of the Waterloo to Weymouth railway. First Poole Harbour had to be crossed by means of an embankment and bridge and then there was a steep climb through Parkstone reaching 1 in 60 at several places. This involved a number of bridges before the summit was reached at Branksome, three miles from Poole. The final section of just under a mile was on the level and took the line to its terminus at Bournemouth West. Had it gone to its intended destination, ¾ mile further on, it would have reached the Square, the heart of the town, and could have truly called itself Central. But, as always, there were those in high places opposed to such an extension, and the story of the railway in Bournemouth, and perhaps of Bournemouth itself, was very different to what it might have been.

Unlike the station on the line from Christchurch the new West was properly funded and met with general approval, being described by one contemporary writer as 'pretty'. It opened on 20 July 1874 and, like Poole, was served at first only by Somerset and Dorset trains. There were nine in and eight out. They connected at Wimborne with the LSW. At this time the Somerset and Dorset was still an independent company. A few weeks after the opening of Bournemouth West it had completed its long hoped for link with the Midland Railway at Bath and now offered a through route from the South Coast to Bristol, the Midlands and the North of England. It might have been a line of strategic importance and financially viable, but for various reasons, not least its winding, undulating route through the pretty but sparsely populated regions of rural Wessex where the only towns of any size were those at its extremities, it never was.

The completion of its main line had drained the Somerset and Dorset and it looked for assistance. Much of its route lay through Great Western territory and it was logical it should approach Paddington. The GW was interested, and in an uncharacteristically conciliatory move asked the London and South Western if it would like to go shares. But Waterloo would have none of it and instead joined forces with the Midland Railway to outbid the GW. In this it was successful and so from 1 November 1875 the Somerset and Dorset Joint Railway came into being. The LSW assumed responsibility for track maintenance, the Midland provided the motive power and carriages, painted in an attractive deep blue livery.

Whilst the railway had been making its tortuous approach to Bournemouth from the west the residents of Pokesdown and Boscombe on the original line to Bournemouth East had not given up

A Somerset and Dorset express at Poole in 1910. The engine is No 71, a Derby-built Class '2' 4-4-0 (Kelland Collection).

hopes of a station. They were continually presenting petitions and the LSW was continually refusing them. There was equal disatisfaction with the inadequate Bournemouth East station.

The predicted population explosion had taken place and in the ten years between 1871 and 1881 it had virtually trebled from 6,000 to 17,000. The LSW had quite simply not kept up with this staggering increase and both station and services were beneath the standards a fine, self-confident resort expected. Exasperated by the South Western's slothful attitude Bournemouth attempted to break its monopoly, first by encouraging the Somerset and Dorset, and then making overtures to another line which had ambitions to link the South Coast with the Midlands and the North. This was the Didcot, Newbury and Southampton Railway which had the encouragement of the GW. At this the LSW at last stirred itself.

The highly indirect route via Ringwood, and the twisty, slow single track through Hurn and Christchurch had to be improved, and shaken by the threat of the Didcot, Newbury and Southampton proposals to cut a line through the New Forest, the London and South Western authorized in 1882 a survey of a direct route from Brockenhurst to Christchurch. This would shorten the journey from Waterloo to Bournemouth East by 8½ miles and make a significant saving in journey time.

Work on the line began the following year. It was part of a complex development programme which went some, although not all, of the way to giving Bournemouth and Poole up-to-date railway facilities. That it fell short was inevitable, given the ambivalent attitude which Bournemouth had always had to the railway. Everyone could see that it made sense to link the two Bournemouth stations and to make the routes east to Southampton and west to Weymouth more direct. But they did not agree on how far into the centre of Bournemouth the railway should be allowed.

There were those like Merton 'Russell'-Coates, the owner of the Bath hotel, the largest in the town, who felt the town was in need of gingering up a bit. He complained of there being 'no attractions whatever in Bournemouth', which was rather an exaggeration, but he did his best to improve upon those that there were. He joined the Town Commissioners (predecessor of the Town Council which came into existence when Bournemouth was created first a municipal borough in 1890 and then a county borough as the new century dawned, by which time the population was approaching 60,000) and was perhaps the greatest force in directing the town's meteoric progress in the last decades of the nineteenth century. He was an ardent supporter of the railway. But other influential citizens, whilst admitting the town's dependence on it, wished it be kept as much out of sight as possible.

Naturally the LSW wished to get as close to the centre as it could and it proposed a new Central terminus which would have been beside the Town Hall. The surviving drawings of it depict an ugly, ill-proportioned Italianate affair, but Bournemouth has cheerfully put up with worse and by now it would probably be listed! But it was not to be, the Commissioners were aghast at the 'rumbling, screeching, vibration and hubbub' which it would contain and refused. A breath of life to some, but not to others.

Defeated on the Central station issue the LSW found itself also under threat with its proposed link line between the East and West stations. The anti-railway lobby, or more accurately the 'not-wanting-to-see-or-hear' the railway lobby, demanded it be as far away from the residential area as possible and didn't care how roundabout this made it. This time the contest was a draw, the actual line not being as direct as the LSW would have liked but not quite as far out as the residents had hoped. The line between Christchurch and Bournemouth was doubled and a fine new station — there would be no complaints this time — was erected west of the old East station. It was designed by William Jacomb, the Company's Chief Engineer, and had a covered roof 350 ft long and 100 ft wide. On the up side was the engine shed, although there were proposals to re-site this at Bournemouth West, which was also in the process of being rebuilt and enlarged. Despite the splendours of

the new Bournemouth East there were those in the town who were not impressed and were glad to note it was built in a cutting and therefore not visible from any great distance.

At the same time Pokesdown at last got its station. The new Bournemouth East opened on 20 July 1885 and Pokesdown a year later. The ever increasing population soon warranted a station between Pokes-down and Bournemouth, at Boscombe, and this opened in 1893. The LSW, acknowledging that it had got as close the middle of the town as it was ever going to, renamed the East station Bournemouth Central.

The line between the East and West stations was inspected and passed fit on 28 September 1886. The most spectacular section was that immediately north-east of Branksome Station where two of the three sides of the triangle linking Branksome with the East and West stations, and these latter with each other, were accommodated on high, handsome yellow brick viaducts. From them one could look down on the Bourne Valley and the gasworks, something else which had been banished to the edge of the town.

One of Beattie's 2-4-0WTs, No 262, at Bournemouth Central in 1889. Behind it stands one of the town's many Victorian churches; note the Hotel Metropole sign immediately below the station nameboard (LPC).

Finally the cut-off line from Brockenhurst to Christchurch came into use on 5 March 1888. William Adams' fine new apple green 4-4-0, No 526, hauled the inaugural express of eleven bogie carriages, including the Director's Saloon, although it did not hurry, the 108 miles taking a leisurely three hours. It did, however, stop several times.

Generally speaking Bournemouth was pretty pleased with itself and reckoned its rail facilities and its service to London could now match any resort in the country. This was not quite true for it lagged far behind in the provision of facilities for day excursionists. This was very much by design and when one Sunday the LSW put on a cheap special Bournemouth got most indignant. The Chairman of the railway chided the town, reminding it that Sunday was 'the only day the working classes get the opportunity of breathing the health-giving ozone', tartly adding that in any case most excursionists 'rather would go to Brighton'.

Right *The Branksome triangle arches. The nearer one carries the main line to Poole and Weymouth, the further that from Bournemouth Central to Bournemouth West.*

Below *Bournemouth station, 17 August 1986. The 'Bournemouth Belle', hauled by No 33008* Eastleigh *newly repainted in its original green livery, arrives from Waterloo.*

Chapter 9
Suburbia

Waterloo was growing ever busier as the nineteenth century approached its final decades. By the early 1860s some 228 trains arrived each weekday. The Company had not yet given up hope of extending towards the Thames and in particular London Bridge, and on 11 January 1864 it got as near as it was ever going to (at least on the surface) when a single track was extended across the concourse to join up with the newly opened Waterloo Junction station on the South Eastern Railway's line from London Bridge to Charing Cross. In theory this meant that through trains could run from Weymouth, Bournemouth and Southampton to London Bridge but nothing of the sort was ever scheduled. There was little demand for such a service and the impracticability of running regular main line trains across the Waterloo concourse and on to SER metals ruled out any such attempt.

The only passenger service to use the connection was an LNWR one from Euston by way of the West London Extension Railway to London Bridge for a period in 1865. It was an ingenious but eccentric notion and, as even Mr Pickwick in the throes of a particularly severe attack of gout could probably have covered the distance in a shorter time on foot, it is not suprising that the service did not survive the summer of that year. After that empty stock and Queen Victoria on her way from Windsor to the Kentish ports had the line to themselves. Which was just as well for a line running through the circulating area was a great inconvenience. Some idea of the problem can be gauged by the road mail vans which have to cross the concourse today to reach platforms 10 and 11. Pedestrians negotiated the rails by way of either ramps down to and up from track level or by a hinged footbridge.

Nevertheless this line might have led to some intriguing developments. A key figure in attempts to link London's railways was Eustace Watkin. In 1860 he was Chairman of three companies, the Manchester, Sheffield and Lincolnshire, the Metropolitan, and the South Eastern. He had plans to join all three railways and thus provide a through route from the North of England across London by way of Charing Cross and Waterloo Junction and on to the Kent

Coast and from there by way of the Channel Tunnel, which was another of his interests, to France and the Continent. As it was, through a combination of social and financial pressures, no main line railway ever extended right across London and not even trams penetrated the centre of the City or the West End. The establishment of the London County Council in 1888 ensured that one overall authority would in future oversee planning within London (apart from the City), and there simply was not space for more railways.

The finest picture of life in slum conditions around the London and South Western Railway's approach to Waterloo and the terminus itself is to be found in George Moore's novel *Esther Waters*. Esther's father is a brutal drunkard, but also a skilled craftsman, 'a painter of engines, a first-rate hand, earning good money, from twenty-five to thirty shillings a week . . . living in a little street off the Vauxhall Bridge Road, near the factory where (he) worked'. As we are later told that the father has 'lost his situation on the railway' it is clear he is employed by the LSW at Nine Elms works. Most of his money goes on drink and on one typical Saturday night he has been brought home 'long after midnight', and after lying in bed until Sunday afternoon, threatening to 'brain anyone who made the least noise' his family wait fearfully for his departure to 'take a penny boat and go for a blow on the river.'

Very likely Esther's father was dismissed by the LSW for being drunk and might be said to have only himself to blame, but this was of no consolation to his family. Drunkenness was a terrible problem in Victorian England and although it was by no means confined to the working classes it was they who chiefly suffered its consequences. Dugald Drummond when he became Locomotive Superintendant of the LSW in 1895 found it rife amongst enginemen. He took the strongest possible measures to stamp it out and was largely successful, although he was compassionate enough to find many of the displaced footplatemen jobs on the Waterloo and City line.

It was easy enough to lose one's job on the railway and the Locomotive Power Committee minute book is full of such instances. On the surface they give the impression that the men fell down on the job but often this was because of faulty equipment and long hours and may well have been outside the unfortunte man's control. It was before the days when the union existed to fight his case and if he could not argue it himself with sufficient skill then there was no appeal. For instance on 10 April 1839 the minutes record 'In consequence of the accident to the Engine No 2 (*Locke*) arising from the neglect of the Engineer William Hall it was ORDERED that he be discharged and fined to the full extent retained of his wages.' An accident at Basingstoke in November 1839 led to the discharge of 'Engineer Gladdon (who) had on previous occasions been negligent'. Nor were senior employees spared for on 11 October 1839 it was resolved that the Superintendent of Engines, one Binafore, be 'removed from his appointment', although what he had done remains obscure. One railwayman who just managed to escape the dismissal was a labourer who had been reported by the Metropolitan Police 'for having some coke in his possession which he had picked up on the line of railway'. He was called in to his superiors, admonished, and then let go on condition that 'he went round to his fellow labourers' warning them of

Waterloo Road, August 1986. The bridge beneath which the bus is passing originally carried the line linking the LSW and SEC stations. It is now used by foot passengers.

the consequences should any attempt a similar misdeed.

George Moore's *Esther Waters* is not all Victorian doom and gloom, which is why it is still in print, and there is a delightful account of a journey from Waterloo through the south-west suburbs of London to the Derby, where Esther's husband, William, who combines the professions of publican and bookmaker, hopes to make a killing. Some of the places described are still easily recognizable today. 'Out of the grey station they rolled into the light, the plate-glass drawing the rays together until they burnt the face and hand. Now they were speeding alongside of the upper windows nearly on a level with the red and yellow chimney-pots. A moment after they were passing by open spaces filled with cranes, old iron, stacks of railway sleepers, pictorial advertisements, sky signs, and great gasometers rising round and black in their iron cages overtopping or nearly the distant church spires. A train steamed along a hundred arch viaduct; and along a black embankment the other trains rushed by in a whirl of wheels, bringing thousands of clerks up from the suburbs.

'The excursion jogged on, stopping for long intervals before strips of sordid garden where shirts and pink petticoats were blowing. Little streets ascended the hillsides; no more trains; buses too had disappeared, and afoot the folk hurried along the lonely pavements of their suburbs. At Clapham Junction betting men had crowded the platform; they all wore

grey overcoats with race-glasses slung over their shoulders. And the train still rolled through the brick wilderness which old John said was all country forty years ago.

'They passed bits of common with cows and stray horse, also a little rural cemetery; but London suddenly began again parish after parish, the same blue roofs, the same tenement houses. The train had passed the first cedar and the first tennis lawn, and knowing it to be a Derby excursion the players paused in their game and looked up. Again the line was blocked; the train stopped, but it had left London behind, and the next stoppage was in front of a thick meadow with a square weather-beaten church showing beneath the spreading trees, and all around green corn, with birds flying in the bright air, and lazy clouds going out, making way for the endless blue of a long summer's day'.

Suburbia, as old John had remarked, was growing at a tremendous rate, spurred on by the railway, and all along the line out of Waterloo, and the many branches which were springing from it, terraces and villas of all descriptions were being built as fast as the land could be bought. Kingston on the Hill, or Surbiton as it became, grew from a population of 387 living in 69 houses in 1841 to 10,500 living in 2,000 houses in 1887. In the words of F. Somner Merryweather: 'Stuccoed villas, pretentious in design and capricious in style rose on all sides. They were mortgaged up to the tiles as soon as built. Many builders failed but others always stepped in'.

Like Bournemouth, Kingston had not originally wanted to know about the railway. Merryweather records that it 'grumbled and fought against it with the obstruction of old conversatism. Hurrah! Its corporation had beaten off the railway! It was just then flushed with a fatal and barren victory. But

steam as a propeller of iron strength was already becoming a recognized power in the work of human progress'. Good for you F. Somner Merryweather! The 'ancient borough' soon recognized its mistake for land values in the upstart Surbiton shot up six fold, and by 1840 seventeen of the 38 malthouses on the river at Kingston were vacant for the railway could bring malt from away much more cheaply and quickly than the barges used to. New shops up on the hill at Surbiton took trade away from the town, and the old conservatism rapidly gave way to a new realism. The LSW was at first reluctant to build a branch into the centre of Kingston so the citizens proposed their own North London Extension Company. This did the trick and on 1 July 1863 a 'first class station' was opened by the LSW in the heart of Kingston, the event being celebrated by a dinner at the Griffin public house.

Kingston-on-Thames has since then not looked back and is one of the most prosperous of London boroughs. Surbiton has done alright for itself too, although with such a name it could hardly avoid becoming the archetype for all the jibes directed at suburbia. Superficially it may appear a nondescript dormitory area, rootless and lacking distinction, the neighbour of East Cheam, famous for Tony Hancock's Railway Cuttings. Yet Surbiton has existed long enough to have acquired a distinct personality. The handsome London and Southampton Hotel, put up in the Georgian style beside the station, may have been replaced by the Southampton, a bow-legged hostlery at the bottom of a dull-looking office block, but many of the handsome villas remain, including just down the road from the station the imposing red brick Surbiton Club (members only).

Epsom station was opened by the LSW in 1859 on the line from Raynes Park to Guildford via Leather-

Top left *Tenements and Battersea power station.*

Middle left *Back gardens running down to the railway embankment, near Raynes Park.*

Left *An up local train passing Earlsfield, c1905. The locomotive is Adams 4-4-2T No 486, the carriages a long rake of close-coupled six-wheelers* (H. Gordon Tidey).

Right *'M7' 0-4-4T No 30043 shunting in Kingston goods yard, 12 March 1959.*

Left *Rivals come together. Two 19th century suburban tank engines, Adams 4-4-2T No 588 of the LSW, built by Neilsons in March 1885, and Stroudley 0-6-0T No 72 Fenchurch of the LBSC, built at Brighton in 1872, in steam together on the Bluebell Railway on 7 September 1986.*

Right *Former LBSC 0-4-4T No B398 passing Chelsea and Fulham station with a Kensington Addison Road to Clapham Junction train, 26 August 1933 (H. C. Casserley).*

Below *Clapham Junction in 1870, looking north. The LBSC lines are on the right, the LSW ones on the left (Battersea Libraries).*

head and took the Derby crowds to within a mile of the course, which was a lot nearer than the crossing with the Kingston to Ewell road to which those first racegoers had flocked back in the second week of the London and Southampton Railway's existence in May 1838. Such a rich source of revenue was not going to be left to LSW monopoly and the LBSC had got to Epsom in 1847; the station became a joint one when the LSW's Leatherhead line was opened. Later the Brighton got even nearer with its Epsom Downs line, opened from Sutton in 1865 and finally the South Eastern Railway finished up almost sharing the saddle with the jockey when it opened its Tattenham Corner branch in 1901. It is this station which the Queen uses when the Royal Train takes her to the Derby.

Branches off the main Waterloo to Weymouth line opened thick and fast through the last decades of the nineteenth century. Two which were particularly popular with excursionists were those to Hampton Court and Windsor. The former opened on 1 February 1849, with the express purpose in the words of the LSW Chairman, W. J. Chaplin, of affording 'cheap and legitimate recreation to the lower classes'. The Great Western just won the race to get to Windsor but the LSW was a good second. It had some trouble obtaining permission to cross Home Park beneath the walls of Windsor Castle, but this was resolved and Tite's rather florid Windsor and Eton Riverside terminus opened on 1 December 1849.

In 1846 Wandsworth station, originally the first on the line out of Nine Elms, was renamed Clapham Common. It was half way to acquiring the title which has made it world famous. Some fifteen years later Common was changed to Junction and thus was born the stuff of which legends are made. Clapham Junction achieved its pre-eminent position chiefly because it was where the South Western and Brighton main lines found themselves running side by side on their approach to London. There is nowhere else in the capital or its environs where two main lines meet in such a convenient manner. The LBSC had opened its city terminus at London Bridge in 1842 but during the year of the Great Exhibition in 1851 and the subsequent removal of the Crystal Palace to the Norwood Heights it had begun to hanker after a West End terminus and thus the West End of London and Crystal Palace Railway was born. A joint venture with the London, Chatham and Dover company, Victoria station was opened in October 1860. The Chatham side was further subdivided, for the Great Western was part owner and five of the six tracks were mixed gauge. Rather extraordinarily the GW maintained its interest until quite modern times, 1932 in fact.

The GWR reached Victoria via the West London Extension Railway which came through Addison Road, Kensington and crossed the Thames at Chelsea and added to the complexity of the layout at Clapham Junction. GW trains, and those from many other companies which used this convenient link between North and South London, had the choice as they came up to Clapham Junction of either turning right and entering the station itself or turning left on to LSW tracks and heading for Nine Elms and Waterloo, or by a series of further junctions, Victoria.

As the quotation from *Esther Waters* suggests, the approach to Clapham Junction afforded a panorama of lines conveying many trains at various levels running parallel or above or below others. In actual fact little use was ever made of the links with the northern railway lines and Waterloo and Victoria, their value has lain chiefly in those southwards on to the LSW, LBSC and SEC routes.

The Brighton side of Clapham Junction and the South Western platforms serving the Weymouth main line and its many branches were built on a curve on the south side of the site, whilst to the north is the Richmond and Windsor station, a straight through layout; between the two are extensive sidings. The convenience of changing from Brighton to South Western trains and vice versa so that travellers could end their journey either at Victoria or Waterloo was quickly realized and Clapham Junction rapidly became a scene of vast movement as office workers made their way from one platform to another. Neither company ever promoted the facility for long distance passengers and neither have their successors right down to the present time. This seems rather unadventurous for there must, for instance, be many travellers from Weymouth, Bournemouth and Southampton who would find arrival in the West End at Victoria more convenient than continuing to Waterloo.

Waterloo needed more and more signalling facilities as its traffic increased. The first signal box was know as the Crow's Nest for the very good reason that it was perched high up on the roof of the

Clapham Junction, c1905. LBSC Stroudley 'D' Class 0-4-2T in the foreground. The tower immediately above it stands on the present platform 10 (Battersea Libraries).

station. This was replaced in 1847 by 'A' Box with 47 levers to deal with the 400 plus daily train movements. In only seven years it was replaced by a new 'A' Box, this time with 109 levers, this also taking over from a 47 lever box on the Windsor side of the station. Within an even shorter time, five years, an ingenious rebuilding saw another box built around the old one, the latter being taken out when the new 144 lever box went into operation at the end of 1879. Still the station was growing, two new platforms were added on the south side in 1879, six on the north side in 1885. To cope with this 'A' Box went up to 200 levers and then was once again replaced, by a 220 lever box in 1892.

There were now some 700 trains in and out of the station, suburban and long distance, each weekday. Saturday 16 July 1892 was probably the busiest day to date when 879 train movements were recorded. By the turn of the century movements were up to 900 daily and sixteen signalmen were employed in controlling them. The concentration needed in the box was considerable as might be imagined and at the age of sixty the men who worked there were allowed to be put out to grass to end their careers at some less busy spot without loss of pay. They did their job well for accidents were rare and not usually serious. There was one at Clapham Junction on 20 August 1892 when the 9.50 pm train to Feltham, hauled by an Adams 4-4-2T, No 374, ran through signals and hit an empty Bournemouth excursion. Gas from the damaged carriages thrown across the engine caught light and the guard of the Bournemouth train died.

Chapter 10
Locomotive power

To handle its rapidly increasing traffic the LSW had to think seriously about improving the motive power situation. Joseph Beattie's celebrated 2-4-0 well tanks of 1863 were, as we have seen, the first specifically designed for suburban work, and were the South Western's equivalent of Stroudley's even more famous Terriers and his D1 tanks which came out almost a decade later on the Brighton. The three classes monopolized the intensive local traffic passing through Clapham Junction during the 1870s and 80s. Good though they were, and examples from each class survived into British Railways days eighty years later, they gradually found the increasing weights of longer trains and more modern stock more than they could handle and they took themselves off to the country to be replaced by something bigger and more powerful.

Joseph Beattie was succeeded by his son, W. George, who during his brief reign from 1871 to his

retirement due to ill health in 1877 continued to build more of his father's well tanks, although for express work he introduced that most popular of passenger types, the 4-4-0. As it turned out his twenty bogie express engines, the '348' Class, were a bit of a disaster and their failure probably contributed to their designer's early departure from Nine Elms.

No engines were built at Nine Elms between June 1860 and December 1862 owing to the works' extensive reconstruction and during this period the Manchester firm of Beyer Peacock was called upon to supply the company's needs. It was to be a famous collaboration, and although it lasted only nineteen years, 230 locomotives resulted from it, including 82 of the 2-4-0WTs and a number of their successors.

The younger Beattie was succeeded by William Adams, who came over from the Great Eastern Railway in 1878. He was the first Southerner to become Locomotive Superintendent of the LSWR. He was also the first, and last, to have ten children! He had been very much at home on the GER for he had been born at Limehouse where his father was resident

Beattie 2-4-0 Styx *at Bournemouth in 1889* (LPC).

Engineer of the East and West India Docks Company. Adams junior had not had far to move to take charge at Stratford having previously been at Bow with the North London Railway for twenty years. This is not to say he had not travelled; as a young man he had worked in France and Italy on steamship construction; he spoke French and Italian fluently.

William Adams continued to patronize Beyer Peacock. The firm had built large numbers of 4-4-0Ts for the Metropolitan and the District underground railways and Adams ordered twelve engines of this wheel arrangement for the LSW, although the design was his own and not unlike his similar engines on the North London Railway. Their most distinctive features were their small, solid bogie wheels and stove pipe chimneys, not elegant perhaps but they gave them an air of purposefulness. In order to increase their coal capacity their bunkers were extended and a pair of radial wheels added early in their careers and as 4-4-2Ts they proved ideal for suburban work upon which they were employed for upwards of thirty years. Inevitably their appearance led to their being nicknamed Steamrollers, although late in their careers some of them had migrated to the Bournemouth area where they were known as Hamworthy Buses. Adams had twelve tender engine versions of the Steamrollers built and with their 5 ft 7 in

driving wheels they were efficient mixed traffic machines.

Following the success of the Steamrollers, Adams brought out what was to become another famous class. This was very similar but was built from the start as a 4-4-2T and was a well tank, although later examples had small additional side tanks. In the short space of four years, 1882-85, 71 were built and they took over London suburban work from the Beattie engines. Apart from their increased size the enginemen welcomed them on account of their commodious cabs. With their big, square rear windows they were particularly suitable for working reverse, of which there was inevitably a good deal. Crews on the Beattie tanks were totally exposed to the elements when working backwards.

Three Adams 4-4-2Ts lasted into British Railways days, quite freakishly, like the three Beattie tanks, long after their compatriots had met the cutter's torch. They were the only locomotives considered suitable to work the sinuous Lyme Regis branch. With their tiny smoke boxes, small boilers and generous boiler fittings they looked every inch the antiquities they were. The elegant 4-4-0s which they resembled had long gone, although they had served the LSWR and its successor the Southern Railway well. Yet there was another class of engine which was scarcely newer than the 4-4-2Ts which was enormously long lived, and although it certainly looked rather elderly by the mid 1960s it quite lacked that air of Victorian antiquity possessed by the other Adams tank engines. This was the 02.

In the late 1880s Adams suddenly seemed to take vehemently against bogies. Well fairly vehemently, he did continue to build 4-4-0s for express passenger work but in his last years all his passenger tanks were 0-4-4s whilst he also built no less than ninety tender engine 0-4-2s, the 'Jubilees', so called because the first came out during the fiftieth anniversary of Queen Victoria's reign. Fifty of the 0-4-4Ts had 5 ft 7 in drivers whilst a further sixty had driving wheels of 4 ft 10 in diameter: the former were classified 'T1's, the latter '02's. Neither class really displaced the older bogie tanks from London suburban work, being chiefly found out in the country.

In his last years poor old William Adams' mind began to go, but that is not to say that there was anything the least eccentric or faulty of his later designs for they were all excellent; very likely his assistant W. F. Pettigrew (who later went on to build some enormous Baltic tanks for the Furness Railway) was largely responsible for them. Much the same situation occurred at Swindon a few years later in the period when Churchward was taking over from Dean. Adams was 72 when he retired from the company and his going was marked by genuine tokens of affection from all he knew and worked for him. He retired to Putney and died some nine years later.

Adams had need of constantly more powerful motive power for during the 1880s there had been great improvement in South Western carriages, each improvement resulting in greater weight for the locomotives to haul. The most noticeable advance was the bogie carriage. Until the last decades of the nineteenth century LSWR carriages had been nothing very special but from now on the company could justly claim that it treated all classes, and especially the humble but prolific third, a good deal better than on many lines. It was a time of prosperity for the South-Western and very decently it shared its good fortune with its customers. All-bogie expresses rapidly became the norm on the Bournemouth line, although they were not provided with quite as many lavatories as were necessary to ensure the comfort of all passengers, given that there were at first no through corridor connections. Interestingly the very first all corridor train built for ordinary service in this country appeared at Weymouth when brand new in June 1891. This was a Great Western innovation and was a fairly modest effort of the three Dean clerestory carriages — a fourth was added later — and its visit to Weymouth was part of an extensive programme of trials before entering regular service. That the company included Weymouth at a very early stage of its tour indicates how seriously the GWR took the Channel Islands traffic, for competition between the GW Weymouth route and the LSWR Southampton one was at its height at this time. And in the next chapter we will look at the development and rivalry of these two ports and the involvement of the two railways in their expansion.

Above *'02' 0-4-4T No 186 and some of the men employed on her overhaul at Nine Elms works, c1905. The gentleman in the bowler hat is surely the foreman* (National Railway Museum).

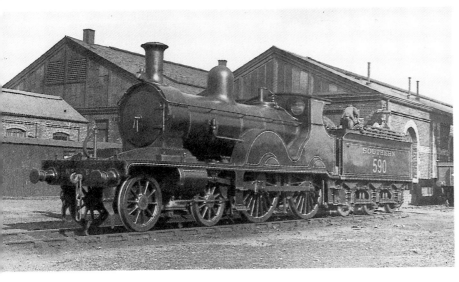

Left *This view at Reading GWR shed in 1925 shows the elegance Adams achieved in his final designs, particularly when rebuilt with a Drummond chimney. 'X2' Class No E590 has just brought in a train from Basingstoke. It is painted in the splendidly-dignified olive green livery the Southern Railway employed from 1923 until the late 1930s* (John Ashman FRPS).

Chapter 11
Maritime matters

The Channel Islands have always played an important role in the fortunes of Weymouth and Southampton. No-one has ever made his fortune from this traffic, yet the rivalry between the two mainland ports has continued for almost 200 years. It is a curious story, as much about the long-standing rivalry between the Great Western and the London and South Western Railways, and of civic pride, as it is of commercial enterprise and maritime venturing. The first packet boat carrying regular mails began between Weymouth and Jersey and Guernsey in February 1794; shortly before this a government sailing cutter had taken up station at Southampton and had commenced regular passage of the 120 miles to the Islands.

Southampton had the advantage over Weymouth in that it was nearer to London and had achieved a rail link some eighteen years earlier. But the sea crossing from Weymouth was shorter and the Dorset port was nearer to Falmouth where the ocean mails docked. The honours were thus about even. In 1841 with through trains running between London and Southampton and Weymouth's rail link in the uncertain future, hearts in the latter port fluttered with the announcement that the Admiralty was looking at the possibility of transferring the packet service away. Although this was a false alarm the stay of execution was only temporary. In 1843 the LSWR took over the Southampton to Channel Islands service, that same year many of the ocean mails were transferred to Southampton from Falmouth, and that was it. On the morning of 26 April 1845 the last mails arrived at Weymouth and on the same evening the first South Western Steam Packet Company boat sailed with the outgoing mails. Weymouth had protested, but in vain. However the citizens of the town were not the only ones who felt that Weymouth still had a role to play and in August 1850 the *South Western*, a paddle steamer with a speed of around 12 knots and normally based at Southampton, owned to all intents and purposes by the LSWR, began a weekly service from Weymouth to Guernsey, Jersey, Granville and St Malo. The South Western had the distinction of establishing the first regular link by a railway steamer with Weymouth and France, but the

enterprise was doomed to failure for the railway had still not got beyond Dorchester and the change to stagecoach for the last section of the journey so discourage prospective passengers that the service folded by the end of the year. The *South Western* returned to Southampton and continued to work from there to the Channel Islands and France until being sold to Japan in 1863.

The long awaited arrival of the railway in Weymouth on 20 January 1857, and in particular of the Great Western, transformed the picture. No-one need be surprised that the LSWR saw little profit in competing with itself but for the Great Western Weymouth offered a golden opportunity to muscle in on the lucrative English Channel traffic. A company called the Weymouth and Channel Islands Steam Packet Ltd was set up in which the GWR had a large number of shares. Two paddle steamers were bought. Admittedly they were not brand new and needed some attention, but they were only three years old and thus well up to standard. They were ready by the late spring and the service was inaugurated on 15 May. However the LSWR had no intention of letting its rival get away unchallenged. It was still operating its Southampton service of course, but it also returned to Weymouth and a month before the GW boats began it stole their thunder, and some of their traffic, with the *Express*. This paddle steamer, dating from 1847 and built on the Thames, sailed for the Channel Islands from Weymouth for the first time on 13 April 1857.

A month and two days later the Great Western service began. Neither company was exactly overwhelmed with the volume of business. The first LSWR service carried seven passengers on its outward voyage and eight on its return whilst the GWR one averaged a rather better twenty. Naturally both Weymouth and the Channel Islands were delighted with what can only be described as a lavish over provision of facilities. Southampton still had the lion's share of the business, to the tune of a ratio of three to one.

Journeying across the Channel was not without its hazards. The *Express* ran on to rocks off Jersey on the morning of 2 September 1859 and had to be

beached. It was unfortunate that there were far more passengers than usual aboard, no less than some 160, most of them bound for Guernsey races. Three panicked and fell overboard but the others were saved, along with three racehorses. Although other boats replaced the *Express* this was only a temporary measure and in December that year the LSWR gave up its Weymouth route. The competition had done neither company any good and had it gone on much longer the GWR backed Steam Packet Company would have probably been forced out of business. The Southampton route was the quicker, 15 hours from Jersey to Waterloo, compared with 16¼ via Weymouth to Paddington, and there was the added disadvantage that if the Weymouth boat missed the train connection, as sometimes happened, then the passengers were stranded until next morning. If the Southampton boat was late then the LSWR inevitably put on a special to get the passengers to London that night.

Nevertheless the Weymouth service, if not exactly prospering, at least survived and business was sufficient to warrant the experiment of a link with France. On 1 August 1878 the first regular service from Weymouth to Cherbourg began. The overall time between Paddington and Paris was some 21 hours. As with the Channel Islands the Weymouth route was in competition with Southampton and was running second. The French showed little enthusiasm for the new venture and although it struggled on into the mid 1880s their withdrawal on 30 June 1885 brought it to an end.

The Channel Islands service was doing little better

and when the steamer *Brighton* struck some rocks approaching Guernsey and sank, fortunately without any loss of life, then the end could not be far away. It came on 29 June 1887. But it was the end only for the Weymouth and Channel Island Steam Packet Company. Despite past experience the GWR was confident that a steamer service between Weymouth and the Channel Islands could be a commercial proposition if only it was properly funded and equipped with up-to-date boats. It set about proving its convictions.

This time the GWR had sole charge of the ships. A provisional service was worked immediately the Steam Packet one ceased, but in August when new, larger ships were available the full, splendid might of the GWR was unveiled. The pier tramway, first built in 1865, had been extended, a new pier constructed and it was possible to leave Paddington at 9.15 pm and be in Guernsey at 7 o'clock next morning; Jersey was reached 2 hours, 20 minutes later. Between 1884 and 1888, during the summer months of May to September the average number of passengers carried each year on LSWR boats to and from Southampton was around 13,000, whilst the GWR supported Weymouth route carried between 5,000 and 6,000 each year. The travelling public's reaction to the GWR improvements was immediately apparent for during the 1889 summer season the Weymouth route increased to 7,776 passengers, whilst the Southampton figures stayed about the same. In August 1889 through trains began to run right along the quayside at Weymouth to the ships' side and in October the overall time between

Guernsey and Paddington was reduced to under twelve hours for the first time ever.

The 1890s was a decade when the GWR reasserted itself as one of the great, perhaps the greatest, of the railway companies of the British Isles. The broad gauge was abolished — the last Weymouth broad gauge train had departed years earlier, in June 1874 — routes were shortened, a generation of revolutionary locomotives began to emerge from Swindon works, and carriages became vastly more comfortable. The first all-corridor train for ordinary service, newly built at Swindon, visited Weymouth in June 1891. In the summer of 1892 the Jersey to Paddington best time was down to 10½ hours, although not even the GWR had control of the weather and this schedule was not always maintained.

The rivalry between the GWR and the LSWR was now at its height. The Southampton and Weymouth night boats were both due in at St Helier at 8 am and the competition to see who would win was reminiscent of the races between London and Scotland over the East and West Coast routes. In such conditions safety wasn't always uppermost in everybody's mind. Disaster struck on 30 March 1899. The *Stella* of the LSWR, on the day service from Southampton and in a hurry to beat the Weymouth boat, had sailed through patchy fog all the way across the Channel. At 4.10 pm she ran at full speed into the Casquet Rocks on Jersey and in eight minutes was gone, along with over a hundred passengers and crew. It was much the greatest loss of life ever suffered on the Channel Islands run. Competition had been so intense that neither the LSWR or the GWR was

Left *0-4-0T on the line linking the Eastern and Western docks, Southampton, 1934. No 3741 was one of a class of ten locomotives built as 2-2-0Ts for rail motor work in 1906. Seven were sold for Government service during World War 1, and the others converted by the LSW to the form seen here for shunting in the docks* (Dr Ian C. Allen).

Below left *A boat train at the Royal Pier, Southampton, c1900. The curious little four-wheeled saddle tank is the* Ritzebuttel *built in Scotland in 1873, sold by the LSW in 1915 and broken up in 1921* (National Railway Museum).

Right *Highlanders returning from the Boer War at Southampton, 1902. The liner in dry dock is the* Carisbrook Castle *of the Union Castle line, built by Fairfields of Glasgow in 1898* (Hampshire Libraries).

making a profit and the *Stella* disaster propelled the companies into a working agreement over which desultory negotiations had been going on for some time. The new century dawned with the LSWR and the GWR each running three times a week on alternate nights in both directions during the winter season, and six times a week from 1 May to 30 September, the LSWR out from Southampton by night, the GWR out from Weymouth by day, both companies returning by day. Receipts were to be pooled on a ratio based on the figures for the years 1897/98, return tickets could be used on either route.

Weymouth could put up a fair fight with Southampton for the Channel Islands traffic but when it came to ocean travel there could only be one winner. The Dorset port had little room for expansion. It consisted of quays on either side of the River Wey and was hemmed in on both sides by houses and increasingly on the east side, as the nineteenth century drew to its end, by boarding houses, hotels and other buildings associated with the holiday business. Indeed there were many in Weymouth who felt that a commercial port in the heart of the resort made fashionable by George IV lowered the tone of the place and were implacably opposed to its existence, let alone expansion.

Southampton had also once had pretentions to resort status but its unique double tides and the possibility of deep water berths with direct access to

the open sea unencumbered by dock gates, yet protected from storms, made its progress towards its eventual pre-eminent position among British passenger ports inevitable. The Channel Islands business was life and death to Weymouth but to Southampton it became increasingly small beer compared to the liner traffic.

From the opening of the first ocean dock in 1843 expansion was almost continuous. Graving docks followed, then the one and only tidal basin, in 1851, just in time to handle the 100,000 men and 20,000 horses which P&O boats took to the Crimea War. As ships grew ever larger so the earliest docks became too small to handle the liners and were given over to railway steamers, whilst new berths were built for the big ships. The still flourishing trade with South Africa was established in the 1870s with the arrival of the Union Steamships Company. In 1891 the Castle Line transferred its South African mail service from Dartmouth to Southampton and nine years later a merger produced the famous Union Castle Line. My Uncle Harry began work in the company's Leadenhall Street City head office in the early years of this century, and to him the name Donald Currie who had founded what was to become the Castle Line in 1862 and had died at the age of 83 in 1909 was one which was heard almost every day in the office until he retired 49 years later in the 1950s. The Boer War resulted in an enormous increase in business, both for Southampton and the Union Castle Line, just as the Crimea had for the P&O nearly fifty years earlier, although once it was over there was a period when no less than fifteen Union-Castle ships were laid up in Southampton Water. Their livery was perhaps the most distinctive of all the lines which regularly called at Southampton, their pale lavender-grey hulls instantly distinguishing them from all others for over 100 years from 1871, until mergers and amalgamations brought about its disappearance around 1980.

The network of railway lines grew within the docks and also extended to the Town Quay and the Royal Pier. The former had been rail connected as early as 1847 by a line which ran along Canute Road on the perimeter of the docks, but trains could not travel direct from LSWR tracks to dock ones for the only connection was by a turntable at Southampton Terminus station. Both the Quay and the Pier served the Isle of Wight steamers and in the 1890s after the Royal Pier had been greatly rebuilt and extended there was an average of five trains a day running right through from the main line to serve the Isle of Wight boats.

However not all was well with the Dock Company. Alternating periods of expansion and stagnation had left it in a frail financial position and it had received considerable support from the LSWR. Events were moving towards a complete take-over by the railway company and on 1 November 1892 the whole of the Southampton Docks became LSWR property.

Chapter 12
Branch lines galore

The fortunes of the railway and the docks at Southampton had been linked for some sixty years. With the absorption of the latter by the former and its becoming part of the family, so to speak, both were about to enter a period of increasing prosperity and to experience much fame as a consequence of playing a part in so many of the great events of the time. But this part of our story belongs to the next century and we have not yet finished with the old. So we will leave Southampton for the moment and return to its rival westwards along the coast. We have seen that this rivalry extended only as far as the Channel Isles, and to a limited extent the Continental traffic for the physical limitations of Weymouth ruled out expansion of the sort possible along Southampton Water.

However across Weymouth Bay there existed harbour facilities which seemed to be ripe for exploitation. The Isle of Portland had been fortified at the beginning of the nineteenth century when attack by Napoleon's navy seemed imminent. Subsequently these fortifications and their naval base had been enlarged several times but there was still room for civilian facilities and from time to time plans to put these in hand had reached a fairly advanced stage. They all came to nothing, chiefly through the hostility of the Admiralty, and also on account of the relative remoteness of Portland. The island did, however, acquire a railway.

Portland in terms of strict geographical accuracy is, like that other Dorset island, Purbeck, not a real island at all, although at times of storms and unusually high tides the sea, even now, can come crashing over Chesil Bank and cut Portland off from Weymouth. Its position, a solid fist of rock jutting far out into the Channel, has over the centuries endowed its inhabitants with many of the characteristics of islanders — independence, hardiness and a wariness of strangers. Today, despite the railway having come and gone, easy road access and the constant clatter of helicopters flying across it, life on Portland still sometimes seems shaped and regulated more by the wild sea and storm torn skies than by the man-made technical innovations of the late twentieth century.

There were rope and hand-worked railways serving the quarries for some time before the Isle of Portland got its first proper railway on 16 October 1865. This started out from a junction with the main line just north of Weymouth Town station and had its own single platform station close by at Melcombe Regis. From there it struck out across the harbour on a lengthy viaduct which, to tell the truth, did nothing to improve the view across the marshes and was something of an eyesore. The new road bridge opened on its site in 1987 is a good deal more handsome. Next it crossed the Abbotsbury Road by way of a level crossing — there was a subway for pedestrians which survived into the 1980s — climbed a high embankment past the football ground, continued through the western suburbs of the town and came out on to Chesil Bank along which it ran to Victoria Square at just about the lowest point on the island next to the naval base. Although the line was nominally independent it was worked from the outset jointly by the GWR and the LSWR. Originally it was provided with broad gauge track, although it is doubtful if much use was ever made of the broad gauge and this was soon taken up.

The branch had ambitions to penetrate the rocky heart of the island and this it eventually did in September 1902 when the 3½ miles on to Easton was blasted out and opened for goods and passenger traffic. For part of its length it incorporated an Admiralty line and clung perilously to the cliff as it wound its way beneath the forbidding gaol and above the water's edge.

It might be argued that Portland was the true terminus of the line from Waterloo for the branch was a southward extension from Weymouth and trains from the London direction could work directly on to it. In reality they almost never did and the

Above right *GWR 0-6-0PT No 3737 climbs through the rocky cutting near Eastham on the Portland branch with a train of SR Bulleid stock, 14 August 1960 (C. L. Caddy collection).*

Right *Clay works near Norden in the Isle of Purbeck (Author's collection).*

Above *Adams '460' Class 4-4-0 No 470 at Swanage with a Wareham and Bournemouth train, c1920 (LPC).*

Below *A Swanage to Wareham train crossing the Studland Road, seen from Corfe Castle, June 1958. Poole Harbour is on the horizon. The locomotive is an 'M7' 0-4-4T, the first two carriages are an ex-LSW push-pull set, regularly employed on the branch, while the Maunsell and Bulleid corridor ones at the rear are through for Waterloo (P. Q. Treloar).*

Below *A Class '50' in Network South East livery and Class '421' 4TC No 8009 at the head of a twelve-coach express about to depart for Bournemouth, Waterloo, 22 November 1986.*

Above *2BIL No 2090, restored to its original green livery, and a Class '411' 4CEP in London and South East livery, Waterloo, 22 November 1986.*

Overleaf *A late autumn sunset at Wareham station, October 1985.*

Above *The restored Venice Simplon Orient Express Pullmans forming the 'Bournemouth Belle', Bournemouth station, August 1986.*

Below *'King Arthur' Class 4-6-0 No 777* Sir Lamiel *about to depart from Marylebone with a Santa Steam Special, 20 December 1986.*

branch tended to be worked as a self-contained affair over which the LSWR and the GWR took turns to provide the motive power and other rolling stock.

Much of the branch's income derived from the stone industry, a characteristic it shared with another Dorset branch, the Swanage one. As on Portland, the Purbeck quarries and the clay pits which lay amongst the heathland were served by their own narrow gauge lines dating back to the early years of the nineteenth century. Swanage, like so many seaside towns, grew greatly in Victorian times, particularly consequent upon the enterprise of its most famous son, John Mowlem, who made his fortune in quarrying and then shipping the stone to London and elsewhere. The firm he founded still exists as the great civil engineering company which bears his name.

The Swanage branch opened on 20 May 1885. Wareham station had to be rebuilt for the original one was too small. Because the inhabitants of Wareham refused to let the branch take the direct route through their town, the Swanage trains had to trundle down the main line in the direction of Weymouth for a mile, pass under the Weymouth and Dorchester road and then out of sight of the town, branch sharply away at Worgret, swing back almost through 90°, cross the water meadows of the Frome, head over the adder-infested heathland until the clay works at Furzbrook were reached, and continue to Corfe Castle. The only intermediate station on the line was situated here in one of the most picturesque settings imaginable under the ruined walls of Dorset's most famous landmark, courtesy of Oliver Cromwell. Then it was on down the valley through the Purbeck Hills to Swanage, 10 miles in all.

As was to be expected Swanage's growth accelerated immediately and the hotel and boarding house business flourished as visitors arrived, not just from stations along the Waterloo line but, by way of the Somerset and Dorset, from Bristol, the Midlands and the North. However this was only in the relatively brief summer season, at other times passenger traffic was mostly local. A daily goods train took out the clay and stone. Through carriages to and from Waterloo began to be worked on to the branch and there were even times when complete trains were run between Waterloo and Swanage. They usually took the Old Road, as the original main line via Wimborne and Ringwood, avoiding Poole and Bournemouth, had by now become known. Trains branched on to it at Hamworthy Junction, whilst those heading for Poole and Bournemouth took the Holes Bay cut-off route, opened on 1 June 1893 across Poole Harbour.

The Swanage branch made travel from the Isle of Purbeck to Poole and Bournemouth much easier, although the route had perforce to be rather indirect. Trains set off from Swanage in a north-westerly direction, turned north-eastwards at Worgret Junction, east at Hamworthy, south at Holes Bay Junction, then finally east at Poole, all this wriggling around being necessary to avoid Poole Harbour. Much the shortest distances were either by paddle steamer across the bay, or by unmade road to the ancient Sandbanks ferry, but only the steamers could compete with the railway for speed.

On most days there are excellent views from Swanage to the Isle of Wight and in summers there was, for many years, a steamer service to Yarmouth. The LSWR took little interest in this traffic, but it did develop a link with the Island some way eastwards along the Hampshire coast.

Lymington is an ancient town and port going back at least as far as Roman times. It was therefore no wonder it felt itself entitled to a railway line. Too remote for a through route, the locals lobbied hard for a branch line and on 12 July 1858 they achieved their ambition when public services began over the 5 miles of single line from Brockenhurst. In actual fact many of the public had had their first ride two months earlier when a special train, ostensibly for the conveyance of such notables as directors and engineers, had arrived at Lymington and caused such excitement that a large proportion of the population had besieged its engine, tender and single carriage, and had proceded up and down the line festooned about the train in a manner more appropriate to a Calcutta tram during the rush-hour than a group of dignified mid-Victorian Hampshire folk!

Steamboats were already operating across the Solent between Lymington and Yarmouth but the railway did not run right up to the quayside, and this situation and the generally unsatisfactory relations between the railway and the ships provoked criticism. Not that Lymington was unique in this respect. Since the first train ran down a quayside with the nominal notion of connecting with an adjacent boat those responsible for this seemingly uncomplicated operation have taken a perverse delight in making it as unpleasant and inconvenient as possible, using a variety of wheezes such as insufficient gangways, unprotected windswept quays and unhelpful or non-existent porters, ticket-collectors and customs officers. A favourite ploy on incoming boats was to wait until most of the passengers had assembled by a gangway and then announce that it would be the one on the deck above or below which would actually be used!

However things did get better at Lymington in 1880 with the incorporation of the Freshwater, Yarmouth and Newport Railway. Although passenger trains didn't start running on it until July 1889 the

Left *A train from Brockenhurst crossing Lymington Harbour, June 1982.*

Right *The preserved 'T9' 4-4-0 No 30120 entering Medstead and Four Marks with a train from Alresford on the Mid-Hants line, March 1985.*

LSWR decided to offer much better facilities in anticipation and built an extension incorporating a viaduct across the harbour to a new station alongside a deep water pier. This opened on 1 May 1884 and four trains a day from Waterloo connected with the boats. A couple of months later the LSWR took over the Solent Steamship Company and its two ships, both paddle steamers, the Lymington-built *Solent* and the Tyneside-built *Mayflower*. Both dated from the 1860s and were to prove long-lived, for the LSWR kept them at work until the early 1900s. The west end of the Isle of Wight has always been less populated with fewer tourist facilities than the east, and consequently the Freshwater, Yarmouth and Newport Railway was run on a shoestring budget. It was worked by the Isle of Wight Central Railway until the pair quarrelled in 1913, after which it had to provide its own, secondhand rolling stock until absorbed by the Southern Railway in 1923. Probably the most interesting locomotive to work the line was LBSCR Terrier, No 40 *Brighton*, built in that town in March 1878. Stroudley shipped her to the Paris Exhibition when new where she was awarded a Gold medal. At the age of 23, with over half a million miles to her credit, she took to sea again, being sold, along with three sisters, to the Isle of Wight Central for £600, becoming their No 11. At 23 she was in the first flush of youth. The Southern Railway named her *Newport*, but the nameplate was removed in 1947 when she was returned to the mainland to work the Hayling Island branch. British Railways eventually withdrew her from service in 1963 but her career was far from over. Yet another seaside resort was to become her home when Butlins bought her and put her on display at Pwllheli. Sold yet again, she came back to the Isle of Wight and was restored to Isle of Wight Central livery in 1975. She is now running on the Isle of Wight Steam Railway.

William Stroudley, the Terrier's designer, like so many of his profession, worked at the Swindon factory of the GWR as a young man. He rose to prominence in Scotland, first as Works Manager of the Edinburgh and Glasgow (later North British) Railway at Cowlairs works and then at the early age of 32 as the Locomotive and Carriage Superintendent of the Highland Railway. At Cowlairs Stroudley formed a lasting friendship with Dugald Drummond, who worked under him both at Inverness and Brighton. In 1875 Drummond got his own superintendantship, back on the North British Railway, and after five years there moved to its great rival the Caledonian. The locomotives he produced were supremely elegant and to many his inside cylinder 4-4-0s and 0-6-0s epitomize the British passenger and goods engine at the heyday of our railway system around the turn of the century. In 1895 Dugald Drummond followed his old chief south to take charge of locomotive affairs on the LSWR, although sadly Stroudley had been dead six years, passing away unexpectedly at the early age of 56 just before Christmas 1889 whilst on a visit to Paris with his express engine *William Blount*.

Drummond's first express engine for the LSWR was a bit of a surprise for whilst superficially resembling the 4-4-0s he had produced in Scotland it was actually a 4-2-2-0, each pair of driving wheels worked independently of the other pair by their own two cylinders. Whilst not as bad as the worst of Francis Webb's divided drive engines being turned out of Crewe at this time, they were fairly useless. Having got them out of his system Drummond went back to the 4-4-0s at which he was unsurpassed. So good were his LSWR engines that all 166 of them were still at work at the end of the Second World War. Some were designed for West Country conditions but many spent most of their careers on the Weymouth line.

The most famous and the most numerous were the 'T9's. There were 66 of them and although they were not especially large, even when new in 1899, their

free running qualities, which were employed to the full on Bournemouth expresses, gained them the nickname 'Greyhounds'.

The final Drummond design of 4-4-0 was the 'D15'. There were only ten, Nos 463 to 472, but they represented the ultimate development of the classic Drummond 4-4-0, 25 years on from its appearance at Cowlairs. Built especially for the Bournemouth line they were superbly powerful looking machines, and their performance on the heavy restaurant car corridor expresses in the twilight of post-Edwardian England immediately before World War 1 equalled their appearance.

Stroudley never went in for 4-4-0s but Drummond's very first engines for the LSWR clearly showed his influence, although they also followed Adams traditions. These were the 'M7' 0-4-4Ts. They were in production virtually the entire seventeen years Drummond was in charge on the LSWR and totalled 105. No class in the history of the company was so numerous. They worked briefly on main line expresses — they were the most powerful 0-4-4Ts in the country — but no front coupled tank engine ever inspired confidence when running at speed and the 'M7', like the Beattie 2-4-0Ts and the Adams 4-4-2Ts before them, found their niche on suburban services. They rapidly became as familiar as part of the southwest London landscape as the leafy avenues of redbrick villas where so many of their regular passengers lived, hauling long rakes of salmon and pink coloured bogie carriages.

The LSWR separated the responsibility of designing locomotives from that of carriages in 1885 so we cannot speak of a typical Drummond coach as we can of his predecessors, Adams and the Beatties. William Panter was the Carriage and Wagon Superintendent from 1885 to 1905 and Surrey Warner (what a perfect name for an LSWR dignitary) from then until the grouping. There was nothing particularly showy about their designs, nothing which

could compete with Swindon's 'Dreadnoughts' or Wolverton's clerestory-roofed, twelve-wheeled diners for example; neither was there anything to be ashamed about even the most ordinary of them and there was no railway, except the Midland, which could make a similar claim, without blushing at its impertinence. It might be argued that Panter ought to have built rather more corridor carriages, although none of the southern companies with their fairly short main lines seemed to think them necessary other than for special occasions. However Warner rapidly repaired this omission, building them in considerable numbers from 1906 onwards.

Throughout the nineteenth century Nine Elms had been the home of the LSWR's locomotive and carriage works and had supplied most of the company's rolling stock, although from time to time outside manufacturers had been called upon, notably Beyer Peacock. Once Nine Elms had been within sight of green fields but by the last two decades of the nineteenth century many of its inhabitants scarcely knew what a cow looked like. Hemmed in by tenements, factories, and mile upon crowded mile of suburbia, there was no room for the expansion which the vastly larger system needing ever more powerful locomotives and more sophisticated carriages demanded. So the directors began to seach for a new site for the carriage works, outside London and close to the centre of operations so there was as little dead mileage as possible. The Great Western had Swindon, the LNWR had Crewe, the Midland had Derby, the Great Northern had Doncaster. Andover or Eastleigh seemed to be the obvious choices for the LSWR and after some deliberation it chose Eastleigh.

Bishopstoke was the name by which Eastleigh was first known when the railway arrived in 1839; in fact the two existed side by side on opposite banks of the River Itchen, but gradually Eastleigh gained the ascendancy. The first railway houses were a small group built by the junction of the Fareham and

Southampton lines in the late 1840s, but when the carriage works were set up here there was naturally a very large expansion, for accommodation had to be found for some 1,500 extra men and their families. The move from Nine Elms took place in 1890 and Eastleigh from then on grew rapidly. Many of the new houses were put up by speculative builders, but the LSWR had one group designed by Ralph Nevill. They were on the model village principle, a forerunner of the new towns of the immediate pre-and post-Second World War period, and their designs were displayed at the 1889 Royal Academy exhibition. They were built of red brick and selentic mortar, whatever that was, tiles and imperial stone windows in such a manner that no exterior woodwork or paint was used, and thus maintenance costs would be reduced.

The houses were grouped around what were described as 'village greens', and each one had an allotment as well as a garden. Downstairs there was a parlour, a kitchen, a scullery and a coal shed off a verandah, and upstairs there were three bedrooms. The cost of each house was kept below £200. All in all the new occupiers could consider themselves tenants of very superior accommodation, even if the washing hanging in the gardens suffered from an excess of coal smuts. Eastleigh had now joined that select band of towns which had either come into existence or grown from very small origins — the latter in the case of Eastleigh — on account of the setting up of a railway works.

Above *A railwayman outside his home in the terrace of railway houses between the depot and the works, Eastleigh, June 1986.*

Below *Eastleigh station, 1900* (Hampshire Libraries).

Chapter 13
The golden years?

The years between 1900 and the outbreak of the First World War are generally regarded as the golden era of Britain's railway companies, when innovations in signalling, operating, motive power, and rolling stock came thick and fast, and travel became ever faster, safer and more luxurious. Like all sweeping generalisations you could find exceptions fairly easily; some of the Brighton line commuters and inhabitants of the remoter parts of Wales, Scotland and East Anglia had a different tale to tell and in the field of labour relations management treatment of labour ranged from benevolent paternalism to downright exploitation with the burgeoning union movement regarded

A view of the Eastern Docks at the time of the grouping, showing part of the extensive rail network. The lines in the centre foreground lead across Canute Road to Northiam. Amongst the liners is the Mauretania *on the far right* (Hampshire Libraries).

almost universally with uncomprehending hostility. Nevertheless on the London and South Western Railway's line from Waterloo to Southampton, Bournemouth and Weymouth the period was certainly one of prosperity and advancement.

The purchase of Southampton Docks by the LSW in 1892 unleashed new funds for expansion and as a consequence more and more shipping lines, both British and foreign, became regular users. The accepted image of Southampton is very much that of a passenger port with freight hardly more than a sideline, but the figures tell a different story. In 1883 400,000 tons was handled whilst by 1903 this had more than doubled to 900,000 tons. It was not to be wondered that the LSW's monopoly of such a rich source of income should be challenged, nor that the challenger should be the old enemy, the Great Western.

In the mid 1870s the LSW had made itself very un-

popular in Southampton. It was considered to be concerned only with profits and to care little for the convenience or interests of the townspeople. Around this time a purely local line was being promoted to link the important Great Western junction station of Didcot with Newbury and Winchester, this to include a connection to Andover and the LSW West of England main line at Whitchurch. But Southampton saw in it a chance to break the LSW stranglehold and sent forth emissaries to persuade the line to seize its opportunity and extend right through to the Channel. So convinced was it by Southampton's eloquence that Didcot, Newbury and Winchester eventually conceived the notion of going the whole hog and aiming for Bournemouth. This wonderfully concentrated the minds of the LSW's directors and they offered to build a 7½ mile long link from Hurstbourne on their West of England main line, a short distance east of Andover, to Fullerton on the Andover to Romsey line. If the Whitchurch connection had been put in this would have got Didcot, Newbury and Winchester trains into Southampton, but over LSW metals. To the LSW this seemed an eminently reasonable solution, saving the upstart the cost of constructing its own line south of Whitchurch.

The GWR was shrewd enough not to invest any money in the Didcot, Newbury and Winchester, but it was extraordinarily generous in its encouragement to go for an independent route to Southampton, and so the LSW's compromise was rejected. It nevertheless went ahead with the Hurstbourne-Fullerton line, chiefly to keep the Didcot line away from Bournemouth so it is said, although studying the railway map of the area it is difficult to see quite how this affected the situation. It certainly brought little benefit to the LSW, although no doubt the half-dozen local inhabitants and their livestock thought it a grand thing. It was singled as early as 1913, closed for passengers in 1931 and finally for goods in 1956, long before Beeching got a chance to throttle it.

So anxious was Southampton to encourage the Didcot, Newbury and Southampton line (as it had become), that it offered it land for a station in the town free of charge. On 10 August 1882 the company was granted powers to extend to Southampton and also to construct a link with the GWR at Aldermaston between Reading and Newbury.

The threat of through trains from Paddington to Southampton (88 miles against 78 miles from Waterloo to Southampton) was now very real and construction began of an embankment at a cost of £100,000 to carry the line to its Southampton terminus. The LSW sued for peace and the Great Western agreed. The latter had never been prepared to put money into the DN&S line, although it had agreed to work it. A treaty was signed in 1884 which meant that Paddington and Waterloo abandoned the DN&S to its own devices.

These were slender. It gave up the connection to the LSW main line at Whitchurch, which was probably a mistake, and pushed on through the chalk downs to Winchester. It entered the city by way of a tunnel and built its terminus at Cheesehill, within a few hundred yards of the cathedral and even closer to King Alfred's statue. But a terminus on a not very

Far left *A carrier's cart outside Winchester station, c1890* (Hampshire Libraries).

Left *Peter Shilton, the Southampton and England goalkeeper, on duty at the Dell, the home of Southampton Football Club and originally the intended terminus of the line from Didcot and Winchester* (Southampton Evening Echo).

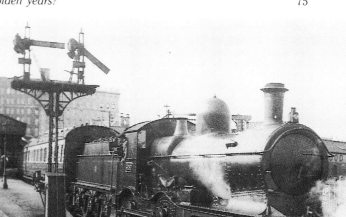

Right *GWR 'Duke' Class 4-4-0 No 3257 leaving Southampton Terminus with a Didcot train, 1936* (C. R. L. Coles).

busy branch line was simply a liability and so the company had to swallow what little pride it had left and accept the LSW's terms for a connection at Shawford, south of Winchester, and thus get its trains into Southampton. There would be no running powers and LSW locomotives would take over all trains at Cheesehill station. The latter quite soon came to be known as Chesil although there are still railwaymen employed on BR who use the old name.

Thus GWR trains finally got to Southampton. And next time you watch Peter Shilton, the Southampton and England goalkeeper, making a daring save, you might care to reflect that had things worked out differently he might be jumping to avoid an HST pulling in from Paddington, for the Dell, the home of Southampton football club, was originally intended as part of the terminus of the Didcot, Newbury and Southampton railway. When this fell through Southampton football club moved in and thus came to celebrate its centenary there in 1985. To this day there is still a Didcot Road and a Newbury Road in the vicinity.

The link between the DN&S and the LSW was made on 1 October 1891. Any threat to South Western interests was minimal, although in a booklet published by John Adams in 1898 entitled *Southampton Docks and its Shipping*, there is an advertisement for the Didcot, Newbury and Southampton line claiming that it is 'the shortest and more direct route... to the Midlands, the North and North Wales.' It goes on somewhat airily to describe 'fast through trains between Southampton, Reading and London' and advises intending passengers that

they 'should ask for tickets via Newbury'. Presumably the odd innocent, sons of the Empire returning to the old country, wide-eyed Southern belles newly disembarked from a White Star liner, and the like, actually took this advice.

It is a fact that the Great Central Railway, following the completion of its London extension in 1899 and its arrival on the scene as one of the great trunk routes, did send through carriages by way of Banbury and Oxford down the DN&S, but the Basingstoke connection always carried the vast proportion of through traffic between the LSW and the GW, and beyond. It was only during the two world wars that the Newbury route really rose above the status of a little used branch line.

Although many shipping lines plied the North Atlantic, the most prestigious were the British-owned Cunard and White Star — which is not to deny the challenge of the Germans in the years immediately before the First World War. Liverpool had traditionally been the principal British transatlantic port but in 1907 the White Star Line, lured by its up-to-date facilities and its closeness to London, transferred its operations to Southampton. It was a blow to Liverpool's pride, and its prosperity, and a tremendous boost for the Hampshire port.

A few years earlier Panter, the LSW Carriage Superintendent, had designed a special train for the transatlantic services already operating out of Southampton, known as the 'American Eagle Express'. The carriages were each 46 ft 6 in long and most ornately furnished and, naturally enough, carried first-class passengers only. Originally without corridor connections, these were fitted in 1900-1901, when second and third class carriages were added to the set. From then on it was not exclusively employed on Southampton duties and thus it was that three of the vehicles came to be destroyed in the never-explained high speed accident at Salisbury on 1 July 1906 when an up Plymouth boat train left the rails on the curve at the east end of the station. After this accident the LSW conceded the Plymouth traffic to the GW and sold that company its clerestory roofed sleeping cars.

The rivalry between Plymouth and Southampton continued and went on until the 1960s when both had to concede victory to the airlines. Although the Cunard and White Star companies never made regular use of the Devon port others, particularly the French, did, and it was possible by disembarking into a Great Western tender in Plymouth Sound and catching an express from Millbay station to reach London several hours ahead of those passengers who had remained on the ship to Southampton. After a brief flirtation with Pullman cars around 1929-30 the GWR built its own magnificent Ocean Saloons for the transatlantic traffic. Five have survived, two being preserved on the Dart Valley Railway and three by the Great Western Society at Didcot.

Just as a disaster brought about the end of the LSW's interest in the Plymouth transatlantic so another, the greatest peacetime shipping disaster there has ever been, proved to be the beginning of the end of the White Star Line.

The Southampton-based *Southern Daily Echo* of 11 April 1912 carried an article about a national coal strike and reported that 'for the present the restricted passenger train service will continue in force but railway officials are hopeful this will be augmented in the course of the next few days'. Boat services to the Channel Islands and France were also reduced and were likely to remain so for at least the next two weeks, but the SS *New York* was the only 'big ocean-going liner' affected by the coal shortage. The previous day, as every day, there was a list of arrivals and departures at the docks, and the latter read as follows. '*Alberta* to Jersey and Honfleur, L&SWR Company. *Titanic* to New York, White Star Line. *Tagus* to West Indies, Eider Hamburg RMSP Co.' And that was it. The only mention in the entire paper of the maiden voyage of the world's largest liner.

The next day in the same column was this brief reference. 'The White Star liner *Titanic* arrived at Cherbourg at seven o'clock this morning.' Elsewhere, tucked away at the bottom of a column and warranting no more than half-a-dozen lines under the heading 'The *Titanic*'s departure — curious incident', was an account of how the SS *New York*, delayed by the coal strike, had been pulled towards the *Titanic*

as she left her berth at No 44 North Dock shortly after noon by the suction created by the White Star liner's propellers and a collision narrowly averted. The *Olympic*, the *Titanic*'s sister ship, which had made her maiden voyage the previous summer, arrived at New York one hour after the *Titanic* left Southampton.

On 13 April the *Southern Daily Echo* reported that the LSW would announce on the following Monday the reinstatement of many services both 'in the London suburban district' and of long distance trains. The shipping news noted '*Titanic*, Southampton for New York, signalled that she was 250 miles west of Brow Head 3.46 am yesterday.'

Then in the issue of 15 April the *Titanic* for the first time hit the headlines. These read '*Titanic* collides with Iceberg in Mid-ocean'. All the passengers were 'reported to be safe'. There is at last a more detailed account of her departure. The crowds, 'if numerically not so large as those assembled to see the sailing of her sister ship the *Olympic*, were no less enthusiastic.' A photograph showed a considerable number watching her pass Netley, but there had been no bands nor special display. It seems curiously low-key, perhaps the coal strike had something to do with the lack of ceremony. Although Southampton was well accustomed to the comings and goings of ocean giants the maiden voyage of the largest of them all, with its glittering passenger list and its 'unsinkable' reputation was surely something out of the ordinary.

Another day passed and by now the full horror was dawning. On 16 April the headlines read 'The Ocean Catastrophe', and 'Consternation in Canute Road'. This dockside thoroughfare housed the headquarters of the recently formed British Seafarers Union, to which all but five per cent of the *Titanic*'s crew belonged. On 17 April the town of Southampton was said to be 'shocked', on the 18th 'A Town of Mourning', although there was still no definitive list of the crew lost, but on 19 April this was published.

'Shortly after half-past seven the list of survivors was posted outside the White Star offices in Canute Road.' Of the 940 crew members, 730 were drowned. Almost all, including Captain Smith who lived in Winn Road, were from Southampton.

Roger Arnold recalled that as a small boy his father, who was a sea captain and a friend of Captain Smith, took himself, his mother and his three brothers and sisters to have lunch on the *Titanic* and to be shown over her by her proud master before she sailed. The family travelled by way of Fareham, in the charge of a 'T9', and came back the same way, hauled by an 'M7'. It is a curiously indirect route between Southampton and London, but again may have been occasioned by the coal strike disrupting

'T9' 4-4-0 No 282 near Earlsfield with an up White Star line boat train from Southampton Docks in the last year of the LSW's existence. The first seven carriages are brand new Ironclad stock (LPC).

services. At Fareham, where they had to change, they encountered Herbert Walker, the newly appointed General Manager of the LSW and its most outstanding figure. The Alton train, which was the last one of the day by which passengers could get to London, was about to depart without making the Southampton connection and Walker threatened both stationmaster and guard with an interview with him in his Waterloo office if they ever tried that trick again. Had Walker been at Southampton to check that the arrangements for the great ship were satisfactory, or perhaps it was on account of the coal strike? We are not told.

Neither do we know the precise formation of the *Titanic* boat trains, but it seems likely that they were hauled by 'T9' 4-4-0s, probably of the 280 series. The second and third class passengers left from platform 12 at Waterloo at 7.30 am (these were the ship designations as there were no third class carriages on the boat trains at this time). The first class passengers, who although all were mercifully unaware of the fact, stood a much better chance of reaching New York, could make more leisurely preparations for their train did not depart until 9.45 am. The 79.2 mile journey took around 1 hour 40 minutes. It cost the first class passengers eleven shillings and the second class ones seven shillings. Some of the 'American Eagle Express' stock may well have been used although it was getting rather elderly and the LSW naturally liked to use its most up-to-date carriages on these prestigious services.

The sense of loss felt in Southampton, and particularly in shipping and railway circles, was acute. The docks, the shipping lines, and the railways were between them far and away the largest employers. The huge crew losses on the coal-fired *Titanic*,

chiefly stokers and stewards, meant that many Southampton families had lost a father, husband or son and various appeal schemes were launched. The *Olympic* docked shortly after midnight on 22 April and the £1,500 raised by her passengers for the dependents of those drowned on her sister ship was added to the relief fund. The *Olympic* had been some 500 miles away when the SOS from the *Titanic* reached her and there had been thoughts of transferring the survivors picked up by the Cunard liner *Carpathia* to her, but when it was realised that in their shocked state they might well imagine that the almost identical *Olympic* was a reincarnation of the ship they had just seen slip beneath the waves this plan was hastily given up. Whilst the *Olympic* was in dock at Southampton frantic efforts went on to improve her safety features, including the installation of sufficient collapsible lifeboats for all the crew and pasengers, before she sailed the following Wednesday.

As a footnote to the tragedy and to bring us back to where we began — the national coal strike — it is perhaps worth recording that at the enquiry into the *Titanic*'s sinking her second officer, Lightoller, when asked if she was perhaps being driven at top speed in order to make a particularly fast crossing, replied that this could not have been so as 'there was a shortage of coal and a number of boilers were shut off'.

As the docks grew so did the town of Southampton (it was not yet a city) and its stations multiplied. Blechynden, the through station immediately west of the tunnel on the main line to Salisbury and Bournemouth, became West End in 1858. By the last decade of the nineteenth century it was no longer adequate for the increased services and much longer trains serving it, so a new station took its place a few hundred yards to the west although the old one lingered on for several decades. Its replacement, which is now the city's principal station, was known as Southampton West. It is an indication of how the

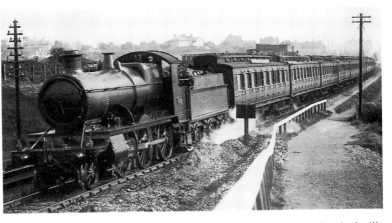

commercial centre of Southampton has moved away from the dock area that this station, which was once on the western, marshy fringes of the town, is now within five minutes walk of the City Hall and the principal shopping street.

Southampton's first station also operated under various titles. It set out simply as Southampton, but this soon got to be confusing, and a trifle presumptious, as others appeared so in 1858 it became Docks, in 1896 Town and Docks, and in 1923 Terminus (for Docks).

By the turn of the century coming down the main line from Eastleigh one encountered stations at Swaythling (the y had been added in 1895), St Denys (which had been Portswood until 1876 and was then renamed owing to the unwary confusing it with Portsmouth), Northiam, which was served only by trains heading for the Town and Docks station, round the bend and through the tunnel to West station, then off again along the shores of the Test through Millbrook and Redbridge, where the Salisbury line continued north-westwards and the Bournemouth line swung south-westwards over the Test with a last view down it to the now distant docks and the wooded shores of the western bank, through Totton and out into the country.

By early 1900s the line had taken on definite leanings towards the literary and artistic. It had all begun at the very beginning when Robert Browning and Elizabeth Barrett eloped from Nine Elms in 1846. Inexplicably neither of them seems to have noted the name or number of the locomotive which played so vital a part in their destinies. George Moore's *Esther Waters* has already been noted, whilst Dickens must have known the LSW in Hampshire well, and quite possibly not cared much for it; he spent unhappy childhood years at Portsmouth. Very likely he got his own back by setting various pieces of villany in its territory for to quote Hamilton Ellis: 'Nine Elms was an out-of-the-way place, in one of those regions of

swamps, pollarded willows and decrepit windmills that Dickens liked to choose for his more macabre scenes'. Trollope's Barchester is an amalgam of the twin cities of Winchester and Salisbury.

Moving towards the twentieth century Bertrand Russell conducted a passionate love affair in Studland, travelling down to Swanage by train and from there by pony and cart to his secluded cottage amongst the pine trees and sand dunes. That archetypal Bohemian and rather second-rate painter Augustus John lived at Fordingbridge on the Salisbury to Bournemouth branch. Whilst on the subject of painters it is worth recalling that both Turner and Constable painted the Dorset coast in the early nineteenth century, but in a period immediately before the railway arrived. That most typical of High Victorian genre painters, W. P. Frith, immortalized Paddington Station in 1863 and although he never attempted the same for Waterloo, his equally famous *Derby Day* would have included many LSW customers. There is a well known painting set at Waterloo around this time, although on a more intimate scale. It is James Collinson's *Return to the Front*, circa 1855 and depicts a soldier setting off for Southampton Docks and the Crimea. Another war, and a picture in the National Railway Museum at York shows a newsgirl, a Highlander, and a crowd of soldiers at what is almost certainly Waterloo in *Return to the Front*, 1917. In the Second World War Waterloo was to inspire some notable pictures, whilst in literary circles we were into the Betjeman era and the world of genteel, seductive, Home Counties sporting heroines from Weybridge and Woking who were equally at home in Southern electric trains and Lagonda sports cars.

Two Dorset literary figures of the early twentieth century who set much of their work several decades earlier, but late enough, nevertheless, to be within the railway era were John Cowper Powys and Thomas Hardy. The latter, if only through the many

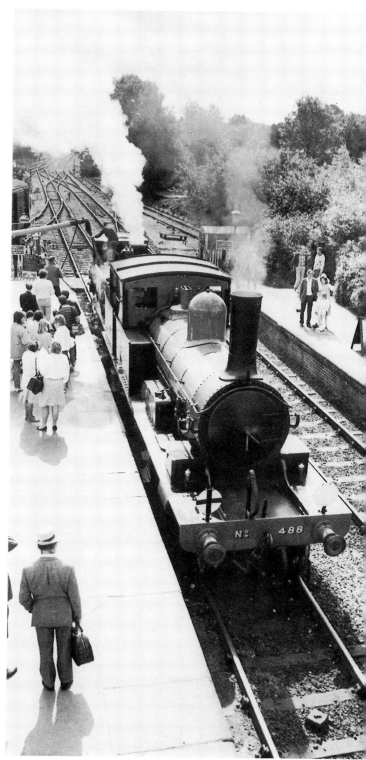

films and television productions of his works, is a household name, but the former, though generally far less well known, is considered by some critics to be of equal stature. There is a fine passage early in his novel *Weymouth Sands*, of the arrival of the Channel Islands boat at Weymouth Quay.

Such is Thomas Hardy's fame, and the demands of the tourist industry, that the final twenty or so miles of the Waterloo to Weymouth line, westwards from Wareham, has become known in certain circles as Hardy Country. The great man himself wished chiefly to be remembered for his poetry, and there are poems of his about railway journeys, but it is his novels which made him famous. Here again railways feature, although not extensively, for the Dorset he writes about, although of the nineteenth century, has an almost medieval air, and the occasional references to rail travel and other innovations brought about by the Industrial Revolution take the reader by surprise.

Some years ago I was on holiday in the Loire Valley and was visiting Richelieu, the town built by the famous Cardinal, and the headquarters of a pre-served steam railway, the Touraine Balade Retro. I was more than a little surprised to come across amongst the former Nord carriages and SNCF steam engines, a little industrial 0-4-0T bearing the initials S&D. I discovered that a few months earlier Ronan Polanski had been filming Thomas Hardy's *Tess of the D'Urbervilles* here. The engine might just have been of British origin, but there was not way I could visualize the typically French station as Egdon Halt somewhere deep in Dorset, which was what it had masqueraded as. However, I have to admit that when I saw the film back in England the episode where Tess drove up in her pony and cart to the wayside halt and loaded the milk churns on to the wagon behind the S&D tank engine could well have been one of the lusher bits of the old Somerset and Dorset somewhere in the Stour Valley. And instead of the charming but quite inappropriate Richelieu some railway buff connected with the film must have persuaded Polanski to send a second unit over to England for the scene involving a passenger train took place at Horsted Keynes, which was a lot nearer the real thing, with an absolutely spot-on Adams 4-4-2T featuring prominently.

Chapter 14

A new century

The London and South Western had long hankered after a terminus in the heart of London. Rising land values, environmental considerations and the sheer impossibility of squeezing such a sizeable piece of property as a railway line into the square mile occupied by the City, which by the last decade of the nineteenth century had become the financial capital of the largest empire the world had seen, had seemed to rule out any chance of an extension beyond Waterloo. London's first tube railway, the City and South London, opened between the City and Southwark and was soon extended southwards to the Elephant and Castle and Stockwell. This brought it virtually within LSW territory and the main line company was not slow to take up the idea of at last achieving its central London terminus by tunnelling under the Thames from Waterloo and approaching from below instead of above. The dream of alighting from a Bournemouth express beside the steps of St. Pauls might be gone for ever, but much more important was the fact that city gents could now travel all the way by LSW from Kingston, Epsom, Wimbledon or wherever direct to their offices.

The City and South London had used locomotives to haul its trains but the LSW was the pioneer in the now universal system of multiple units. These it had to obtain from the USA, from Jackson and Sharp of

Wilmington, the power equipment being supplied by Siemens Brothers. There were five four-car trains and an additional four single power cars for off-peak use and these latter came from Dick Kerr & Co of Preston, well-known suppliers of tramcars. The tunnelling was entrusted to John Mowlem, the civil engineering firm founded by Swanage's favourite son, and one still to be seen at work in the City, as well as many other parts of the world. The Waterloo and City was nominally independent but was wholly backed by the LSW and absorbed by it in 1907. It opened on 8 August 1898 and was a great success from the start, cutting a journey which could take 20 minutes or more to 5 minutes.

The original rolling stock worked until October 1940 when it was replaced by twenty-eight new carriages, twelve motor cars and sixteen trailers, built by English Electric. They bore some resemblance to contemporary London Transport tube stock, although the windows were smaller. Nearly fifty years later they are still at work, bumping and grinding the 1 mile, 46 chains beneath the Thames, the only British Rail owned tube trains in London and the oldest passenger stock in regular use on BR apart from their cousins, the even more antiquated former tube cars which the Isle of Wight has to suffer. Very much for use of City workers, they do not run

Left *A District Line train leaving Kew Gardens station on the Richmond to Acton line built by the LSW, September 1985.*

Right *A three-car electric multiple converted by the Southern Railway from ex-LSW steam stock speeds through Honor Oak Park on a Tadworth and Tattenham Court working* (LPC).

between lunchtime on Saturdays and 06.45 on Mondays.

With electrification schemes proliferating in many cities in Britain and throughout the world, the success of the Waterloo and City line, and competition from the tramways, no-one was surprised when the LSWR decided to begin electrification of its suburban system; for some years it had been very much a question of when rather than whether. The LBSCR was already operating electric trains through Clapham Junction. It used the single-phase, alternating current system at 6,600 volts, collecting from overhead wires and it might have been thought that the LSWR would choose to be compatible with this. but this notion was soon dismissed. The company's electrical engineer had been sent to the USA to study how our American cousins dealt with suburban electrification — it will be recalled that the Waterloo and City carriages were built by the American firm of Jackson and Sharp. Three rail was the norm there. Similar systems were also operating successfully on the Liverpool Overhead and Mersey Railways, on the Lancashire and Yorkshire out of Liverpool and Manchester, on the North Eastern Railway on Tyneside and LNWR plans for Euston and Broad Street were far advanced — and Herbert Walker had moved from the LNWR to become the LSW's General Manager on 1 January 1912. Closest of all was the Metropolitan and District Railway which on 27 August 1905 began operating on the third and fourth rail system over the LSW's own tracks from Putney to Wimbledon.

Construction of the LBSC scheme had been protracted, and acceleration of the trains, one of the chief selling points of electrification, was not very good. Finally much of the equipment was supplied by AEG of Berlin and by 1913, when Herbert Walker announced LSWR electrification, no-one with a modicum of business and political acumen was placing any long term contracts with a country we were likely to be at war with sooner rather than later, although this didn't stop the South Eastern & Chatham Railway ordering ten 'L' Class 4-4-0s from another Berlin firm, Borsig, in Decembr 1913, because no British manufacturer could guarantee a delivery date of August 1914. Did Borsig and the SECR known something the rest of Europe didn't? In fact all the locomotives arrived by mid-June, some two months before the outbreak of the War.

So a direct current, 660 volt, third rail system was chosen and the first trains went into public service between Waterloo and Wimbledon via East Putney in October 1915. Despite the war other routes followed rapidly; the Kingston and Shepperton lines in January 1916, the Hounslow loop two months later and the Hampton Court branch in June of that year. It was the true beginning of the greatest suburban electric railway in the world, which by 1949 covered 1,769 miles, for although the LBSC electrification was first in the field, the Southern Railway converted it to the LSW system between 1925 and 1929.

Modern, but not brand new, units were provided for the inauguration of the LSW scheme, 84 sets in all. The carriages were recently-built non-corridor, wooden-bodied vehicles, formed into three-car sets with a rebuilt motor coach at each end. These latter had highly distinctive, rounded noses, with a head-code panel in the centre and two large windows either side. They set the standard for all subsequent Southern electrical multiple units right down to the 1960s and were some of the most handsome ever produced. Indeed their careers were not all finished even by the 1950s and the underframes and bogies of some were reused with new bodies, which is why it is still possible to see EMUs at work with LSW embossed on their axleboxes. Whether such vener-

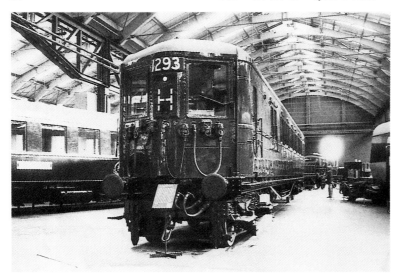

Left *The preserved 1925-built EMU motor coach, based on the original LSW design, in the National Railway Museum, York.*

Below right *'Paddlebox' 4-6-0 No 443 at Waterloo 1912. To the right is the new station, to the left the as-yet-unrebuilt original station* (National Railway Museum).

able equipment ought not by then have been laid to rest is a moot point. Certainly they performed efficiently for some forty years and although none have survived in their original form (and one ventures to suggest that such a significant landmark in the development of rail travel had a prior claim to preservation compared to many of the steam engines which are still with us) a motor coach built by the Southern Railway in 1925 to virtually identical specfications save for flush steel-panelled sides was fortunately saved and is now on display in its original livery — which again was almost identical to that of the LSW electrics — in the National Railway Museum.

One of the first publicity films made by a railway company was put out by the LSW in 1917 and called *The Making of the South Western Electric* and it proved a great hit in the picture palaces of the time. Passengers certainly came thronging back to the railways with the advent of the new trains, to such an extent that additional two-car, non-powered units had to be provided for rush-hour work, enabling trains of eight carriages, that is two, powered, three-car units and a two-car trailer, to be run.

Thus Southampton, Bournemouth and Weymouth expresses dashed past not only LSW electrics at Wimbledon, but also District line ones. One wonders if the crews of the 'Paddleboxes' or the 'D15's in charge of them ever wondered if their charges would one day be superceded by electric traction. The LBSC certainly claimed to be interested in electrifying its Brighton main line, which would inevitably have led to extending electric traction to Eastbourne, Worthing and Portsmouth, the latter would have put it in competition with the LSW, so who knows? But no mention, as far as can be discovered, was ever made

of main line electrification by an LSW official.

With the electrics came a new livery, a darkish olive green. Until then all LSW carriages had for many years had their lower panels painted brown and their upper ones a salmon pink. They must have looked rather attractive, but it was a livery which didn't weather too well and soon looked rather shabby. An LSW train could look a bit piebald with every carriage weathered to a different degree. The fierce arguments which rage over the precise shades of long vanished liveries for which no colour photographic evidence exists — as if that could be of any precise help — are all rather pointless for such learned discussions take into account neither weathering, lighting conditions, nor the fact that at least one third of mankind is to some degree colour blind. So the best we can do in describing LSW carriage livery is to state that it is generally agreed it was dark brown and salmon pink and leave the model-makers, historians and pedants to define what precisely that means. It was not a livery which was to survive to the end of the company's days, for with the advent of the electrics the olive green which they were painted began to be applied to other stock, although not to all carriages straight away.

We have seen that the very first electrics to run over LSW tracks were actually underground trains of the Metropolitan District Railway. There were several locations in west London where this occurred and one where there was a most peculiar situation in that trains of two companies, neither of which was the LSW, operated electric trains over LSW lines. This was between Acton and Richmond. The Metropolitan District electrics began between Whitechapel, Turnham Green and Richmond on 1 August 1905 and the LNW ones over the North London line from

Broad Street via Hampstead Heath and Acton in October 1916, a few months after LSW electrics had begun to work through Richmond. Curiously it was not until the 1980s that Southern Region multiple units finally took up regular operation on the Richmond to Acton line.

The London underground and tube network has always been less extensive south of the river compared to the north, chiefly because electrification came to the southern surface lines first and grew much faster. Generally relations between the main line and the underground companies were fairly amicable, hence the working agreements the LSW entered into, but there were occasions when the LSW felt its interests threatened. Sometimes these were more in the nature of prods by local pressure groups, hoping to nag the LSW into providing a better service, rather than serious proposals — the attempt on Chertsey was one such — but one which did worry the LSW was the Wimbledon and Sutton Railway. This was a 5½ mile long line which received the Royal Assent on 26 July 1910 and was to be worked by the Metropolitan District Railway. However funds were not at this stage forthcoming. Later the City and South London tube proposed an extension from its terminus at Clapham Common to the Wimbledon and Sutton at Morden. The outcome of these proposed excursions into LSW territory takes us into Southern Railway days, and we will look at them later.

By 1900 Waterloo was probably the most inconvenient and out of date terminus in London (although Euston ran it close) and passengers, company servants, managers and directors were in total agreement that something fairly drastic had to be done. Done it was, but it was a fair time coming; it was never the LSW's habit to rush into anything.

Like Churchward on the Great Western the LSW had considerable respect for the American way of doing things and J. W. Jacomb-Wood, the Chief Engineer between 1901 and 1914, was sent to the USA to study some of the great termini, just as A. W. Szlumper was to go a few years later to look at their suburban electrification schemes. Jacomb-Wood came back with a plan for a brand new station of 23 platforms, a terminus which would surpass all others in the country for convenience of handling both trains and passengers. Whether it would rival the architectural glories of St Pancras, Paddington and Kings Cross was another matter. The responsibility for designing great railway stations has always been divided between engineers and architects. So it was with the new Waterloo. It is largely Jacomb-Wood's station, and though J. R. Scott is credited with being the architect one suspects that his involvement was only at a fairly late stage.

More space was needed for the new station and All Saints' church had to go, along with its school, which combined with the neighbouring St John's. The foundations on the south side were ready by 1905 and at last the general public began to be aware that the long promised wonderful new station was indeed beginning to materialize. But it was a slow business and it was not until 1910 that the first five new plat-

forms came into service.

On New Year's day 1912 Herbert Walker became General Manager of the LSW. He soon established himself in the words of C. F. Klapper as the 'outstanding General Manager of the pre-nationalization railway set-up' and one of his first acts was to speed up the rebuilding of Waterloo. It was decided that the total number of platforms would be reduced to 21 (still the greatest of any London termini) and that the Windsor line section could be retained, it was not more than thirty years old and in sound condition, and these are the present platforms 16 to 21. By 1914 eleven of the new platforms were in use with their fine new cantilevered roofs. The war naturally slowed things down again but at last on 22 March 1922 the official opening ceremony was conducted by Queen Mary. King George V should have been with her but was suffering from a chill, however the Queen brought him to have a look later that year and made a point of showing the various details of J. R. Scott's great Victory Arch. Many millions have followed their majesties' example down the years, gazing at Bellona, the Goddess of War with the inscription 1914 on the left of the arch, and Peace, above 1918, on the right, whilst inside is inscribed the hideously long list of 'Company Servants' who died between those dates.

Waterloo is not normally reckoned as the finest of London's great railway stations, certainly not in the Paddington and St Pancras league. Pevsner, for example, dismisses it as 'sadly timid, no arches, no wide spaces'. With all due respect to the great man this strikes the author as pure nonsense. One wonders in just which direction Pevsner was looking when he wrote this, for Waterloo has the widest spaces of any London terminus, the concourse being a perfect example of how such features should be planned with room for queues, for other passengers to get round them, for yet more to stand and stare at the arrival and departure indicators, for bookstalls, for kiosks, for the staff to go about their work, everything being performed under bright, even lighting both day and night. O. S. Nock, whose experience of all aspects of railways world-wide is pretty well unrivalled, calls Waterloo 'one of the really great stations of the world', whilst John Betjeman whose love both for railways and architecture was always discerning admits that although Waterloo 'may be temporarily unfashionable' it is 'practical and airy'. In my view Waterloo is a station which works supremely well and gradually impresses its architectural qualities upon the traveller in an unspectacular but nevertheless lasting manner.

Chapter 15
The end of the LSW

The First World War was, of course, a watershed in the story of the Waterloo to Weymouth line as it was for almost every corner of the British Isles. By a fortunate chance a little guide book which provides a cameo of the line through the New Forest to Weymouth and Portland in the last spring of peacetime has survived. Philip F. Groves's *Railway and Travel Monthly* somewhat puzzlingly didn't publish the facts and figures for May 1914 until the middle of 1916 but no doubt wartime restrictions had delayed its appearance.

Lyndhurst Road was served by fourteen down and thirteen up trains, Beaulieu Road by eleven each way, and Brockenhurst, the junction for the Lymington and the Isle of Wight, by fourteen up and thirteen down London trains and eleven up and ten down locals. On the western fringe of the forest New Milton served Barton-on-Sea and Milton-on-Sea, 'villages' it was noted, but increasing in popularity as resorts.

Christchurch goods depot was 200 yards up the Ringwood branch — it still is, the building that is, although the branch is long gone. Apart from Hurn the only station was the private one at Avon Lodge.

There were five trains each weekday, plus a rail-motor, on the branch.

The ancient town of Christchurch could consider itself highly honoured, for the 2 pm out of Waterloo ran the 104½ miles non-stop in 1 hour, 58 minutes, and was very nearly the fastest run of over 100 miles on the LSW system. The actual holder of the title was the 4.10 pm from Waterloo which took exactly 2 hours to reach Bournemouth. Pokesdown consisted of an 'island platform in a cutting', whilst Boscombe, the last station before Bournemouth Central, was very well served by 33 trains each way daily, only the fastest expresses and one or two 'freaks', whatever they were, failing to call. Today Pokesdown in its cutting still does quite good business, but the once highly favoured Boscombe has vanished.

At Bournemouth Central Grove informs us that 'the through lines are largely used as sidings, though goods trains pass over them when they are unoccu-

Brighton Atlantic No 32422 North Foreland *crosses a heathland section of the New Forest near Sway with the Brighton to Bournemouth train in the summer of 1956 (Dr Ian C. Allen).*

Left '*A12*' '*Jubilee*' *Class 0-4-2 No 537 passing a typical LSW signal box at New Milton with an up goods in 1911* (A. L. P. Reavil, NRM).

Right *A GWR steam railmotor at Upwey Wishing Well Halt, 1912* (Lens of Sutton).

pied'. The method of dealing with up passenger trains was that the Bournemouth West section would arrive first and park itself at the main platform. Its engine would uncouple and proceed eastwards. The second section, from Poole and Weymouth, would then appear at a trot along the through line, come to a halt, and then its engine, either a 'Jubilee' 0-4-2 or a small Adams or Drummond 4-4-0, would reverse it on to the first portion. Being only a supporting player the Weymouth engine would then bow out and leave the stage to the star, the locomotive which had brought in the Bournemouth West section. This would be either one of Drummond's impressive looking but not terribly efficient 'T14' 4-6-0s of 1911, or, most likely, a 'D15'. These latter appeared in 1912 and were the biggest and best of all Drummond's many and excellent 4-4-0s. Either class was expected to cope with the crack trains of the day which covered the 108 miles in 2 hours non-stop. It wasn't so much the speed which proved taxing as the necessity to make the run on one tenderful of water, for the LSW never laid down troughs and even with the massive 4,500 gallon 'watercart' tenders, distinctive vehicles with the unusual arrangement of inside bearings on all their eight wheels, it required skilful driving to get the eight-coach trains, of just over 200 tons tare, to their destination without running dry.

That higher speeds were possible was demonstrated by a trial run done in 110 minutes, but such excesses were considered too risky for everyday schedules. Connoisseurs wishing to study a real live watercart tender are referred to the Watercress Line where the preserved 'T9' is attached to one, No 295, which began its career behind sister engine No 728. Bournemouth Central was 'now a closed station' with 'penny-in-the-slot' platform ticket machines, which

implies that it had until recently been open, as it became once again in 1985. There was a curious 0-2-2T which came out of retirement with one or two six-wheel carriages when the scheduled railmotor was out of action. These were just about the the only non-bogie carriages in the Bournemouth area, other than some on the Somerset and Dorset Joint line. On the north side on the station, at the Weymouth end, was the engine shed, home of around forty locomotives.

Beyond the Central station was Meyrick Park, a halt which at this time did a brisk business whenever flying meetings or other sporting activities were being held in the park. Further on the line crossed the Hampshire/Dorset border just before the gasworks junction and the handsome brick viaduct which took Bournemouth West trains to their destination. The third side of the Branksome triangle brought them out again; within it was the Somerset and Dorset engine shed. There had been plans to transfer the LSW's Bournemouth one to this site and approval had been given in 1908 but it was a move which never took place.

Bournemouth West possessed six platform faces and a number of carriage sidings. An interesting, not to say hazardous-sounding technique had been perfected for dealing with empty stock — the locomotive reversed its train out of the station, uncoupled and hastened out of its way whilst it rolled in a dignified manner down the slope back into the station. It seemed to work well enough for there are no accounts of runaways bursting through the buffer stops and fulfilling the company's long held ambition of reaching the town centre. The slower trains from the Central station to points west went via the West station, faster ones gave it a miss.

It was downhill all the way through Branksome and Parkstone stations, a mile long private siding at the latter led to a pottery which possessed its own locomotive, and so across the causeway to Poole. At this time 0-4-0T No 92 was the Poole Quay shunter. Groves remarks that the paddle steamers between Bournemouth, Poole and Swanage took 'much less time than the trains', and having just watched the *Waverley* purposefully heading across Swanage Bay and round Old Harry I can well believe it.

Wareham, the junction for Swanage, for some reason gets no mention, but we are told that the rather less important stations of Wool and Moreton each had eight down and seven up trains on weekdays. The LSW station at Dorchester was served by twelve trains in each direction, although its curious layout meant that there were many more locomotive movements than this. Not the least of its complications was the approach to the engine shed which was off the down main line and took locomotives directly inside, and meant that this road could not be used for storage. Its allocation was chiefly 'T9' 4-4-0s and 'O2' 0-4-4Ts which worked passenger trains to Bournemouth and Weymouth, goods and passenger ones over the old road via Wimborne, and were also employed as bankers on the steep approaches to Bincombe tunnel.

The stations — well halts actually — either side of Bincombe, Monkton and Came Golf Links to the north and Upwey Wishing Well to the south, were ignored by LSW trains, GW railmotors had a monopoly of their business. Further down the bank below Upwey Wishing Well Halt was Upwey station, which had previously been known as Broadwey. Considering that it was equidistant from each village, and nowadays is named after both, one is at a loss

to account for the renaming and Groves does not enlighten us.

Upwey was the junction for a six mile long GW branch line which had opened in November 1885 and served the picturesque villages of Portesham and Abbotsbury. It had been built by a local company, chiefly in the hope of exploiting iron ore and stone, but in the event had to rely on passengers. These, though keen, were not numerous and the GW had to bail out the company in 1896. Abbotsbury, with the extensive ruins of its ancient monastery and its swannery was, and is, something of a tourist attraction. It is equidistant between Weymouth and Bridport and whilst rail links to the former were good, to the latter they were not. The distance by road along the clifftops with magnificent views across Chesil Beach was seven miles, whilst by rail it was 27 and involved two changes, at Upwey Junction and Maiden Newton.

The Bridport branch had opened as a broad gauge line, worked, but not owned, by the Great Western Railway, in November 1857. It ran from a junction with the Weymouth to Yeovil line at Maiden Newton for nine and a quarter miles through Toller (for Toller Percorum) and Powerstock — what names! — and was extended down to Bridport Harbour and West Bay station in March 1884. Neither the harbour nor the beach, such as it was, provided much business. The coastal scenery all around Bridport is very fine but not the sort to attract the day tripper, and although the GWR did run excursions to West Bay by no stretch of the imagintion could it really by called a resort.

However Bridport itself was a busy little town and provided steady business for the railway. Mrs E. J. Broadhurst on a visit from Australia in 1980, fifty

Above *The viaduct carrying the Port-land branch over Weymouth harbour, 1912. The swans remain today, but the railway bridge has been replaced by a new one for the Weymouth ring road* (British Railways).

Below *Drummond 'L11' Class 4-4-0 No 412 passing Basingstoke with a down military special made up of former Great Eastern Railway corridor stock, c1930* (Dr Ian C. Allen).

Below right *'B4' Class 0-4-0T No 91 crossing Canute Road with a train of cattle trucks from the Docks, Southampton 1910* (Hampshire Libraries).

years after the last passenger train had run to West Bay, wrote these recollections of her birthplace:

'You'd never know there was once a railway there,
Memories crowd.
Excitement.
The train puffing into the small country station.
A warm black body barking at the carriage door.
A little girl calling "Jackie, Jackie".
As she clutched her Grandma's dog.

'Happy to be returning once again to her ancestral hometown,
After many, many years had passed her by
She found there was no railway,
But an ugly road with whizzing cars flashing by,
Not only taking away a people's railroad
But destroying carefree environment

'Where is Happy Island where we picnicked?
Where is the clear stream full of tiddlers?
Where we paddled on our way home from school?
No longer there.
Where once a group of happy, laughing youngsters,
Loaded with towels, buckets and spades
Talked to a friendly train-driver,
Watched, with glee as the fireman stoked the glowing coals,
And then were carried, gleefully to the sea,
A confusing roundabout draws the snarling traffic seawards'.

Groves describes Melcombe Regis on the Portland branch and beside Weymouth Town stations as 'recently built' (it was first used on 29 May 1909). No trains ran regularly off the branch to reverse into the Town station at this time. The buildings all along the branch were of GW design but the GW and the LSW each worked the line for a five year period. The final section from Portland to Easton was three miles by rail and 1⅜ miles direct. The ruling gradient was 1 in 44 practically all the way and Groves was certainly not exaggerating when he described this very last section of line along the cliff side as 'spectacular'. There were four passenger trains in each direction.

The war meant an enormous increase in military traffic, possibly more than on any line on the country, for not only was there the vast military area in south-west Surrey and north-east Hampshire around Farnborough and Aldershot, but there were other bases near Wool, at Blandford and up towards Salisbury Plain, whilst the ports of Weymouth, Poole and above all Southampton were crucial in supplying the military machine which was devouring so many men and materials in Flanders.

The War Office gave the Railway Executive — which had taken over the operation of the railways — sixty hours from midnight on 4/5 August 1914 to get sufficient locomotives and trains ready to embark the British Expeditionary Force at Southampton to go to the aid of Belgium. The task was achieved within 48 hours and at 7 o'clock on the evening Sunday 9 August, the first troops began to go aboard the ships. By 31 August it was over; 130,176 soldiers, 38,805 horses, 277 motors, 1,820 motor-cycles, 344 heavy guns, 1,574 other limbered vehicles and 6,406 tons of stores arrived in 711 trains. The busiest day was Saturday 22 August when 73 trains pulled into Southampton.

Left *'Paddlebox' 4-6-0 No 446 passing Surbiton with a down express in 1910* (Lens of Sutton).

Right *One of the first Bedford coaches climbs the steep hill out of Fortuneswell on the Isle of Portland on the annual Chesil Run for preserved buses and coaches, organized for many years by the Dorset Transport Circle.*

Before the last troops had embarked the return traffic of wounded, which was to number well over one million before the carnage was over, had got under way, the GWR's SS *St Andrew* arriving with the first wounded from the retreat from Mons on 28 August.

Once the terrible stalemate of the trenches had been established a vast organization came into being to cope with the casualties. Eight ambulance trains were assembled, one each from the London and North Western, Great Western, Midland, Great Central, Great Eastern and Lancashire and Yorkshire companies and two from the London and South Western. A standard ten coach train had six wards, a pharmacy car and kitchen and staff quarters and was manned by twelve Royal Army Medical Corps personnel, two cooks and two nursing sisters. There was room for twenty patients in each ward, or thirty if the lower cots had sitting patients. A headquarters was set up at Southampton Docks station and the movement of each ambulance train was charted there. 1916 was the bloodiest year of all and after the Battle of the Somme at least 155 ambulance trains left Southampton in the seven days ending 9 July, carrying 30,006 casualties. The heaviest day of all was 7 July when 6,174 wounded passed through. They went to destinations all over the country, from Netley on Southampton Water to Scotland. Throughout the war 7,822 ambulance trains left Southampton carrying 1,234,248 wounded.

Southampton was the principal supply port for the British forces in France and locomotives, carriages and wagons from practically every railway company in England, Scotland and Wales appeared on military specials at the docks at sometime or other. Some British rolling stock went abroad, carried by three Great Eastern train ferries which normally worked out of Harwich, or in a strange looking contraption,

'Train Ferry 4' which had a sort of double deck arrangement and had been built by Cammel Lairds of Birkenhead in 1913 for work on the St Lawrence. It never went back to Canada, being converted to a tanker by Shell after the war and was broken up in 1927. Fifty Adams 0-6-0s and 0-4-2s were sent to work in various theatres of the war, including France and Egypt, my father recalled seeing an '0395' being unloaded at Port Said. He was also involved in a mutiny which ended at Southampton Docks in 1919.

He had volunteered at the outbreak of the war and as qualified mechanic and driver in an army which still depended greatly on horses and mules but was to rapidly find them outmoded, his skills were in some demand. He served all over North Africa and the Middle East and when the war came to an end he was stationed near Cairo. But demobilization seemed no nearer for there was unrest in the city and British troops were sent on patrol to keep the peace. Every so often one would get shot at and sometimes killed. Having survived the war the men made it clear to their officers that they had no desire to die in a cause for which they felt no commitment or responsibility. The junior officers were sympathetic but the senior ones less so. Therefore one dusk when patrols were due to set off they refused to go. No soldier could be found who would obey the order and despite various threats they made it clear that they would perform no more duties until a boat was sent to take them back to England. This eventually was done and when they got to Southampton they were given a short lecture on the dockside by a General who told them they were to say nothing of what had happened and were demobbed on the spot. I went to several reunions of my father's old company and never heard mention of the incident and it was only when he was in his eighties that he told me, so it must have been a well kept secret.

Several LSW ships were lost during the war. The *Normandy* was torpedoed on her regular run to Cherbourg on 25 January 1918, the *South Western* met a similar fate on her way from Southampton to St Malo two months later, the *Sarnia* was torpedoed on war service in the Mediterranean right at the end of the war on 12 September 1918, the *Duchess of Richmond*, a Portsmouth to Ryde ferry, was sunk by a wartime mine in the Mediterranean on 28 June 1919, and the cargo boat *Guernsey* was wrecked on rocks off Cape La Hogue on 9 January 1915 because war conditions prevented the usual warning light showing. Of the 24,270 men who were employed by the LSW in 1914 6,552 joined up and 585 did not come back.

With the end of the war the railways began to move back to peacetime conditions. But the world had changed in many ways and for the railways the monopoly which they had enjoyed up to 1914 was gone for good. The war had given a tremendous boost to the motor vehicle and with many ex-soldiers hard put to find a job and large numbers of war surplus lorries available, one man haulage businesses sprang up everywhere. Some converted their lorries to primitive buses and although many went broke almost instantly others survived and prospered. The Hants & Dorset bus company was formed on 27 July 1920 and rapidly developed an intricate network of services in the Southampton, Bournemouth and Poole areas, and the famous Royal Blue company owned by the Elliot Brothers bought fourteen army lorries from a military depot in Le Havre in 1921, shipped them back to England and had them rebodied by the well known firm of Dodsons as dual purpose charabancs and buses with convertible canvas roofs.

Inflation has soared during the war and there was much agitation over wages and conditions culminating in a railway strike in 1919. Royal Blue had built up their fleet to 25 and during the strike they used the best of these vehicles on an experimental Bournemouth to London service. So successful was it that a regular service was begun in 1920 and a year later this became daily. Pneumatic tyres came in in 1922 and with virtually no controls there was a mad free for all until 1930. Although far stricter safety standards were (and still are) imposed on the railways than on road operators, and although the motor coaches could not match the trains for speed they did open a whole new market, just as today the double deck Rapides have their part to play although they still fall far behind the railways in comfort, speed, and safety.

The LSW was a pioneer itself in the operation of buses, putting its first vehicles to work in Devon and between Lyndhurst and Lyndhurst Road station in

1904. They were unreliable and did not last long, but some vehicles bought from the famous Basingstoke firm of Thornycroft were better, although one of the earliest of these is remembered chiefly for a sad accident on the Totton to Fawley route on 12 May 1908 when the conductor fell from his platform and was killed. In 1912 the LSW operated a joint service with the Great Western in Weymouth and this survived right through World War 1.

Towards the end of the 1920s some order began to grow out of the free for all which had persisted since 1918 and in 1929 the Southern Railway obtained a financial interest in the largest bus and coach companies working within its territory. These included Hants and Dorset and Royal Blue. Two new companies, whose names survive today, were set up in 1929. These were the Western National, a joint SR/NOTC concern. The very last wholly railway owned buses were those in Weymouth which became part of the Southern National's empire on 1 January 1934.

Although the railway companies original interest in buses was as feeders for railway services they gradually became aware, indeed rapidly in 1918-19, that they offered stiff competition, particularly to the less well patronized branch lines, and inevitably there would be closures and contractions.

Other things had changed since 1914. It was seen that central control of the railways had much to recommend it in terms of efficiency and co-operation. Herbert Walker, who had been in charge of the executive running the railways between 1914 and 1919, made no secret of his opinion that nationalization or amalgamation was inevitable. Many agreed with him and thus on the last day of 1922 the LSW went out of existence and on New Year's Day 1923 the Waterloo to Weymouth line found itself part of the Southern Railway.

Chapter 16

The Southern Railway

The LSWR handed over to the Southern Railway an efficient and up-to-date locomotive stud and an equally modern carriage fleet, and both were to form the basis of Southern Railway practice. The LSWR's system of suburban electrification would spread to the former LBSCR and SECR systems, and with Sir Herbert Walker (knighted for his war service) as general manager there could be no doubt that the LSWR was going to be the dominating influence. But it would be a benign one. Few from the LBSCR or the SECR felt their noses particularly put out of joint and there was not the rivalry and in-fighting which so beset the LMS and to a lesser extent the LNER.

The last Chief Mechanical Engineer of the LSWR was Robert Urie, who had been works manager under Drummond. He had taken over in 1912 when Drummond had suffered a foot infection which turned to gangrene and resulted in his death from the shock of amputation. Three years earlier he had presided over the move of the locomotive works from Nine Elms to Eastleigh. The carriage works had moved there in 1890 and when the widening of the approach lines to Waterloo necessitated the demolition of part of the locomotive works it made sense to move the whole show out to Eastleigh and start afresh, leaving Nine Elms to serve as the company's principal running shed.

The new works opened in 1909 and Drummond declared; 'This transfer has been accomplished without an employee of the department being one hour out of work or the output of work interfered with'. Not one hour out of work? It was an extraordinary claim, but then Dugald Drummond was not the sort of man even the chairman of the board would pick an argument with. Drummond went on: 'I have no hesitation in saying that the company possesses the most complete and up-to-date works owned by any railway company'. Houses were built by the company for the new influx of workers, between the works and the running depot, known locally as Spike Island. The town of Eastleigh grew, and during the First World War many of the inhabitants, both those employed in the works and elsewhere, were engaged in work of military importance in one form or another.

Robert Urie, like his predecessor, was a Scot and had worked with Drummond for many years, following him from the Caledonian Railway where he had been chief draughtsman. He had time to bring out just ten locomotives before the war intervened and the works had to concentrate on military matters. These locomotives, Class 'H15', were of high distinction, or perhaps more accurately high promise, for they were the precursors of a whole family of mixed traffic, goods and express passenger 4-6-0s which would serve the Southern main lines until the end of steam.

Unlike Drummond's complicated and unsuccessful four cylinder 4-6-0s, Urie's engines of the same wheel arrangement had but two cylinders, with outside Walschaerts' valve gear. They were massive looking, with high running plates and their working parts easily accessible, very much of the twentieth century. Intended for mixed traffic work, they spent most of the war in charge of expresses and the original one, No 486, ran for seven years before being called in for general overhaul, a remarkable achievement and one which, under war conditions, was extremely valuable. They were not much seen on the Bournemouth line in their early years, although they worked military traffic to and from Southampton Docks.

With the end of the war Urie was able to bring out his long awaited express passenger engines, the 'N15' two-cylinder design with 6 ft 7 in driving wheels. Ten were built between the latter part of 1918 and November 1919 and some were immediately put to work on the Bournemouth line. Finally, at least in the 4-6-0 line, came twenty almost identical looking locomotives but with the smallest diameter coupled wheels of the three classes, 5 ft 7 in. These were the 'S15's and were intended for goods work. They certainly made a speciality of the heavy freight trains to and from Southampton Docks, but like so many LSWR engines down the years which were officially classified as goods, they actually performed much passenger service.

Urie designed two classes of tank locomotives, massive engines and clearly related to his 4-6-0s. They were built in conjunction with a bold scheme the LSWR initiated immediately after World War 1 to

Above *The LSW works at Eastleigh, c1912* (Hampshire Libraries).

Right *The first Urie design of 4-6-0 was the 'H15'. No 331 seen here entering Basingstoke in 1930 with a Bournemouth line local train was a 1924 rebuild of a Drummond '330' Class engine. The reconstruction was pretty drastic, from four to two cylinders, but the Drummond boiler was retained. No 331 had not yet been fitted with smoke deflectors* (Dr Ian C. Allen).

Right *The first 'S15' Class 4-6-0, No 497 of 1920, passing Battledown with a Nine Elms to Southampton Docks goods in 1936. No 497 has its original, ugly stove pipe chimney, although this has by now lost its capuchon, and it has acquired smoke deflectors, as did all Southern Railway 4-6-0s. Beginning its career at Nine Elms, No 497 was working from Feltham shed by the time this picture was taken and it spent the rest of its career there, except for a period during World War 2 when it was loaned to the GWR. It was withdrawn in July 1963 and broken up the following year* (Dr Ian C. Allen).

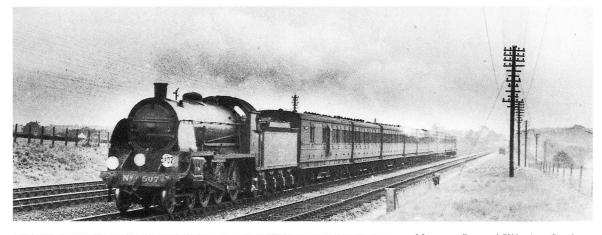

Above *Pure LSW in Southern Railway days. An 'S15' 4-6-0 No 507, with stove pipe chimney, approaching Basingstoke with a down stopping train composed of nine non-corridor carriages (Dr Ian C. Allen).*

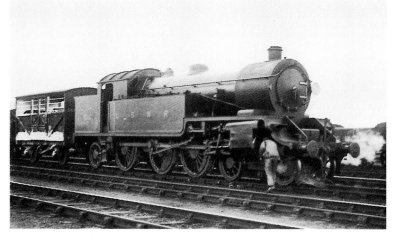

Left *Brand new Urie 'H16' 4-6-2T No 516 at Feltham in 1921 (LPC).*

Left *A member of the last and most powerful class of LSW 4-4-0, 'D15' No 463, was specially built for the Bournemouth expresses. She is seen here in Southern Railway livery at Waterloo with the old A signalbox in the background (P. Ransome Wallis, NRM).*

rationalize the handling of goods traffic between the northern lines, Southampton Docks, and the rest of the LSWR system. This was at Feltham, some 14½ miles from Waterloo on the Reading line. The yard was controlled by two all-electric signal boxes and had eight up and six down reception sidings, sixteen up and seventeen down sorting lines, plus eight flat sidings for down trains to be shunted into station order. The reception and sorting lines were approached over humps and hump shunting began on 1 May 1921. The first locomotives which carried out the hump shunting were a most interesting and unique collection of a type which had never before been regularly employed on any of the southern lines and never would be again, although it was common elsewhere. This was the 2-8-0.

With the inefficient overproduction so typical of wartime conditions Robinson 2-8-0s ordered by the Railway Operating Division of the British Army went on being turned out for months after it was obvious that no more were needed. They were taken to and brought back from France by way of Richborough, Kent and many were dumped on the LSWR at Winchester and Brockenhurst after the war. The LSWR decided to hire seventeen of them, and a number were put to work shunting the new yard at Feltham. Others were employed on main line freights, but tender engines have never made good shunters and slow-moving, if powerful, purely goods engines have never been able to find full employment in the south of England, and so after a few months the 2-8-0s were returned to the Government.

At Feltham they were replaced by four purpose-built Urie tank engines. These were the 'G16' 4-8-0Ts and they spent practically all their careers at Feltham shed on these duties. Feltham took over from Strawberry Hill depot although ironically many of the original buildings at Strawberry Hill remain, for after losing its steam allocation in 1924 it became an electrical multiple unit depot which it still is, whilst its successor, Feltham, has vanished. I always feel that with such a name Strawberry Hill ought to be a bit special, a touch of rural lushness amongst suburbia — in the manner of Primrose Hill beneath which trains to and from Euston pass — but I fear it is not.

Very close relations to the 'G16's were the five 'H16' 4-6-2Ts which came out of Eastleigh at the same time. These were designed to haul transfer freights from Feltham to other yards in London and were thus regularly seen on foreign metals at Willesden Junction and elsewhere in north and west London. For some curious reason they were given full lined-out passenger livery, unlike the 4-8-0Ts, although the only passenger work they ever performed was Ascot race specials and occasionally,

later in their careers, empty stock workings between Waterloo and Clapham Junction.

The railways made a much quicker recovery from the strains and deprivations of the First World War than they did after the Second, and with the introduction of the 1921 summer timetable the LSWR was able to restore a Waterloo to Bournemouth service which was in some respects an advance on 1914 standards. Regular interval trains departed every hour from 7.30 am, and the remarkable thing is that they still do. The 11.30 am, 12.30 pm, 4.30 pm and 6.30 pm included five car pantry sets for teas and light refreshments — the LSWR and the SR were very keen on pantries — whilst tables could be erected in the compartments of the 2.30 pm and the 3.30 pm for snacks. The last non-corridor carriages disappeared from regular Bournemouth line expresses — LBSCR and SECR patrons wouldn't have believed such avant garde situations could exist — and the trains were painted in the new green livery introduced with the electrics. Four of the five-coach sets were built to a design which was to become Southern Railway standard. These were the 'Ironclads', so called because they were steel clad with none of the detailed panelling familiar on all-wooden stock and of far plainer and more modern aspect than any previous LSWR carriages. Again, remarkably, some still survive at Bournemouth, in departmental service in the carriage sidings on the approach to what used to be the West station.

At grouping Bournemouth expresses were still largely in the charge of the 'D15', 'L12' and 'T9' 4-4-0s, all rebuilt and superheated by Urie, although Drummond and Urie 4-6-0s were sometimes seen. There were no regular non-stop runs, nor are there now, Southampton being too important for any train to pass. The best trains were allowed 92 minutes for the 79.3 miles between Waterloo and Southampton West (as the present Southampton station was then called), and 36 minutes for the final 28.7 miles to Bournemouth Central. Ten more 'H15' 4-6-0s were built, with 'N15' boilers, in 1924 and a number of them were sent to Bournemouth Shed to work the London expresses. One would have expected these powerful-looking machines to put the much smaller 4-4-0s firmly in their places, but although the first batch of 'H15's had been timed up to 80 mph so it was known they could run, as well as exert considerable power, O. S. Nock in his travels behind them on the Bournemouth line was 'not all impressed' and reckoned that the 'D15' 4-4-0s 'could run the proverbial rings round them'.

Urie retired at Grouping, as did Billington, the Chief Mechanical Engineer of the LBSCR, and that left the way clear for R. E. L. Maunsell of the SECR to take charge of locomotive design on the Southern

Left *Still on top link duties after thirty years, a Urie 'N15' 4-6-0, No 30751 Etarre, pulls out of Waterloo with a Bournemouth express. It passes Urie 'H16' 4-6-2T No 30520 with empty stock for Clapham Yard and a 4COR EMU on a Portsmouth working, 23 August 1952 (Brian Morrison).*

Right *The Cunard White Star Line's Aquitania in the Solent with a seaplane off her starboard side (Author's collection).*

Far right *The Short Sandringham flying boat Beachcomber (now in the Hall of Aviation, Southampton) in the Solent in 1981 (Southern Evening Echo).*

Railway. Because of weight restrictions on bridges long overdue for reconstruction Ashford had never been called upon to build engines as big as the Urie 4-6-0s or the Brighton Baltic tanks, but under Maunsell a series of excellent mixed traffic 2-6-0s had been turned out.

Maunsell, who was Irish born and had come from Inchicore, the works of the Great Southern and Western, the largest of the Irish railway companies, gathered around him on his appointment to Ashford in 1913 a team dominated by Great Western men. His 2-6-0s incorporated many Swindon features, and were immediately successful, and although intended primarily for goods traffic, soon proved themselves invaluable passenger engines, as had the Churchward 'Moguls' on the GWR.

Immediately on its formation the infant Southern Railway fell foul of the popular press. Just why this should have been so is difficult to say, though it should surprise no-one for there are sections of the so-called popular press to whom logic and fair play are quite beyond their intellectual and moral grasp. Many Fleet Street journalists lived on the Southern, and although crimes far worse than its relatively minor indiscretions of occasional unpunctuality and not terribly clean suburban carriages were being committed elsewhere on the British railway system, these were not noticed, or at least not reported. It was certainly true that the South Eastern suburban services left much to be desired and Sir Herbert Walker was pushing through plans for electrification which had first been formulated in 1903, but elsewhere on the Southern there was much that was admirable, not least the main line and suburban services out of Waterloo.

Walker decided to play the papers at their own game and build up a highly sophisticated publicity machine. He put it in the charge of a young man of 26, John Elliot, who as assistant editor of the *Evening*

Standard had been one of his chief tormentors. Elliot quickly decided that one of the principal reasons why nobody loved the Southern Railway and everyone loved the Great Western was that the latter had lots of engines with names and the former very few. It was true that the LSWR, after the glories and eccentricities of the Gooch and Beattie era, had quite given up the practice; neither was it one the SECR favoured. Elliot wasn't such a fool as to imagine that a few well chosen names could change the Southern Railway's image overnight, but he was certainly correct in thinking that if the company's first brand new express engines were to be named after those legendary heroes of Wessex and the West Country, King Arthur and his knights, and launched with a suitable flourish this would be no bad thing.

The engines weren't really, in design terms, new at all. New express engines were urgently needed on both the Eastern Section, as the former SECR lines were now known, and the Western, the former LSW system. Bridge strengthening was now under way on the Kent Coast main lines so that bigger engines, 4-6-0s for instance, could be used and the obvious choice was the Urie 'N15'. It was by no means perfect but there was potential for development and improvement and Maunsell and his team immediately set about this, concentrating on the smokebox area of the existing former LSW engines. Satisfied with his efforts Maunsell went ahead with his modified 'N15' and the first, No 453, came out of Eastleigh early in 1925. It, and its nine brothers, were officially replacements for ten Drummond 'G14' 4-6-0s and received their eight wheel water cart tenders. Their chimneys were far more elegant than the austere Urie version and an outwardly visible clue to their redesigned front end was their outside steam pipes, but their cabs were still the distinctive Eastleigh pattern with the strengthening ribs on the outside; they were very much in the LSWR tradition.

No 453 went on show to the press at Waterloo bearing the name *King Arthur*. It was a splendidly proportioned, impressive-looking machine in dignified lined olive green livery with the bold 'Southern' and gold numbers on the tender and the red backed brass nameplate on the single continuous splasher over the big driving wheels. H. V. Morton, who never passed up a purple phrase if it could be avoided, wrote thus of one of the 'King Arthur's, No 772 *Sir Percivale* in his *Nights of London*, published in 1926:

'He stands covered with the sweat of his run, his six-foot-seven driving wheels moist with green oil, his great connecting and side rods silver with effort, his pistons bright, the flanges of his bogie wheels white as new shillings... *Sir Percivale*, with a mighty snort and a puff of sudden steam, backs his long leanness out into that place where all engines go at night to be fussed and washed and patted and bathed and made ready for new miles.'

The *Sir Percivale* in question was one of twenty 'King Arthur's built in Glasgow by the North British Locomotive Company. As the Eastleigh pattern cab was outside the Eastern Section loading gauge the 'Scotch Arthurs', as they instantly became known, were given modified ones, reminiscent of those on Maunsell's 2-6-0s, and thus could work on both Eastern and Western Sections. The Maunsell cabs certainly didn't detract from the engines' looks although being without side windows they were hardly up-to-date for the mid-1920s. The twenty original LSWR 'N15's, now modified by Maunsell, also became part of the 'King Arthur' Class, and it was completed by fourteen final engines; Nos 793-806, built at Eastleigh between March 1926 and January 1927. They were identical to the Scotsmen, save for their tenders which were six-wheelers, thus enabling the locomotives to work on the Central Section of the former LBSCR lines where the length of turntables was restricted.

The last twenty of the 'Scotch Arthurs' went to the Western Section, Nos 773-782 to Nine Elms where they worked both to Salisbury and to Bournemouth, and Nos 783-792 to Bournemouth Shed. Such an influx of 4-6-0s meant that the 'King Arthur's had a virtual monopoly of the Waterloo to Southampton and Bournemouth expresses, and the long reign of 4-4-0s on these trains was at last over — or so it seemed.

Southampton Docks had piled up some impressive statistics by the end of the First World War. Over 7½ million soldiers, sailors and airmen had passed through, along with 850,000 horses and mules, but only 175,000 vehicles, whilst 16,291 ships had come and gone. Recovery from war conditions was rapid and by 1923 more passengers than ever before were handled, 420,000, an increase of 40,000 on 1913. In 1920 the White Star Line's great rival, Cunard, quit Liverpool and transferred its most prestigious services to Southampton, the Blue Ribband holder *Mauretania* making her first regular run from there to New York on 6 March 1920. The LSWR was well aware of the great asset it had in Southampton and was not slow to invest in it. On 27 June 1924 the Prince of Wales performed the opening ceremony of the largest floating dock in the world there and watched the four-funnelled Union Castle liner *Arundel Castle* steam into it, bunting flying from her masts.

Arundel Castle, at 19,118 tons, was the biggest ship her owners had ever possessed when she made her maiden voyage from Southampton in 1921, but she looked almost toy-like compared to the three ex-German giants which were such a familiar sight at Southampton in the 1920s and 30s. The oldest by a few months was the 52,226 ton Cunarder, *Berengaria*. Built at Hamburg as the *Imperator*, she had made her maiden voyage from there via Southampton to New York in 1913. She was taken over by Cunard in 1920 and made her first voyage as the *Berengaria* from Southampton to New York on 16 April 1921. Virtual sister ships were the White Star Line's *Majestic* and the United States Line's *Leviathan*, known somewhat disrespectfully but affectionately as the 'Levi Nathan'. Both owners claimed them as the biggest liners in the world.

The 1920s and 30s saw the building of yet greater and faster transatlantic liners; the German *Bremen* and *Europa* which would finally take the Blue riband from the veteran Cunarder *Mauretania*, the *Rex*, the only Italian liner to hold the trophy, then the beautiful French giant, *Normandie* and finally the most famous of them all, the *Queen Mary*. But there were rivals, both on the Atlantic and elsewhere. The Germans made many Atlantic crossings with the *Graf Zeppelin* airship and its successor the *Hindenburg* looked to have established airship travel until her destruction by fire. More successful was the flying boat.

Routes operated by the Railway Air Services in August 1937 (British Railways).

Southampton and the Solent area had been associated with the aircraft industry, and seaplanes and flying boats in particular, since the first years of the century. Most famous of all was the series of Supermarine seaplanes designed by R. J. Mitchell, culminating in the S6B which won the Schneider trophy outright for Britain in 1931 off Cowes and which captured the world speed record of 407.8 mph. Mitchell developed the S6B into the land based Spitfire, the prototype of which made its first flight from Eastleigh in 1936.

The heyday of the flying boat was brief but whilst it lasted the privileged passengers who made their way from Southampton eastwards and southwards to the furthest reaches of the Empire enjoyed a more civilized and comfortable form of commercial flight than any before or since. It began on 29 June 1937 with the departure of an Empire flying boat for South Africa. Its capacity of 24 (sixteen at night) meant that nothing more substantial than a Pullman and a baggage van, hauled by a 'T9' was needed to bring the passengers from London to the Eastern Docks. Because Imperial Airways terminal was in Buckingham Palace Road the train which connected with the flying boats left from Victoria station and to this day it remains the sole example of a regular passenger service from the old LBSC terminus down the former LSW main line. The final few hundred yards to the aircraft was by fast motor launch, which must have provided an exciting and appropriately nautical prelude to the flight.

The Supermarine works at Hythe became the maintenance base and so popular did the flying boats become that by 1938 there were seven weekly flights to Egypt, four to India, three to East Africa and two to South Africa, Malaya and Australia. The threat to the mail contracts held by the shipping companies was by now very real, although the huge discrepancy between the passenger capacity of an ocean liner and that of an aeroplane of the 1930s seemed to preclude serious competition in this sector of the business.

War was looming and the authorities, justifiably, decided that Southampton Water was too vulnerable a target and plans were put in hand to move the flying boat base along the coast, and down the line, to Poole. The Royal Assent to the amalgamation of Imperial Airways and British Airlines, henceforward to be known as British Overseas Airways Corporation, was granted in July 1939. In the meantime a number of experimental flights had been made across the Atlantic to New York, but before regular services could begin War broke out. Nevertheless flying boats, both civil and military, continued to operate from Southampton and Poole throughout the years 1939 to 1945.

Chapter 17
Rival powers

The Southern Railway's emphasis on electrification did not mean that steam locomotive development stopped. Whilst it is true that the Southern never built a suburban tank engine or a heavy long distance freight one, designs for a successor to the 'King Arthur' Class were in hand whilst these engines were still in production.

The Liverpool and Manchester 125th anniversary celebrations at Bold Colliery in 1980. Prominent are former Somerset and Dorset 2-8-0 No 13809 and Southern Railway 4-6-0 No 850 Lord Nelson, *as rebuilt by Bulleid with a multiple jet blastpipe.*

No 850 *Lord Nelson* emerged from Eastleigh in August 1926. It was a handsome engine, with four cylinders and billed as 'the most powerful British locomotive'. There were certain Swindon influences, although the greatest resemblance was to the LMS 'Royal Scot's, which was not surprising as Eastleigh had loaned the LMS a complete set of 'Nelson' drawings. In all sixteen were built, the last coming out in 1929. At first they were not much seen on the Bournemouth line, although later the entire class was concentrated there. Sixteen was an awkward number; it would have been virtually doubled but

'King Arthur' Class 4-6-0 No 778 Sir Pelleas *at Waterloo with the 'Bournemouth Belle'* (F. E. Box, NRM).

orders for a further fifteen were cancelled and the money transferred to further electrification. Because they were such a small class any tasks they were allocated had also to be within the capacity of a 'King Arthur' and thus they were seldom stretched. Even so in their early years, although they were free-running and fast, the 'Lord Nelsons' seldom gave the impression that they were much in advance of the older 4-6-0s. The Bournemouth line service with which the 'Lord Nelson's were chiefly associated in the 1930s was the most glamorous the line had yet seen.

The London, Brighton and South Coast and the South Eastern and Chatham Railways had been enthusiastic users of Pullman cars, but the London and South Western, perhaps because its own coaching stock was of a much higher standard than those of the other two Southern constituents, had not. The Southern Railway whole-heartedly embraced the Pullman ethos, and used the chocolate and cream cars lavishly, almost in the way other companies used restaurant cars. Early in 1931 the company placed a number in service on the Southampton Docks Ocean Liner expresses and in the summer of that year, on 5 July, a complete train of Pullmans began to run between Waterloo and Bournemouth.

This was the 'Bournemouth Belle', a companion to the Victoria to Brighton 'Southern Belle' and the Victoria to Dover Marine 'Golden Arrow'.

At first the 'Bournemouth Belle' ran only on week-days during the summer and at weekends throughout the year but from the beginning of 1936 it became a daily service. Not surprisingly the press was much taken with it and devoted it many columns which must have greatly pleased the Southern's publicity department. They certainly couldn't have bettered the fulsome comments of the *Bournemouth Daily Echo*. In the issue of 2 January 1936 under a three column picture of the train, it waxed enthusiastic. 'When the mighty *Lord Collingwood* engine steamed into Bournemouth West station yesterday at the end of its run it had inaugurated the latest enterprise of the Southern Railway Company... Public appreciation of this lovely train with its magnificent Pullman cars, with unlimited comfort and facilities had led the company to make the decision (to operate daily).' In the matter of speed the paper was very easily pleased: 'During the run down lunch was served on board while the train flashed through the New Forest at 50 mph'. Apart from various newspapermen the BBC was also on board, as were the Mayors of Southampton and Bournemouth and the Southern's traffic manager, E. C. Cox. The following day there was another picture, depicting the two mayors and various other bowler and trilby-hatted dignitaries standing in front of one of the Pullmans before being taken on a tour organized by Bournemouth Corporation of the 'winter attractions'. One of these included the Westover Ice Rink (which has barely changed in the intervening fifty years); the motor coach tour ended with tea at the Pavilion.

Still the *Bournemouth Echo* had not finished with its new wonder and in the edition of 4 January 1936 the following perceptive reflections appeared in the comment column: 'The extent to which Bournemouth's destiny has always been allied with railway enterprise is perhaps hardly sufficiently realized. The town's distance from London would prove a handicap but for the attention which in the early days the LSWR gave to inaugurating and maintaining a quick, frequent and comfortable service of express trains. The supply helped to create the demand and proved one of the circumstances that enabled *The Times* this week to assert that Bournemouth is one of the few seaside towns in the country which have really become all-the-year-round resorts... as a recognition of the municipality's enterprise the Southern Railway has decided that during 1936 the all Pullman express known as the "Bournemouth Belle" is to run daily.'

The all Pullman train took exactly 2 hours 2

Below *'Merchant Navy' Pacific No 35015* Rotterdam Lloyd *in blue livery pulls out of Bournemouth West with the Waterloo-bound 'Bournemouth Belle' in the summer of 1949* (Colour Rail).

Above *Holidaymakers arrive at Weymouth, August 1986.*

Overleaf *Adams 4-4-2T No 488 being prepared for the day's work, coupled to LBSCR Terrier No 72* Fenchurch *at Sheffield Park in September 1986.*

Above *The down 'Bournemouth Belle' in the charge of a 'Merchant Navy' Pacific passing Basingstoke in the summer of 1948* (Colour Rail).

Below *The restaurant car centenary train, made up of a variety of historic restaurant, kitchen and buffet cars, arriving at Weymouth, September 1979.*

A poster put out jointly by the four main line companies in the 1930s (British Railways).

The 'Bournemouth Limited' near Weybridge in 1937, hauled by 'Schools' Class 4-4-0 No 925 Cheltenham *(Kelland Collection).*

minutes to reach Bournemouth Central from Waterloo, stopping at Southampton. It left Waterloo at the curious time of 10.38 in the morning, reached Southampton at 11.58, and Bournemouth West at 12.40 pm. Coming back it departed from the West station at 4.35 pm, Bournemouth Central ten minutes later, Southampton at 5.25 pm and arrived at Waterloo at 6.55 pm.

The Southern did not neglect the ordinary Bournemouth line services and the late 1930s marked a highpoint, as on so many main lines, which was not to be surpassed until well after World War 2. Updated versions of the LSW designed 'Ironclad' stock had been introduced throughout the 1920s and for the 1929 summer service a new named express made up of the latest coaches was introduced. This was the 'Bournemouth Limited'. It left Bournemouth Central at 8.40 am and travelled to Waterloo non-stop arriving at 10.40 am. The return journey began at 4.30 pm and the train arrived back at 6.30 pm. In the words of the *Railway Magazine* a 'brightly coloured poster' was produced featuring a 'couple of hour glass figures — no doubt to add force to the slogan "108 miles, non-stop in two hours".' The poster also depicts what looks rather like a 'King Arthur', but in a report two issues later on the inaugural trial trip on 4 July the thirteen coach train was hauled by the 'Lord Nelson' Class locomotive *Lord Hawke*. Despite various slacks

the two hour schedule was bettered by 1½ minutes. The report adds that 'throughout the travelling was extremely smooth, and was particularly noticeable when the fastest running was being attained'.

Later in the same report there is a reference to further 'new corridor trains', one of ten carriages, including a diner, for the Bournemouth, Birkenhead and Manchester service, which alternated with GWR stock, the other of eight carriages, again one a diner, for the Bournemouth to Leeds, Bradford, and Newcastle route. This alternated with an LNER train and meant that, taking into account the Somerset and Dorset trains, carriages of all four main line companies were now regularly seen at Bournemouth. The variety was further added to by the motive power, for although LNER locomotives were not seen, those of the LMS had long been familiar, whilst GWR ones regularly worked through expresses south from Basingstoke into Bournemouth.

At the start of the 1938 summer timetable the 'Bournemouth Limited', was provided with two new eleven coach trains. Well, although the Southern Railway claimed they were new, this wasn't strictly true for the carriages had already seen some main line service. However they looked new, which presumably was what mattered as far as the customers were concerned. Outside they were painted in what was variously described as Bulleid, Bournemouth, or malachite green. It was very much brighter than the previous shade, inherited from the LSW, and to go with it lining was abolished, class designations were applied in numerals LMS and LNER fashion instead of words, and a new style of lettering was used for 'Southern'. Whether you thought it an improvement was purely a matter of opinion; the Southern obviously did for eventually malachite became the standard green for all carriages and the larger loco-motives. Internally varnished wood disappeared, to be replaced by rexine, pale stone in the third class, pale yellow in the first, whilst new, shaped seats, in pale green upholstery in the first class, pale pink in the third, became standard. A nice touch of luxury was floor rugs in all compartments. There were echoes of this decor in the contemporary Bulleid 2HAL EMUs, then entering service on the Medway and Reading routes, which were austere in the extreme, but on the 'Bournemouth Limited' it was applied with a good deal more sensitivity, and achieved a sense of airy modernity.

The Southern Railway was anxious that its new trains were kept immaculate and to this end an additional gang of cleaners was taken on at Wey-mouth to look after it, a welcome move where un-employment, whilst nowhere near as bad as that in

the industrial areas of Britain, was far from neg-ligible. It was common practice for the Southern Railway to lay off quite large numbers of staff, including those in the motive power department, at the end of each summer timetable right through the 1930s.

The 'Bournemouth Limited' conveyed through car-riages for Swanage and Weymouth and these vehicles were turned out in the new livery. A two-coach set left Swanage at 7.44 am, attached to the branch's regular ex-LSW wooden-bodied non-corridors, reached Wareham at 8.06 and left at 8.14, now attached to a three-coach set which had departed from Weymouth at 7.42. This got to Bournemouth Central at 8.35 and there the five coaches were attached to a six-coach set, including a dining car, which had started its journey at Bournemouth West at 8.20. The complete eleven coach train left Bournemouth Central at 8.40 and ran non-stop to Waterloo, arriving at 10.38. After a 2 hour stopover, giving plenty of time for an 'M7' to run the train to Clapham yard and back for a brush and trim — Bournemouth line express stock has always required notably less effort from cleaning staff than that on many other routes — the 'Bournemouth Limited' set off home at 12.30 pm. This time it stopped at Southampton and consequently took 2 hours 9 minutes to reach Bournemouth Central. The eleven coaches did a third journey before the day

Weymouth station between the wars (British Railways).

'Schools' No 928 Stowe *as preserved in olive green livery on the Bluebell Railway, 1986.*

was out, getting back to Waterloo at ten minutes to nine in the evening.

Next morning the set worked a diagram which enabled it to get to Bournemouth and back ready to make a final journey to Bournemouth, Swanage and Weymouth, leaving Waterloo at 4.30 pm. This and the 10.38 arrival at Waterloo were the only runs which the two sets of carriages made when they bore 'Bournemouth Limited' headboards.

Surprisingly the regular motive power of the new 'Bournemouth Limited' was neither a 'Lord Nelson' nor a 'King Arthur'. It was in fact the very last in the long line of 4-4-0s which had been in charge of Bournemouth line expresses since the days of William Adams. Maunsell's 'Schools' Class had been introduced in 1930 for the restricted conditions of the Hastings line, but it soon proved itself a splendid express locomotive for almost every Southern Railway main line. Nominally and in reality the 'Schools' were the most powerful 4-4-0s in Europe, and along with the not dissimilar post-war three-cylinder 'VS's of the Great Northern Railway of Ireland, were by general agreement the finest locomotives of that wheel arrangement ever seen. Not even electrification could prevent a total of forty being built, one of the latter batches going on to the Waterloo to

Portsmouth line. With its imminent electrification No 929 *Malvern* was transferred to Bournemouth shed at the beginning of 1936.

The big 4-4-0 instantly endeared itself to Bournemouth crews, with their fond memories of Drummonds 'D15's, and by July 1937 the entire batch of ten locomotives, Nos 924-933, which had gone new to Fratton in 1934, was at Bournemouth. Remarkably they ousted the 'Lord Nelson's and the 'King Arthur's from all the top link duties other than the 'Bournemouth Belle' and the through expresses to Oxford. The GWR claimed it was 'unused to such large four-coupled engines' for which fiction someone should have been struck dumb or at least made to write out a thousand times 'What about the "French Atlantics" and the "County" 4-4-0s?'.

The 'Schools' were both powerful and fast. O. S. Nock recorded No 926 *Repton* keeping time between Waterloo and Southampton with no less than fifteen bogies totalling 525 tons and noted that it was 'no isolated effort' whilst at the other extreme No 928 *Stowe* attained the highest speed ever recorded on Southern lines prior to the Bulleid Pacifics when she hurtled through Wool one afternoon in 1938 with four coaches at 95 mph. The level 14 mile 7.9 chain run from Dorchester to Wareham was always a favourite racing stretch and in LSW days one train had been scheduled to cover it in 15 minutes, 3 seconds with 165 tons gross, and this at a time when

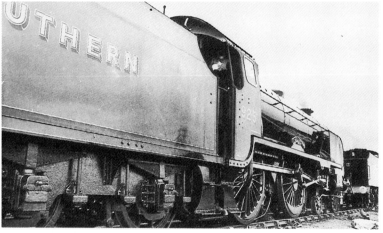

Above *A lightweight train from Weymouth speeds through Wool behind a 'T9' Class 4-4-0 in 1935* (Dr Ian C. Allen).

Left Cheltenham *as preserved in malachite green livery at Rainhill, 1980.*

Left *A Waterloo-bound 4SUB leaving Vauxhall with Lambeth Bridge, The Houses of Parliament and Big Ben in the background.*

high speed was far from the order of the day anywhere on Britain' railways. Many's the time I've waited at the level crossing at Wool for a train to pass; nowadays with the growth of the village and the nearby nuclear power station and army camps there is sufficient traffic for nearly all trains to stop, but to stand at the gates inches away from a steam engine hurtling past at close on 100 mph must have been quite an experience.

In order to match the new livery of the 'Bournemouth Limited' six of the Bournemouth 'Schools' were repainted in malachite green with white lining and black edging and the famous sunshine style of lettering. A 'Schools' so adorned at the head of the newly outshopped 'Bournemouth Limited' must have been a splendid sight, and whilst it is one that is impossible to recreate in its entirety today we are most fortunate that two of the Bournemouth 'Schools' have been preserved in working order. The 95 mph No 928 *Stowe* is at the Bluebell Railway and is in her original dark green livery, whilst No 925 *Cheltenham* (which once cut the Waterloo to Southampton schedule by 2 minutes with fourteen coaches behind her) was restored to working order by the National Railway Museum for the 1980 Rainhill celebrations and is painted in the 1938 malachite shade of green; both engines look magnificent.

It was the electrification of the direct Portsmouth line in June 1937 which had brought about the transfer of the 'Schools' Class engines from Fratton shed to Bournemouth, and that electrification mean that for the first time steam-hauled passenger trains were banished from a former LSW main line. The third rail had reached the Solent and expresses for Portsmouth Harbour bore the roofboards 'Waterloo, Portsmouth and the Isle of Wight'. I'm sure I wasn't the only small boy who assumed this meant they travelled across on a ferry and resumed their journey down Ryde Pier and on to Sandown, Shanklin and Ventnor.

Electrification now extended 25 miles down the Waterloo to Weymouth main line as far as Woking. The completion of the Portsmouth line electrification coincided with the retirement of Sir Herbert Walker. He had been General Manager, first of the LSW and then of the Southern Railway for a total of 25 years.

Sir Herbert was a dynamic figure who had initiated many changes, not least the completion of the lengthy rebuilding of Waterloo and the establishment of Southampton as the principal port in the United Kingdom for ocean passenger travel. But probably his greatest achievement was the creation of the largest electrified network in the world, one which extended far beyond suburbia to the Sussex and Hampshire coasts. Sir Herbert's philosophy was that both suburban and long distance electric services should be frequent and reliable, rather than particu-

larly fast. It was one which appealed to the public and with each extension of the electrified network so more and more speculative estates of mock Tudor semi-detacheds went up, covering the Surrey valleys and hillsides and, by 1937, extending into the Hampshire heathlands.

John Betjeman, better than any other writer, captured the essence of the comfortable, middle class, easily mocked and much envied (if secretly) way of life enjoyed by those fortunate enough to live in this outer suburbia which the Southern Electric had done much to create. In his *Love in a Valley*, published in 1937, there are these lines:

'White down the valley curves the living rail,
Tall, tall, above me, olive spikes the pinewoods,
Olive against blue-black, moving in the gale.'

Betjeman loved everything to do with railways and certainly didn't limit his affection to the steam engine; the especial atmosphere of the electric railway had equal appeal for him, take this for example:

'Early Electric! With what radiant hope
Men formed this many-branched electrolier,
Twisted the flex around the iron rope
And let the dazzling vacuum globes hang clear...'

Almost all of Betjeman's sports-loving, clear-eyed, clean-limbed seductive heroines are Home Counties born and bred. Pam in *Pot Pourri for a Surrey Garden*, published in 1940, is a perfect example. After being told that her 'Old Malvernian brother... Although he's playing for Woking can't stand up to her wonderful backhand drive', there follows one of the most deliciously erotic passages Betjeman ever wrote:

'See the strength of her arm, as firm and as hairy as Hendren's;
See the size of her thighs, the pout of her lips as, cross,
And full of pent-up strength, she swipes at the rhododendrons,
Lucky the rhododendrons,
And flings her arrogant love-lock
Back with a petulant toss.'

Although written nearly fifty years ago life on the Surrey/Hampshire border has changed little in essence since Betjeman captured it so perfectly. Take almost any Bournemouth stopping service out of Waterloo, first stop Surbiton, then all stations to Woking, between 10 am and 4 pm and if there isn't a sprinkling of bank manager's wives, retired colonels, preparatory schoolboys and straw-hatted girls and Duchess of York look-alikes (the former Sarah Ferguson's nearest station was Basingstoke) then you are on the wrong train.

Chapter 18
Progress and decline

The branch lines serving the Waterloo to Weymouth route came into existence for a variety of reasons, usually to serve a local need and usually promoted by local people, although often financed from outside. Sometimes they were part of a through route and sometimes they had had ambitions in this direction which they did not achieve. If not owned by the LSW from the start then they were nearly always worked by the main line company. The reasons for their decline were far less complicated and in the years between the two world wars, when this decline set in, there was really only one — competition from road transport.

This competition did not affect all lines. Many continued to prosper, or at least do quite well, and one area is totally exempt from any reference to hard times. In the London suburbs and their hinterland electrification continued steadily and there was even a new line built, which was electrified from the start. This was the one from Wimbledon south-eastwards to Sutton through territory where the Underground had once been so keen to stake a claim. Some five miles in length it passed through a district which was purely twentieth century development and included the huge London County Council St Helier estate. The nearest London Underground passengers ever got to it was on the Northern Line to Morden; strictly speaking the trains themselves got, and get, nearer still for they emerge from what every schoolboy knows is the longest tunnel in the world into the open air on the far side of the station forecourt. It was here that all the 281 wartime Daimler buses which London Transport owned congregated at one time or another in the late 1940s and early 50s, for all lived at Merton and Sutton garages. I know this for my friend Hicks copped the lot; I didn't, one of the chief reasons being I could seldom resist the lure of Raynes Park Station ten minutes ride away and would often desert my allotted task of adding to my list of D types for the sight of a Urie 'King Arthur' on an Ocean Liner express or a 'Lord Nelson' on the 5.30 pm Waterloo to Bournemouth.

I digress. The tube trains come out of their tunnel in order to get to their depot which is within a few hundred yards of Morden South station. It was

opened, along with the complete Wimbledon to Sutton line, by the Southern Railway on 5 January 1930. A remarkable feature of the line was that some of the trains which used it started their journeys at London Bridge and finished them at Holborn Viaduct and thus managed to travel over former LBSC, LSW and SEC metals.

A little over two years after the Wimbledon to Sutton line opened another branch with a short, but highly eventful history and one which had a greater footage of cinefilm exposed on it than any other, closed. This was the Basingstoke to Alton line. It had been removed to France during the First World War, and had only been relaid after a court case. It closed to passengers for good on 12 September 1932, although sections at either end remained open for goods traffic.

Four years earlier the climax of an almost forgotten film (forgotten that is except by railway buffs) called *The Wrecker* was staged on the branch on Sunday 19 January 1928 at Salter's Crossing, Lasham. The Southern Railway sold an old South Eastern Stirling 4-4-0 No A148 and six SEC bogies to the film makers. A Fowler steam lorry was driven on to the level crossing, filled with dynamite, the track beyond loosened and the train set off. The local police were out in strength to control the crowds, who had been issued with passes. A most satisfying (except for lovers of Stirling 4-4-0s and SEC carriages) holocaust resulted, at a cost of around £7,000. The remains were cleared up by two steam cranes from Eastleigh and Nine Elms, ready for the 3.25 pm from Basingstoke to Alton the next day.

Nine years later the film-makers returned and this time the result was a classic. The character that Will Hay created on the screen, and repeated many times with slight variations, was not a particularly admirable one. There was more than a hint of Hancock in his noisy, overbearing, bumbling incompetence. Will Hay himself is said to have been subject to fits of introspection. On the screen the chemistry he created with his side-kicks, the Old Man and the Fat Boy, both equally incompetent and inclined to panic at the earliest opportunity, sparked off magic. The film they made on the Basingstoke to Alton line,

Oh Mr Porter, transformed in imagination to Buggleskelly on the borders of Southern and Northern Ireland, was gloriously funny. Hay was the stationmaster, transferred there so as to be as far away from Head Office as possible — the latter presumably being loosely based on Euston and Buggleskelly being somewhere on the Northern Counties Committee of the LMS. There any resemblance to fact and logic was mercifully abandoned for the locomotives used bore little likeness to anything Irish, being a Hawthorn Leslie 2-4-0T, No 2 *Northiam* from the Kent and East Sussex Railway, and two former LSW Adams engines, 'X2' 4-4-0 No 657 and '0395' 0-6-0 No 3509. The final frenetic chase took the action out on to the main line and into some very un-Irish settings, notably Clapham Junction.

Although the Basingstoke to Alton line was open to passenger traffic for the extraordinarily brief span of 23 years, goods traffic continued to work over a short stretch from Alton to Treloars Hospital for well over double this time, until July 1967. At the

northern end was the Thornycroft lorry and engine works and goods traffic continued to serve it after passenger services ended. Thornycroft lorries and buses were used both by the LSW and the Southern Railways. A Thornycroft bus operated in the Lymington area as early as 1904, others worked at Farnham and along Southampton Water. Curiously when the Alton to Basingstoke line was lifted during World War 1 a Karrier rather than a Thornycroft lorry was used to carry the milk which had formerly gone by train.

LSW and Southern Railway patronage of Thornycroft was limited and of all the railways it was the Great Western, owners of the Reading to Basingstoke line, which was far and away the biggest purchaser of Thornycroft vehicles. Very few railway-owned motor vehicles have been preserved, but it is appropriate that the only former Great Western one in running order should be a 3 ton Nippy platform lorry, built by Thornycroft in 1938, owned by the London Group of the Great Western Society and first shown to the public at the 25th anniversary of the British Trolleybus Society at Didcot on Sunday 15 June 1986.

The Alton line actually passed right through the Thornycroft works, which sounds a trifle hazardous, but the only serious accident would seem to have occurred in 1928 when a train cut a lorry in half, fortunately without any serious injury to the driver.

A splendid collection of London Transport 'E1' and 'E3' Class trams, ST and STL buses and horse and motor powered commercial vehicles, but not a single private car, negotiate the complex of junctions around Vauxhall station in July 1934 (London Transport).

The works is now the ETN Transmission Division; a few hundred yards of the line still exists, curving away as a rusty siding beside the waterworks on the down side of the main line south of Bastingstoke station, whilst a road occupies the track bed further on.

In 1937 electrification reached Alton at the same time as the Portsmouth route was electrified. This meant the virtual end of regular through trains on this alternative route between Waterloo and Winchester, although it retained its usefulness as a relief line right down to electrification of the main line in 1967. From 1937 trains south of Alton were 'M7' powered push-pulls which terminated either at Eastleigh or Southampton Terminus. There was, however, one most curious through service which survived until the Second World War. This was a single coach which worked between Sandwich and Bournemouth. Its journey was a fascinating one, not least for the number of times it was attached and detached at various junctions in Kent, Surrey and Hampshire. It set off just after breakfast at 9.13 am and, travelling by way of Dover and Folkestone, reached Ashford where it joined the 9.18 am Margate to Birkenhead. The combined train, complete with restaurant car, departed from Ashford at 10.33 am, reversed at Redhill, and got to Guildford at 13 minutes past midday. The Bournemouth coach left 10 minutes later. The local timetable for the Alton to Winchester line notes that it is a through coach, so possibly it was worked in solitary state, although it would seem more likely that other carriages were added for local

passengers. Departure from Alton was at 1.04 pm and arrival at Winchester (noted as being '1 mile from Cheesehill Station') at 1.37 pm. Bournemouth Central was reached at 3.04 pm and journey's end, Bournemouth West at 3.16 pm. Here again it is recorded as a through train, so it must surely have had other vehicles attached. On summer Saturdays it ran as a complete train all the way which meant passengers could leave Sandwich 35 minutes later and get to Bournemouth West only 9 minutes later: but they didn't get the benefit of the restaurant car. I think I'd have gladly forsaken the 26 minute advantage on the 6 hour, 3 minute journey for the sake of a cup of Southern Railway tea and a pork pie between Ashford and Guildford. (It could equally well have been Great Western fare for the two companies provided the coaching stock on the Margate to Birkenhead train on alternate days.)

Mention of the Fawley bus route a few paragraphs back is a reminder that a branch line was opened by the Southern Railway from Totton to serve stations at Marchwood, Hythe and Fawley in 1925. There was also goods traffic to, amongst other sites, the Agwi Petroleum Corporation, out of which was to grow the enormous Fawley refinery.

To return to branch closures, one took place on 28 September 1935 of a by then quiet and little used line which had once been of vastly more importance. This was the line from Ringwood to Christchurch. When built in 1870 it had formed part of the through route from Waterloo to Weymouth but had long been by-passed. It was little used in its last years and soon

forgotten. Not even the construction of Hurn aero-drome during World War 2 prompted any serious consideration of its revival. However the goods yard on the curve at Christchurch survived for thirty years and at Hurn the station has become a pub. In 1971 it was bought by the Parker family who set about restoring it and adding all sorts of railway para-phenalia, culminating in 1979 in the arrival of a full-sized Pullman car. This was No 340, one of the Metro-Cammell cars dating from 1960 and of the batch which form the restored train normally pro-vided for SLOA steam runs on various parts of the BR network. One can thus eat and drink in a Pullman car on its own section of track beside the platform at Hurn station, which is an advance on anything the LSW or Southern Railway ever offered passengers on the branch. The only drawback is it doesn't actually go anywhere. Still it's a pleasant and nostalgic experience to sit and reflect as one listens to the distant rumble of the traffic on the main A338 Bournemouth to London road beyond the pine trees, or as a jet roars overhead taking off or landing at Hurn airport, that neither mode of travel can approach the comfort of a Pullman car, whether stationary or on the move.

Military lines connected with the Waterloo to Wey-mouth line, or came close to it at several points. One which had a short life was that linking Wool station and Bovington Camp. It disappeared shortly after the First World War and thus never had the distinction of conveying Lawrence of Arabia, T. E. Lawrence, who was stationed at Bovington in the 1920s and was killed in an accident whilst on his way by motor-cycle from his Cloud's Hill home to Wool post office. The tiny Cloud's Hill cottage now belongs to the National Trust and is open to the public. The most famous of the military lines was the Longmoor Rail-way. Its southern end connected with the Waterloo to Portsmouth line, its northern with the Waterloo to Alton, Alresford and Winchester. Originally known as the Woolmer Instructional Military Railway, it opened in 1907 and was linked to the LSW network by way of the Bentley to Bordon branch, which had come into use two years earlier. In its time some fascinating locomotives, carriages and wagons worked over it, some discards from the LSW, Southern and other railways, others built especially for military service. The Longmoor Military Railway reached its greatest extent during World War 2, when there were 71 miles of track, and after a period of steady decline, it closed in 1971. In its final years as an abortive preservation centre its fate, and that of its rolling stock, was all part of the story of the preserva-tion of locomotives, carriages and wagons representative of those employed between Waterloo and Weymouth.

Military railways bring us inexorably to September 1939 and the all but six years when the Southern Railway was to all intents and purposes to become one enormous network of lines serving the needs of the Army, the Navy and the Royal Air Force.

Left *Former LBSC 'H1' Class Atlantic No 2041* Peveril Point *after overhaul at Eastleigh in 1935. The engine received its name in Southern Railway days, Peveril Point being a headland off Swanage. Although Brighton Atlantics worked regularly into Bournemouth there is no record of one ever coming down the Swanage branch* (Author's collection).

Right *A former LBSCR Baltic tank at Eastleigh after rebuilding as an N15X 4-6-0 (Author's Collection).*

Chapter 19

War again

The LSW had carried a greater volume of military traffic than any other railway during World War 1, and during World War 2 its successor, the Southern Railway, was called upon to make a similar effort; given that it had a virtual monopoly of the Channel ports it could hardly have been otherwise. Up to a point the Southern could draw upon the experiences of a generation earlier, but there was much that was new, and even more demanding and horrific; not least the involvement of the entire population of South-Eastern England in the front line through bombing, and the total loss of France to the enemy between 1940 and 1944, thus making redundant Southampton's role as the principal supply port to the front in that country.

I was two years old when war broke out and what must be my earliest memory is of hearing the air raid sirens sounding when my parents and I were waiting on Richmond station for a train to take us back to Clapham Junction after a day out on the river. It was a hot Sunday afternoon, 3 September 1939, and war had been declared a few hours earlier. As it happened it was a false alarm but the panic of those all around certainly communicated itself to me.

That panic, or, to put it more politely, uncertainty, was experienced at all levels and no wonder, for bombs and poison gas were expected to rain down on British cities within days, if not hours. The railways, as in 1914, were put under government control on 1 September 1939 when it had become certain that war could not be avoided, and within days services were reduced, Pullmans and restaurant cars withdrawn, and plans drawn up for large scale evacuation of children and other civilians from London and other areas which might be expected to be in the front line. Huge numbers of children left London for the country, and Waterloo and suburban stations on the Western Section, Earlsfield for example, saw many painful scenes as the bewildered evacuees were ushered with their teachers and other adults, but not their parents, aboard trains for unknown destinations in Hampshire, Dorset and the

Left A poster issued by the Railway Executive Committee in 1940 (British Railways).

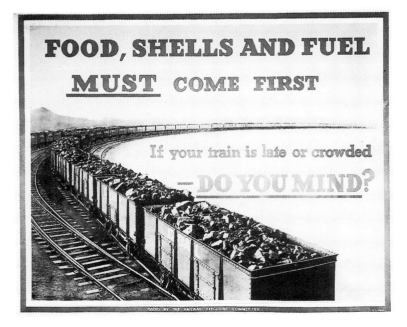

Right Wagons built by the GWR in 1940 loaded with steel from Belgium at Hamworthy Quay in 1985.

West Country. This was the period of the Phoney War when Hitler held his hand and the RAF frantically built up its squadrons of Hurricanes and Southampton designed Spitfires, and many of the children drifted back home. When the blitz arrived in the autumn of 1940 the evacuee trains headed southwestwards again, in some cases passing those bringing French, Channel Island and other refugees who had escaped the German advance and had been landed at Southampton or Weymouth. There was yet a third evacuation when the V1 flying bombs and then the V2 rockets (in effect missiles) began raining down on London. It was one my parents and I were involved in, for our house in Croydon was badly damaged. My father, who worked for NAAFI, was transferred to a hotel on the clifftops at Bournemouth which his organization had taken over, and he, my mother and I travelled from Waterloo to Bournemouth in a fish van. We hadn't meant to but the train was so full that there was no space to be found anywhere else. As far as I recall the fish had already got out but there was no mistaking they'd been there. It was dark when we reached Southampton, the journey took an interminable time and the train stopped frequently, so I could not see the docks, which would have been a spectacular sight packed with passenger and naval craft of every description.

At Bournemouth Central we thankfully alighted and finished our journey in a No 25 trolleybus. We spent the next year living in a not very comfortable flat over a grocer's shop just up the hill from the Square, listening to our landlord's assertion that the Luftwaffe would ''ave one more go at Bournemouth' before the war was over. Compared to what we had become used to in South London there seemed absolutely no evidence of its previous 'go' so we were not very impressed. The town was bursting to the seams with American soldiers on their way to Normandy and most days an aircraft towing a target would fly over the sea parallel to the promenade and all the guns set up there would blaze away at it (the target not the plane). I could never tell whether any hits were scored but it seemed to be an enormously risky business flying that plane (it still does). There must have been a fascinating variety of carriages and engines which brought the Americans to Bournemouth, and took them away again to Southampton and Weymouth for embarkation and the war, but I saw little railway activity in the town during this period, most of our travel being by Corporation trolley or Hants and Dorset bus.

The latter we used once a week to visit my grandmother who was living with an uncle who owned a shoeshop in Poole High Street. I saw a good deal more of the railway there though I chiefly remember the dark passage at the back of the shop which squelched at high tide and frightened me no end.

One day I ventured out the back way and down one of the alleys which lead to the quay and found myself dwarfed by the towering, rust-stained sides of a cargo steamer which had survived an Atlantic convoy. Another time I saw a Sunderland flying boat cutting through the water, spray curving away from

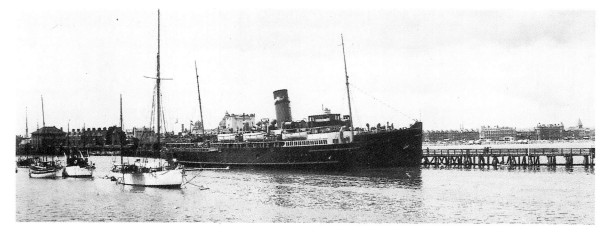

its hull as it sped across the harbour in front of Brownsea Island, and slowly rose into the air. That was a thrilling sight. But the most familiar spectacle was the little saddle tank which shunted up and down the quay and sometimes ventured out on to the main road and puffed off to the main line station. I'd never seen anything like this before and my father had some difficulty in explaining to me why it could make do with what seemed to be grooves cut into the road surface rather than needing proper rails. I don't see why this should have been such a puzzle, back home in Croydon trams ran past the end of our road and I never wondered about their needing rails. One of the saddle tanks which worked on Poole Quay, a Robert Stephenson Hawthorne *Bonnie Prince Charlie*, later went to Southampton Docks and is now preserved by the Great Western Society at Didcot.

Although the greatest number of evacuees came from the London area thousands of children also left other cities which were expected to be targets of the German bombers and this inevitably included Southampton. The first group assembled at the Central station at 6.30 in the morning on 31 August 1939 and others rapidly joined them. One particularly sad sight was a school which had been caught in the rain with their carrier bags, the contents of which fell through the soggy paper on to the ground. In all 37 per cent of the city's schoolchildren, a total of 32,000, left on Thursday 31 August and Friday 1 September.

Many are the views on evacuation. For some, like the war itself, it was the experience of a lifetime, for others it was something which had to be endured, both by those evacuated and those who made a home for them. Not all did this willingly. When one group of 281 Southampton children arrived at Romsey 93 of them finished up spending the night in a school in Station Road. The local people came to the station, picked those they thought looked pre-

sentable, and refused to have anything to do with the rest. Such an experience was a common one. Local facialities were often overwhelmed by the numbers involved. There were other reasons why the children were not always welcome. Some were verminous, others it was discovered, were literally sewn into their clothes.

The way of life some city children were used to was very different to those of the people who were expected to take them in. A welfare officer in Bournemouth commented that many evacuees wanted only fish and chips or something out of a tin and a piece of bread, which they could eat out in the street. They often passed on diseases. Some of their mothers took the train from Southampton to Bournemouth, not so much to visit their offspring it was said but 'with the idea of having a holiday'.

We may well throw our hands up in horror at such fecklessness. I kept the greatest possible distance from such families. But then, although we considered ourselves far from well off we managed a holiday every year, even during the war, actually travelling in trains instead of watching them go by and perhaps chucking the odd stone in their direction. My first years of education were in private schools and when I finally did go to a state primary school I was appalled at the number of children whose behinds were literally hanging out of their shorts, and this in a basically middle class area. I joined the infant Ian Allan Locospotters Club, along with my friends; it never occurred to me then what an essentially middle class activity this was, for you needed to be literate and in receipt of regular pocket money to indulge such a hobby, and in the 1940s there were millions of under tens who were neither.

Southampton in the 1930s was a relatively prosperous city, certainly compared with those of the North of England, of South Wales and Scotland. Nevertheless 4,000 out of the total labour force of

Left *The* SS St Julien, *built for the GWR by John Brown of Clydebank in 1926, leaving Weymouth for the Channel Islands in August 1929. The* St Julien *served throughout World War 2 as a hospital ship and then returned to the Channel Islands service, making her last voyage from Guernsey to Weymouth at the end of the 1960 season* (British Railways).

Right *An airliner from the Channel Islands passing over Eastleigh works as it lands at Southampton Airport, August 1986.*

69,000 was unemployed, whilst 19 per cent of the population was living below the poverty line — and the poverty line was drawn very low, at 42 shillings per week. 20 per cent of the population earned over £4 per week.

A greater percentage of the population of Southampton was employed in dock-orientated occupations, 179 out of every 1,000 working men, than in any other large harbour town; the next highest was Liverpool with 138 then Hull with 137. Very few families of dock workers could afford anything more than days out and the 29 mile journey to Bournemouth would have been a great adventure. We may therefore perhaps better understand why those mothers who followed their offspring took the chance to indulge in what in many cases was the first opportunity they had ever had for a holiday.

Some children were evacuated under Government schemes very much greater distances, to the United States and Canada, whilst others whose families could afford it sent their children independently to friends and relations on the other side of the Atlantic — the first sailing of the *Empress of Canada* from Southampton after the outbreak of war carried more than double the usual number of children.

The occupation of the Channel Islands coincided with the end of the Phoney War and the long-feared bombing of British cities. Travel from both Southampton and Weymouth to Guernsey and Jersey had boomed during the 1930s, even though air services had begun to compete. From 1934 Weymouth had provided the fastest service all the year round, although it remained true, as it had always really done, that it was only in June, July and August that the service made a significant profit. In July 1933 the Prince of Wales had opened the extension to the quay at Weymouth and trains from Birmingham, as well as London, came alongside the ships. Cargo had dropped away a little but the passenger traffic,

including day excursions, was increasing. In many ways the last full peacetime season of 1938 was a record one.

After 9 September 1939 all regular sailings between Weymouth and the Channel Islands ended. Cargo continued to be carried but Southampton had a monopoly of passenger traffic. Many of the ships, as in the First World War, were called up. For eleven days in 1940, between 20 and 30 June, passenger sailings from Guernsey and Jersey to Weymouth were resumed to bring out all those who wished to get away from the German occupation, but after that there were no more sailings of any sort to either Southampton or Weymouth until the Islands were free again in the spring of 1945.

At the same time refugees were pouring into Southampton from France. The plight of one bewildered group of children so touched the stevedores on duty that they had a whip-round and raised £3 10 shillings to buy sweets and other comforts, which may not sound a lot until one realises that a Mars bar, if you could get one, cost 2d.

On 19 June 1940 Southampton suffered its first air raid. Altogether there would be 1,605 alerts before the war ended. The worst night was that of 31 November-1 December 1940. The *Southern Daily Echo* described 'a blazing furnace in which every living thing seemed doomed to perish'. 160 engines, from as far away as Nottingham, fought the fires. Of the 631 people who were killed in Southampton during the war, 370 died on those two nights. For a period normal life almost came to an end and the administration of Southampton broke down. 9,600 people left each evening; the Mayor, it was noted, was anxious to get away on the 3 pm train otherwise he would have to wait until 7 pm. The docks and the various factories, particularly the Supermarine Spitfire works, were the chief targets and all were hit, although the railway works at Eastleigh escaped.

London was the principal target of the Luftwaffe during the later stages of the Battle of Britain and afterwards, and many railway installations on the Waterloo line were hit, including Dursnford Road power station and Waterloo station itself. The final 2¼ miles of the main line, from Queens Road, Battersea to Waterloo, was the most heavily attacked section of railway in the country, being bombed no less than 92 times between September 1940 and May 1941. One of the most severe raids was on 16 April and during this the Necropolis station and its train were virtually destroyed, the station was never rebuilt and the train never ran again. Nine Elms depot was also hit resulting in a number of deaths and the destruction of 'Paddlebox' 'T14' 4-6-0 No 458.

Another casualty was Brooklands. This most famous of car racing circuits had been built alongside the railway at Byfleet on land owned by an enthusiast, H. F. Locke-King, the actual work being under the charge of 'Mr Donaldson, a skilled railway engineer', to quote a contemporary account. This went on 'by December 1906 travellers on the South-Western main line could see clearly the beginnings of the Railway straight'. The River Wey was diverted to flow under a seven arch viaduct under the main line and on the site itself 2,000 navvies were at work. These men, many of whom travelled from London each day, certainly earned their money. Dr Reginald Farrar in a report to Parliament in 1907 noted that 'a large number of navvies travelled between East London and Weybridge on cheap day tickets but the weekly cost of these was still 4s 6d out of a wage of about 24s.' Seven miles of track, using 25,000 sleepers, were laid within the site to help the con-

struction of the massive banking and 'eighty truck loads of gravel and cement arrived daily hauled by six locomotives'. This massive undertaking was finished in July 1907 and the first meeting held on the 6th of that month.

The last race meeting took place on 7 August 1939. Immediately on the outbreak of war the racecourse came under Government control. It was used for a variety of experimental purposes, which involved breaching the banking and after the war it was sold to the Government for £330,000. Sections of the banking may still be seen from passing trains, particularly in winter time when they are less obscured by foliage.

Apart from being on the receiving end during the Battle of Britain the Waterloo to Weymouth line carried many personnel and thousands of tons of supplies to RAF establishments in Surrey, Hampshire and Dorset. Farnborough was the home of a research establishment where, after the war, the famous air show at which the latest products of the British aeronautical industry would be on display. Many Spitfires made their first flight from Eastleigh, and Hurn Aerodrome was opened on 1 August 1941. It was a mile from the site of the station on the closed Ringwood to Bournemouth branch, but there seems to have been no serious consideration given to re-opening it and passengers and freight for Hurn Aerodrome were handled either at Christchurch or Bournemouth Central. Although it was too late to take part in the Battle of Britain, Hurn served a vital role during the rest of the war, operating Lysanders to fields in France to send in and bring back secret agents and generally assist the Resistance. There was also a small airfield at Christchurch but much of its experimental work was transferred to Hurn when this opened. Winston Churchill's own personal Liberator was kept at Hurn and the aerodrome provided flights for many VIPs, including General Eisenhower, particularly from October 1943 when the USAF virtually took it over, until the period immediately before D-Day, when Fighter Command assumed control.

The most westerly of all the RAF stations which supplied squadrons for the Battle of Britain was Warmwell. This was beside the railway west of Moreton station. It was a Moreton Whirlwind fighter which was the first aircraft to land at Hurn, or rather crash land for it hit an obstruction on the uncompleted runway, injuring the pilot. Today Hurn is a commercial airport owned by Bournemouth Corporation whilst Warmwell has reverted to farmland, the only clues to its military past being a section of broken concrete beside the fence separating it from the railway line, which was once a hardstanding for Spitfires and Hurricanes, and two or three brick huts where their crews waited at dispersal for the next call

Left *'Paddlebox' 'T14' 4-6-0 No 458 near Hook on 16 April 1939 with a Waterloo to Basingstoke train. A year later No 458 was destroyed in the bombing of Nine Elms depot* (National Railway Museum).

Right *Three Spitfires flying over Eastleigh Airport to commemorate the fiftieth anniversary of the first flight of the prototype in 1935* (Southern Daily Echo).

Below *The second 'Merchant Navy' Class to be built, No 35002* Union Castle, *passing Raynes Park with a down Waterloo to West of England express, September 1955.*

to intercept the Messerschmidts, Heinkels and Focke-Wulfs coming in over Lulworth and Weymouth Bay.

Yet the war did not bring all normal activity to an end and extraordinary though it might seem at a time when so much of the nation's energy was devoted to national survival and little else, Eastleigh works managed to continue with the design of a revolutionary new express engine, the very first Pacific to work on Southern lines.

Maunsell's 'Lord Nelson's had not initially proved to be much of an advance over the 'King Arthur's. However when O. V. S. Bulleid came from Doncaster in 1937 to take over as the CME of the Southern Railway after Maunsell's retirement he rebuilt the 'Lord Nelson' front end and transformed the sixteen engines so that they were every bit as good as the LMS rebuilt 'Royal Scot's and the GWR 'Castle's, if not the 'King's. But Bulleid wanted his very own

express engine and in May 1938 the Board of Directors had given him authority to build ten. With the exploits of the Doncaster-built 'P2' 2-8-2 express engines clearly in his thoughts Bulleid considered an eight-coupled engine but on the advice of the Civil Engineer settled for a 4-6-2. Despite the war the work continued — Bulleid claimed the new engines were suitable for mixed traffic duties and thus got away with it. In fact they were out and out express passenger ones although ironically in their early days they often worked goods trains whilst their teething troubles were being sorted out.

In February 1941 the first, No 21C1, was completed. Bulleid called it air-smoothed, although only he knew the difference between this and streamlined. On 22 February it worked a twenty coach test train from Eastleigh to Bournemouth and back and on 10 March, despite the war, a ceremony

took place in the works yard at Eastleigh at which Lieutenant Colonel J. T. C. Moore-Brabazon, the Minister of Transport, and incidentally the holder of pilot's licence No 1, named the engine *Channel Packet*. That it, and its ten companions, should have been allowed to have been built during the war is extraordinary enough, but that there should have been a naming ceremony to boot borders on the bizarre. The main revolutionary features of the 'Merchant Navy' Class are too well known for them to be detailed here, suffice it to say that they caused many problems in the war years and until 1944 they were largely restricted to working west of Salisbury, often on goods trains. One cannot but conclude that the Southern would have been better served if their introduction had been delayed until after the war and that Eastleigh had occupied itself in building either more modified 'Lord Nelson's or Maunsell 2-6-0s.

As remarkable in appearance as the Pacifics were the 'Q1' 0-6-0s, designed, but not built at Eastleigh; they were however far simpler in construction. Simplest of all and ideal for the rigours of war work were the 23 Stanier 2-8-0s which Eastleigh built between December 1942 and June 1944.

As the war progressed into 1942 so the bombing raids slackened and the pressure on the Southern Railway eased. 68 engines were lent to other railways including seven to the Longmoor Military Railway and six of the seven 'Remembrance' Class engines to the GWR. These latter had once been the pride and joy of the LBSC and had been built as 4-6-4Ts. They were perhaps the most handsome tank engines ever to run in Britain, but electrification had rendered them redundant and so between December 1934 and April 1936 Eastleigh had rebuilt them as 4-6-0s. They were classified 'N15X' and it was briefly supposed by some that they were a superior breed of 'King Arthur'. But they were not and the sparkle they had shown as Baltic tanks on the Brighton line seemed to have vanished with their rebuilding. A reproduction

of one in its original form graces the sign of the pub outside Winchester station. They worked as 4-6-0s for some twenty years, apart from their wartime evacuation, on the Bournemouth line but were only entrusted with important expresses when nothing else was available.

In the two years leading up to the Normandy landings preparations were building up to the extent that the southern counties from Kent to Dorset were virtually one entire fortified camp. Many of the gliders which landed behind the lines were built at Christchurch and flown from Hurn, whilst huge numbers of landing craft and ships were assembled at Weymouth and Southampton, the troops manning them being brought by a succession of trains from camps on Salisbury Plain, the Aldershot area and elsewhere.

The variety of locomotives, carriages, and wagons seen on the Waterloo to Weymouth line at this period in its history was as great as that during the First World War and quite unequalled in peacetime. Unfortunately wartime conditions, and restrictions on photography — films had disappeared from the chemists' shelves 'for the duration' — meant that most of it went unrecorded. One lunchtime my father, returning from work, remarked he had popped into Bournemouth West station to the bookstall and had noticed a tank engine quite unlike anything he had seen there before. He took no more than a passing interest in railways but this was sufficiently out of the ordinary to attract his attention. It was very large, painted black and carried no indication of ownership on its tank or bunker sides. My father was sufficiently knowledgeable to know it wasn't of Great Western origin. I've often puzzled over what it could have been, perhaps a Fowler or Stanier 2-6-4T from the Somerset and Dorset, or even more exotic, maybe an ex-Great Central 4-6-2T come down on a special by way of Banbury and Oxford? It can only be guesswork, just one more small, unsolved mystery from those troubled years.

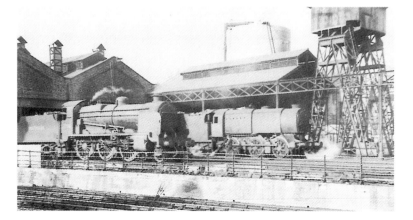

A Bulleid 'Q1' Class 0-6-0 and a Maunsell 'U' Class 2-6-0, rebuilt from a 'River' Class 2-6-4T, at Bournemouth shed in 1947 (Kelland Collection).

Chapter 20
The end of the war

Inevitably not everything in the build-up to D-Day went smoothly. Many of the trains travelled great distances and the crews found themselves in unfamiliar territory as they approached Southampton or Weymouth. With the tremendous demands on manpower pilots were not always available and delays occurred. Then the sheer volume of traffic created problems. Woking turntable, for instance, was not able to cope with all the demands put upon it and engines had to be sent to Addlestone to turn on the triangle there.

Ensuring that everyone was properly fed on a journey which might extend over two days was a huge undertaking. Resources and people were stretched to breaking point, and sometimes beyond. Even in wartime there are limits beyond which the participants are not prepared to push themselves. Such a situation arose at Basingstoke. Bernard Darwin in his *War on the Line*, published by the Southern Railway in 1946, put it down to a 'question of red tape and guaranteed payment', but one suspects war weariness and a reluctance to perform unlimited unpaid overtime played their part. The problem was resolved partly by the Mayor who raised £500, £100 of it from the staff of Thornycroft, by the efforts of the bakers and provision merchants in the town, and a hundred lady helpers and other volunteers who between them saw that all the troops were fed and watered.

Just as they had been thirty years earlier the railways were called upon to provide ambulance trains — six Bournemouth line restaurant cars were converted for the use of the US forces — and the first casualties from the Normandy beaches reached Southampton on 7 June 1944. 104 ambulance trains left Southampton Docks in June and 113 the following month.

The Control Office had charge of the enormous job of seeing that these trains, as well as all the other wartime traffic, and the normal scheduled services got safely to their destinations. It had been established at Southampton in 1913 and covered an area bounded by Portsmouth, Alton, Basingstoke, Newbury, Salisbury, Bath, Burnham-on-Sea, Weymouth and Portland.

The Didcot, Newbury and Winchester line and the Midland and Great Western Joint were busier then they had ever been, or would be again, and so to a lesser extent was the Somerset and Dorset Joint. Sections of the DN&S were doubled and extra loops put in elsewhere and signalboxes on the MGW were manned continuously, day and night, to speed the troop trains from the camps on Salisbury Plain to the Channel ports.

The floating Mulberry Harbour, which probably made all the difference between the failure and success of the Normandy landings, was built at Southampton and towed across so that supplies could be poured in to back up the first invasion assault. A few sections of it still exist and are preserved off the French coast.

By the end of 1944 one million United States military personnel had sailed from Southampton for France. Such a figure is difficult to visualize in human terms. It takes on meaning if one had met and spoken to some of those GIs. To a seven year old such as myself they were all grown men but many were still in their teens, thousands of miles away from home in a land, where although the inhabitants spoke approximately the same language as themselves, they were certainly foreigners and which was in any case merely a staging post to the war and, perhaps, mutilation or death. The word nostalgia entered my vocabulary when I overheard it used by one American to another who was talking about his home on the upper deck of a Bournemouth bus. The first black men I ever saw were American soldiers and on Christmas morning 1944 one handed me a bar of chocolate as I was coming out of church with my parents. Rubber balls were always being washed up on the beach from life rafts off sunken ships and one got pretty blase about these but a real find was the fuselage and wing of a model aeroplane with American markings. My father replaced the missing parts from bits of scrap wood and when it was ready I took it to a group of GIs who were sitting on the cliff walk near Alum Chine; the argument got quite heated in their attempts to identify it.

My first encounter with the narrow gauge took place at Bournemouth in the summer of 1944,

Top *A USA 0-6-0T shunts empty stock in front of the impressive Solent Flour Mills, Southampton, on 2 June 1962 (Stanley Creer).*

Above *One of the 'H15's built in 1924, No 30475 of Eastleigh shed, storms up Parkstone Bank with a Weymouth to Bournemouth West train in 1961 (Dr Ian C. Allen).*

Left *Nine Elms Shed in 1949 with not-yet renumbered 'T14' Class 4-6-0s Nos 444 and 443, alongside 'West Country' Class light Pacific No 34023 Blackmore Vale. The latter, after beginning its preservation career t Longmoor, is now on the Bluebell Railway (P. Ransome-Wallis, NRM).*

unlikely though that may seem. We are about to score a first here with the entry into print of a hitherto unrecorded railway line. It was not very long, around one hundred yards, a bit more some days, a bit less others. It conveyed hand-propelled tipper wagons, the motive power sometimes being yours truly, and was used in the rebuilding of a section of the promenade. I quickly ingratiated myself with the operators, a gang of navvies, and spent most of the gloriously sunny month of August 1944 assisting in this vital piece of war work, although there were a couple of occasions when I abandoned it to consort with General Montgomery's nephew who was staying in a hotel where my mother sometimes worked as a cook.

Journeys on proper trains in the year we lived at Bournemouth were rare. Once during a bus strike — yes there were strikes in wartime — we came back from Poole by train and I have a notion our engine was a 'U' Class 2-6-0, though why I should think this I cannot say for it was not the glamorous sort of engine which got itself into the few railway books for boys then available and there was no-one to tell me what it was. We also went to Weymouth by train and did that Limerick Junction type shuffle into and out of Dorchester station on the way back. Our one visit to Swanage was by bus. The only memories I have of this are not of the 'M7's which worked the branch but of the towering ruin of Corfe Castle and that the single deck bus had an engine which stuck out at the front. Then there was the time my father and I were shooed away from the sidings on Hamworthy Quay by a sentry when we were exploring amongst the wagons, beachcombing for more rubber balls or model aeroplanes.

My mother and I were walking down Richmond Hill past the *Bournemouth Echo* offices the afternoon the end of the war in Europe was announced. We knew it had happened for a Union Jack appeared out of an upper window of the newspaper offices, followed by flags of many hues and allegiances, but all more or less on our side, from offices and shops all over the centre of Bournemouth. It was time to take the train back to Waterloo and the Feltham tram home to Thornton Heath.

I'd missed the VE day street party but was in time for the VJ day one. The first railway books specifically aimed at young train-spotters had appeared and armed with vastly more information than had previously been available Wadham, Gillham and I set off to cop 'Nelsons', 'Arthurs' and the ever-increasing ranks of Bulleid Pacifics.

Ten more 'Merchant Navy's came out of Eastleigh in the final months of the war. Not all the problems which the initial ten had revealed were yet solved. O. S. Nock recounts one incident when a big end

failed (a not infrequent happening) on the level crossing at Brockenhurst, of all places, on a summer Saturday and no road or rail traffic could move until the drastic solution of cutting away the offending parts was resorted to and the engine towed away in disgrace. Despite such incidents Bulleid got authority not only to build twenty more 'Merchant Navy's — the final ten came out immediately after nationalization in 1948 — but to introduce a lightweight version, the 'West Country' and 'Battle of Britain' Class. The first of these appeared in June 1945 and by October 1947 no less than seventy were at work.

The 'Merchant Navy' Class bore splendid names, the majority of them associated with Southampton Docks, but some of the smaller Pacifics were saddled with distinctly curious appellations. The various squadrons commemorated no doubt had splendid war records but a long list of numbers hardly stirred the imagination, whilst it was difficult to stifle a snigger when confronted with 21C125 *Whimple* immediately followed by 21C126 *Yes Tor*. I don't suppose many trains ever got right through to *Lundy* (No 21C129), whilst there are those who would claim that if *Swanage* (No 34105 — it was never a Southern Railway engine) qualified as West Country why not Bournemouth?

Be that as it may, whenever we visited Waterloo or Clapham Junction there were yet more shiny new Bulleid Pacifics to be seen, some not yet named, until it seemed that even the postal workers train to Kensington Olympia must be taken over by them. That never happened but the construction of no less than 110 Pacifics between 1945 and 1950 found the operating authorities hard pressed to keep them occupied and they could frequently be seen pottering about with trains which had previously been the concern of ancient 4-4-0s, 0-6-0s and 0-4-4Ts.

Not the least interesting feature of the 'West Country' and 'Battle of Britain' Pacifics was that, although designed at Eastleigh, only six of them, Nos 34095, 34097, 34099, 34101, 34102 and 34104, of the final batch were built there. All the rest came out of Brighton, a works that had given up building, so it was generally assumed, soon after the amalgamation.

Whether or not the Southern needed such a sudden deluge of powerful, if not totally reliable, and certainly distinctive Pacifics will long be argued. But it was true that the company had a very high proportion of elderly passenger engines, chiefly 4-4-0s, which could not be expected to soldier on much longer, even if more electrification was in the offing. The first priority in the immediate post-war period was to catch up on the backlog of maintenance and the general neglect of the 1939 to 1945 years, extension of the electrified network would have to wait until this was achieved.

Amongst the classes which had disappeared by August 1945 were the last of the Adams 4-4-0s. No 563, a 'T3' built at Nine Elms in March 1893, had actually been withdrawn in March 1939, having spent her last years working down to Bournemouth on slow trains from Salisbury by way of Fording-bridge and Broadstone, or else pottering about East-leigh. But the outbreak of war meant a reprieve and she was overhauled and sent to work from Basing-stoke shed on van trains and similar light but very necessary duties. With the end of the war old 563 was once again withdrawn and dumped first at East-leigh and then near Romsey. Being one of many engines which the end of the war and the advent of the Bulleid Pacifics had made redundant, the cutters torch hadn't got round to her some two and a half years later. Waterloo station celebrated its centenary in 1948 and it was thought it would be rather nice if some vintage rolling stock could be put on display to mark the occasion. What could be more delightfully vintage and appropriate than No 563? So once again she was rescued from the edge of extinction and towed back to Eastleigh.

On 11 June 1948 she steamed up to Waterloo at a gentle 25 mph in order not to strain her tired old fire-box. She had had various original Adams-type fittings restored, including a stovepipe chimney and had been repainted in 1903 LSW livery. With her, most happily, went a 1903 carriage, also restored to original condition. This was a non-corridor brake tri-composite, originally No 847. In SR days it was renumbered 6474 and for some curious reason kept this number when it was taken out of passenger ser-vice in May 1948 and put back into LSW livery for the Waterloo centenary celebrations.

The exhibition lasted from 14 to 25 June 1948. The stars were undoubtedly the LSW engine and carriage; the supporting cast was the Brighton Terrier *Boxhill* and West Country Pacific No 34017 *Ilfracombe*.

The Adams 4-4-0 was the first locomotive from a Southern constituent to be preserved officially, although the Stephenson Locomotive Society had bought the celebrated LBSC express engine *Gladstone* in 1927, and after restoration at Brighton Works the LNER had found a place for her in their York Museum. The two Southern locomotives would eventually come to rest side by side in the National Railway Museum at York, but before that the LSW locomotive appeared at Eastleigh Works open days, was stored in a variety of locations and then, after a second restoration to original Adams 1893 condition, was put on display at the British Transport Museum at Clapham. When this closed she was towed to York in April 1975 and there she may seen to-day. The LSW carriage also eventually went to York, but unfortunately it was not put on display as some restoration work was needed. Part of this has been completed and it is very much hoped No 847 will shortly reappear for it is the only LSW bogie carriage to be preserved in original condition; the salmon and pink livery would be a welcome addition to the kaleidoscope of colours at York.

Bulleid's carriages, if not quite such a revolution-ary break with Southern Railway traditions as his locomotives, were certainly unmistakably different to anything which had gone before. The Southern, far more than the other three main line companies, liked to organize its carriages into sets and Bulleid and his Technical Assistant (Carriage and Wagons) L. Lynes had the designs for a number of six-car sets and up to 150 carriages in all for the Bournemouth line ready before the outbreak of World War 2. As with his Pacifics this would seem to by a distinct case of overkill for Bulleid's 150 carriages would have seen off all others, including the only just refurbished and very modern 'Bournemouth Limited' sets. Construc-tion of some of the underframes began at Lancing in 1939 but none were completed at that time, and it wasn't until November 1945 that Bulleid's first main line carriages, using the 1939 underframes, emerged from Eastleigh Works; Maunsell vehicles continued to be found on Bournemouth expresses, if in steadily decreasing numbers, until the mid-1960s.

The interiors of the new carriages were surpris-ingly conservative, very reminiscent of Maunsell practice rather than the Bulleid refurbishments of the 1938 'Bournemouth Limited' stock. They also had the traditional separate doors to each compartment, a feature which the other three main line companies had abandoned, although they did have contin-uously curved bodysides and toplights above the

doors. These last two characteristics gave the carriages a close similarity to Bulleid electric stock, although they were much better appointed. They were not, however, the real precursors of Bulleid's express carriages, rather an interim stage between what was possible at the end of the war and what was hoped would become the norm in the prosperous years to follow.

The real prototype came out as a one-off from Eastleigh at the end of 1945. A composite vehicle, at 64 ft 6 in long over end panels it was 5 ft longer than the previous SR standard; there were the usual four three-a-side first class compartments and three four-a-side 3rd class ones and two lavatories which meant there was more space all round. Seats were more comfortable with the curved bodysides giving more room at shoulder level, big windows with sliding ventilators were provided with external doors only at

the end and in the centre. Unlike the electric stock the body frames were of wood, the panelling was steel, whilst a curiously old-fashioned feature was the canvas-covered roof. The carriage, No 5751, was exhibited during October 1945 at Waterloo and other London termini and the public — no less than 25,000 visited it — asked for their reactions. These were largely favourable, although there was a strong preference for individual reading lamps which it had not been possible to fit, and more sensitive heating.

Soon Bulleid corridor coaches were rolling off the production line. In August 1947 the *Southern Daily Echo* reported that 'No 1 of the Southern Railways new luxury trains will be put into service on the Waterloo to Bournemouth run. With their new-style restaurants and revolutionary heating and ventilation these trains will be the most sumptuous running in Britain. Heat-wave footnote. For the first time on any

Left *'Battle of Britain' Pacific No 34073* 249 Squadron *speeds through Worting Junction with the 1 pm Waterloo to West of England express, 22 May 1961.*

Above *A Waterloo to Bournemouth express speeds through Clapham Junction behind Urie 'N15' 'King Arthur' 4-6-0 No 30751 Etarre on 23 June 1951. To the left is a brand new Bulleid corridor first, to the right Bulleid 4SUB EMUs* (Brian Morrison).

Right *The preserved Adams 4-4-0 No 563, in the National Railway Museum, York.*

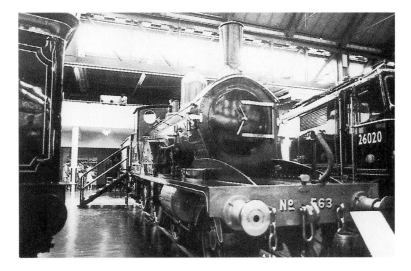

British train, iced lager and REALLY cold bottled beer will be on sale.' The reporter had rather gone over the top regarding the heating and ventilation, which were perfectly ordinary, unlike the air-conditioning experiments being carried out by the GWR and the LNER, and I doubt if even the Southern's well-oiled publicity department would have used sumptious with quite such abandon, but nevertheless the citizens of Bournemouth could consider themselves pretty well provided for in Bulleid's new carriages.

Although the prototype had an all-compartment layout and the questionnaire which those visiting it were asked to fill in had indicated a preference for this, fashion was moving inexorably towards open carriages and a distinctive design which incorporated both compartments and a saloon section was a brake third. There were more of them than any other Bulleid type, 205, built between the end of 1946 and June 1951. I never thought Bulleid carriages possessed particularly handsome exteriors but the first one I travelled in, a brake third, between Sandwich

A railwayman at work on his allotment at Eastleigh, in front of a Bulleid-designed 4EPB Class 415/1 electric multiple unit.

and Ashford in the summer of 1947, made a great impression with its light and spacious interior. I still get the opportunity to repeat the experience, when the preserved No 4365, a brake third built in 1947, comes puffing up from Swanage behind the school where I teach.

No 4365 when new was formed into 'Bournemouth Dining Set' No 298. There were eleven such sets, Nos 290-300, each of six carriages, thus going a long way to fulfilling the pre-war intention of monopolizing the Bournemouth and Weymouth route with Bulleid vehicles. The new carriages were to be found all over the Southern network, although they took a little while to become commonplace on the Central Section, but they were particularly associated with the Bournemouth line. Elsewhere on British Railways pre-nationalization design carriages had largely disappeared from the top rank duties by around 1960 but on the Bournemouth line the Bulleids refused to be ousted by BR Mark 1s and they remained a commonplace sight on Waterloo to Southampton, Bournemouth and Weymouth trains right up to electrification in 1967.

Bulleid seldom adopted a conventional approach to any problem if it could be avoided, but even he must have been taken aback by the furore which erupted over sixteen carriages which went into service in the summer of 1949. These were the Tavern Cars. They were not, in truth, a very significant part of Bulleid's output and as they didn't run regulaly over the Bournemouth line in their original form, although they were built at Eastleigh, we mustn't devote too much space to them. The idea was to recreate the atmosphere of a cosy English pub, with mock-Tudor woodwork, whitewashed ceilings — and stainless steel and plastic bars. They were even painted on the outsides with inn signs and imitation brickwork. It could have all been rather jolly and amusing but where it went disastrously wrong was in the absence of any windows in the dining cars, save small ones set too high to see out of. Apparently the idea behind this piece of idiocy was that diners would not dawdle over the view but rapidly vacate their seats so that others could take them and profits would increase. Of course the opposite happened as the oppressive atmosphere drove customers away and they did not hesitate to say so. The press had a real field day and within months the Tavern Cars began to retreat in disgrace. The dining cars were all rebuilt as conventional vehicles by June 1951, but the bar and kitchen cars needed less drastic surgery to make them acceptable and although they quickly lost their imitation brickwork and signs, other features remained. By 1952 one Tavern Car with a rebuilt dining trailer was regularly at work between Waterloo and Weymouth in the 'Royal Wessex'.

Chapter 21
The Bulleid years

In the years immediately after the Second World War Southampton Docks became busier than ever. One by one the liners which had survived the war re-entered regular civilian service, and these included the three Cunard giants, *Queen Elizabeth, Queen Mary* and *Aquitania*. The war had taken the *Queen Elizabeth* into waters her builders could never have envisaged the flagship of the Cunard's transatlantic fleet becoming acquainted with and between 1940 and 1946 she had carried 800,000 military personnel. On 16 October 1946 she at last set off on her maiden peacetime voyage from Southampton to New York. It was an occasion for national rejoicing — she was the largest ship in the world, though not the fastest and she never captured the Blue Riband from the *Queen Mary* — a BBC radio commentator travelled with her, broadcasting her progress and her triumphant arrival back to the millions listening in at home.

A month earlier her sister ship had ended her trooping career and on 31 July 1947 the *Queen Mary* too went back on the transatlantic run between Southampton and New York. Each of the 'Queens' post-war maiden voyages had been the occasion for special trains from Waterloo and with regular ocean travel resuming around a world where more and more people were on the move, over 300 boat trains a month were operating to and from Southampton and Waterloo.

The *Aquitania* was the only transatlantic liner to work right through the two wars. By now she was also the only four-funnelled passenger ship in service, a reminder of the days of Edwardian confidence and opulence, although there was little evidence of this latter by the time she finished nine years of trooping in the spring of 1948. With the two 'Queens' providing the regular weekly departure for New York the old *Aquitania* spent her last eighteen months working out of Southampton carrying migrants and war brides across the Atlantic to Canada. On 1 December 1949 she arrived at Southampton for the last time and when she sailed shortly afterwards for the Clyde to be broken up thousands turned out to say goodbye. The press and the newsreels were there and photographic technology had advanced sufficiently for a dramatic

record to be made in colour transparencies of the last of the great four-funnellers steaming down the Solent on a cold clear January morning.

In 1948 590,000 passengers passed through Southampton, the greatest number so far in the port's history, exceeding that of 1938 by 30,000.

Perhaps the most obvious outward sign that wartime days had been left behind and that Southampton was prospering as never before came on 31 July 1950 when the Prime Minister, Clement Attlee, opened the Ocean Terminal. Planned by the Southern Railway who had begun demolition of the

The Queen Mary *leaving Southampton for New York.*

existing, partly-bombed, buildings at the Ocean Dock at the end of 1946 in order to make way for it, nationalization on 1 January 1948 meant that the British Transport Commission were the proud owners when the first users of it, 1,400 passengers for the *Queen Elizabeth*, passed through on 1 August, 1950. Two days later the *Queen Mary* was the first inbound liner to use the terminal, 1,000 of her passengers passing through on to the three boat trains in two hours, the first getting away within 90 minutes of the liner's docking.

Designed as 1,297½ ft long (I don't know if anyone ever checked that extra half), with a 100 ft high tower at the seaward end, it was certainly an impressive-looking structure. It was very much of its period, steel framed, clad in concrete, (brick would have been used had it not been in short supply) with a curved glass end. It always seemed to me a gloomy old barn of a place, but it was highly thought of at the time, and it certainly provided plenty of up-to-date facilities, with lifts and escalators, as well as stairs, to and from the 1,011 ft long island platform. Embarkation and disembarkation was greatly speeded up with the provision of six telescopic gangways, but then there was need of it for a full complement of passengers for one of the 'Queens' required five boat trains.

The fastest liner ever to use the Ocean Terminal called for the first time two years after its opening in July 1952. This was the *United States* and she captured the Blue Riband from the *Queen Mary* on her maiden voyage, achieving a remarkable average of 35.39 knots. Although laid up for many years now, despite persistent rumours of her return as a cruise liner, she remains the holder and unless some totally unforseeable event drives every airliner from the sky and great liners once again race across the Atlantic, her record is likely to stand for ever. Richard Branson's efforts have nothing to do with the Blue

Riband, a souped-up speedboat which has to be refuelled several times and can only sail in the most favourable conditions bearing no comparison with a floating community of 3,000 and more souls designed to make hundreds of crossings in perfect safety spring, summer, autumn and winter.

By the mid 1950s the airlines had captured a significant proportion of the transatlantic, and indeed the worldwide travel market. The last BOAC flying boats had made their final flights from Poole in 1949 and although some found further employment on the Berlin airlift and elsewhere, many were broken up on Southampton Water and at Poole. A dying fall was provided by the giant ten-engined Princess flying boat which made its first flight from Cowes on 22 August 1952, but it simply could not compete with the American-built, land-based Constellations, Skymasters and Stratocruisers, and it never carried a fare-paying passenger. Nevertheless so rapidly was the total number of travellers across the Atlantic, emigrants to Australia, and holidaymakers to the Continent and elsewhere increasing that in 1955 Southampton handled 690,000 passengers, its highest total ever.

In July 1945 regular sailings to the Channel Islands began again from Southampton, and two months later GWR boats restarted from Weymouth, although initially the latter were cargo only, passenger sailings not recommencing until June of the following year. With unemployment virtually non-existent, and a relatively affluent society chafing under the restrictions of rationing, there was more money available for spending on holidays than there had ever been before and travel to the Channel Islands boomed in 1947. Much of it went by way of Southampton and Weymouth, but an increasing proportion flew from Eastleigh airport.

Freight traffic through Southampton, whilst attracting nothing like the publicity of the glamorous passenger side of the port's activities, was nevertheless big business. In 1953 it amounted to 1,100,000 tons, a figure roughly equivalent to that of both 1928 and 1938. It had dipped following the slump to 900,000 in 1933 and after the Second World War to 800,000 in 1948. As with the passenger trafic not all of it entered or left the docks by rail but a vast amount of it did.

'S15' 4-6-0s provided the principal motive power for the heavy goods trains between Southampton and Feltham and Nine Elms whilst within the docks a fleet of shunters was kept busy. The long reign of the Adams 'B4' 0-4-0Ts had come to an end during 1947 when they were replaced by fourteen engines every bit as remarkable as the Bulleid Pacifics then also entering service. These were the 'USA's.

Huge numbers of locomotives were built in the

Left *Urie 'H15' Class 4-6-0 No 30485 of Nine Elms shed crossing Battledown flyover wreathed in smoke and steam with a Bournemouth to Waterloo parcels train, 8 August 1952. The need for smoke deflectors on the big boilered, small chimneyed Urie and Maunsell 4-6-0s is abundantly obvious from this picture although in this particular instance nothing short of a giant pair of bellows would seem to be called for (Brian Morrison).*

Right *Successor to the 'B4's, USA 0-6-0T No 30064 at Sheffield Park, March 1983.*

United States and Canada during the Second World War years and immediately after for service all over the world. Many of the 2-8-0s worked for a brief period in Britain before being shipped off elsewhere, whilst perhaps the most famous were the '141R's which virtually kept the railways of France running single-handed whilst they were recovering from the Occupation, and which could be found on boat trains to the Channel ports until 1970. The only American built engines which took up permanent residence in Britain were fourteen 0-6-0T shunters built by the firms of Porter and Vulcan in 1942-43. These were bought by the Southern Railway specifically for work in Southampton Docks, classified logically enough as the 'USA's, and being powerful little engines with a short wheelbase they proved ideal for the job and virtually monopolized it until the end of steam. Many of the withdrawn Adams engines were sold for industrial use and eleven remained in service with the Southern. Of these latter there was always one to be seen on Poole Quay, another at Winchester, a third around Southampton Terminus and others at Eastleigh.

One of the most welcome signs that peacetime had returned was the reinstatement of Pullmans, both on certain Southampton boat trains, and on the 'Bournemouth Belle'. The latter made its first post-war run on 7 October 1946. Departure from Waterloo was at 12.30 pm; Southampton, where there was a civic reception, was reached at 1.57 and Bournemouth, where there was another reception, at 2.35. 'Lord Nelson's had been replaced by 'Merchant Navy's, which were to be the train's regular motive power for some twenty years. The average speed, including the stop at Southampton was a respectable but certainly not spectacular 51 mph. The 'Schools' 4-4-0s had departed from the Bournemouth line early in the war years, and although there was still plenty of work for

the 'Lord Nelson's, and to a lesser extent the 'King Arthur's, it was largely of a secondary nature, both varieties of Bulleid Pacifics monopolizing top link workings. At the lowest end of the scale a heavy slaughter of Drummond 4-4-0s took place, the forty 'K10's, a similar number of 'L11's, nineteen of the twenty 'S11's and eighteen of the twenty 'L12's all being taken out of service and broken up by the end of 1952. Urie's 4-6-0s would last for a little longer but the Drummond 'Paddleboxes' all disappeared into Eastleigh for scrapping by late 1951.

Perhaps surprisingly the seven 'N15X' 'Remembrance' 4-6-0s were all still at work between Waterloo, Basingstoke and Eastleigh after the last Bulleid Pacifics had entered service. Indeed on summer Saturdays, when in the late 1940s and the early 1950s the railways could barely cope with the demands made on them, many elderly engines found themselves briefly restored to long distance passenger work and on successive weekends in August 1950 'Remembrance' Class locomotives were noted working right through from Bournemouth to Banbury on expresses for Sheffield and beyond; they returned home in a sedate manner on goods trains.

The 'Bournemouth Limited' did not return after the war, the carriages which worked it being dispersed throughout the system, but a new named express, the 'Royal Wessex', made its appearance in the Festival of Britain Year of 1951. This was largely formed of BR standard carriages, and as such was untypical of Bournemouth and Weymouth expresses where Bulleid stock held the ascendancy throughout the 1950s.

On 31 December 1947, at midnight, the Southern Railway, along with its ancient rival the GWR, and the LMS and the LNER, ceased to exist. As from New Year's Day 1948 it became the Southern Region of British Railways.

Chapter 22
Nationalization

On none of the Big Four main line companies did nationalization mean the instant disappearance of their individual identities. There was much talk, a good deal of it with humorous undertones, of 'our' railways, now that they belonged to the nation, flights of such fancies as wandering into one's nearest station and ordering a private train, à la Duke of Wellington, or of civil service railwaymen painstakingly making out tickets in triplicate and bringing business to a standstill for teabreaks. There is a story told of a carter called Champion who was employed by the Southern at Basingstoke. In 1948 many local deliveries from stations all over the country were still carried out by horse and cart. In order to obtain access to one particular customer in the town it was necessary for Mr Champion to place his horse and cart on the pavement. This was too much for a certain Home Counties lady who haughtily informed the carter that as the railways were now nationalized he was in her employ and that he had best shift, horse and cart. After looking her up and down Champion made his way to the nether quarters of his animal, plucked a hair from its tail, and handed it to the lady with the words: 'Here, madam, is your share'.

The first obvious signs of the new order were in the liveries of the rolling stock, the road vehicles, changes in titles, publicity material etc. More importantly the headquarters of the Railway Executive was set up behind the terracotta facade of the Great Central Hotel adjoining Marylebone Station, and the chairmanship, after first being offered to and refused by Sir James Milne of the GWR, was then offered to and accepted by Sir Eustace Missenden of the Southern. It was shortly after this that I came across a brand new Bulleid Pacific at Waterloo, No 34090, bearing the title *Sir Eustace Missenden, Southern Railway,* and wondered how this related either to the West Country or the Battle of Britain. But then the GWR quite happily gave members of its 'Castle' Class such names as *Hurricane, Spitfire* and *Defiant,* and the LMS called a 'Patriot' 4-6-0 *Bunsen;* anyone expecting logic in the nomenclature of railway engines has little sense of history or an understanding of the deviousness of those who have the much-envied task of picking the names.

For a while the regions retained a large degree of autonomy. An organization as enormous as British Railways needed time to sort itself out and decide where its priorities lay and there was still a huge backlog of maintenance to catch up on following the ravages of war. One area where a unified system could quickly bring advantages in operation and a saving of money was in a more logical distribution of lines in the border areas between the regions. This did not necessarily please the railwayman on the spot whose allegiance, for example, had always been to the Great Western and now found himself in the employ of the scorned South Western rival. No good telling him that it was all now British Railways, old loyalties died hard. From 2 April 1950 the Paddington to Weymouth main line south of Sparkford, first station out of Castle Cary, passed to the Southern Region. Perhaps even more traumatic was the transfer of the shipping services at Weymouth to the Southern. The whole of the old Midland and South West Junction line south of Savernake was now Southern property as was the Didcot to Winchester line south of Newbury, the Westbury to Salisbury, and the Reading to Basingstoke lines. In actual fact these were largely administrative moves and former GWR locomotives and carriages continued to work much as they had formerly done; certainly the Channel Islands boat train still ran to and from Paddington and Southern engines were to all intents and purposes quite unknown north of Dorchester and would remain so to the end of steam. Swindon-built 2-6-2Ts and Pannier tanks continued to work the Bridport branch and the Abbotsbury one was the preserve of a 14XX from Weymouth shed with its autocoach.

Two Dorset branches closed in the early 1950s, the aforementioned Abbotsbury one, which went in November 1952, and the Portland one for passengers in March of the same year. A short section of the Abbotsbury line remained open as far as Upwey for a while longer for goods traffic and the whole of the Portland line continued in use for this purpose.

In many ways the Southern was less affected by nationalization than any of the old companies. The war had brought the spread of the electrified network to a halt, but it was only a temporary one, and it would resume in the 1950s, still using what was now the outdated third-rail system with rolling stock of essentially Southern design in the familiar green livery. On the non-electrified lines most long distance passenger trains were in the hands of Bulleid Pacifics, the most modern locomotives in the country, and after nationalization a further fifty were brought out from Brighton and Eastleigh works. The first BR designed carriages entered service in 1951 with a curved profile which was pure Bulleid so that visually they closely resembled the final designs of the Southern Railway, although their all-metal construction and buck-eye couplers were notable advances. They appeared none too soon in the opinion of the *Southern Daily Echo,* for on 24 March 1950 it noted that 'railway passengers who leave Southampton by express have usually clean, comfortable carriages to take them to Bournemouth or Waterloo. But the local trains...are extremely scruffy.' These latter were largely the preserve of LSW non-corridors, dating back to Edwardian times. They were no better or worse than those found on secondary steam services anywhere else on the Southern, or indeed on the rest of BR at that time, but it was true that they were old-fashioned and shabby. For the enthusiast they had period charm, but their dust-laden seats, off-white, wood-beamed ceilings and ancient lighting held little appeal for the ordinary customers. They were gradually going for scrap but

it was a slow process and a few survived into the 1960s.

The *Echo's* solution was 'an electric suburban service', although it should be noted that there were plenty of pre-grouping carriages at work in the London suburban electric multiple units. It is true that they were a good deal cleaner, inevitably, than steam-hauled stock. The *Echo* continued: 'The present haphazardly-timed service is not much use to local travellers...obviously if the plea is ever taken up, it will not be for a long time'. It all depends what you mean by a long time for although the Romsey and Fareham lines are still not electrified, within seven years diesel-electric multiple units were to appear on these services.

In 1951 the Festival of Britain was held on the south bank of the Thames and direct access was provided to the site from Waterloo station. Whilst casting an affectionate look at the past the Festival was essentially an exhilarating prophecy of the future. Amongst the railway exhibits was one of the new BR standard 'Britannia' Class Pacifics, No 70004 *William Shakespeare,* which in concept owed something to Bulleid's light Pacifics. No 70004 was to become famous as the regular engine for the 'Golden Arrow', along with sister No 70014, but 'Britannia's worked on the Bournemouth line only in emergency when the 'Merchant Navy's were temporarily withdrawn due to problems with their driving axles. By then Bulleid had left the Southern, but in the immediate post-nationalization period when the CME's of the

A London Transport LT type bus on the special service between Wimbledon station and the Lawn Tennis Championships, June 1949 (Alan B. Cross).

The 12.30 pm Weymouth express at Paddington in the charge of No 4962 Ragley Hall *of Old Oak Common shed, July 1935* (C. B. Mullinger).

Left *Brand new 'Britannia' Class Pacific No 70009* Alfred the Great *makes a brief appearance on the 'Bournemouth Belle', although this duty was shortly handed back to the Bulleid Pacifics with which it remained for another fifteen years. Clapham Junction, 23 June 1951 (Brian Morrison).*

Below left *The one and only 'Leader' Class tank engine to be put in steam, No 36001, at Eastleigh in 1969 whilst undergoing trials (Kelland Collection).*

Below *GWR built 'Manor' Class 4-6-0 No 7808* Cookham Manor *approaching Eastleigh past a Hants and Dorset Bristol/ECW double-decker with a train of wooden-bodied open wagons for the Midland and South Western Joint line, 2 July 1954. In 1966* Cookham Manor *was bought out of service from BR for the Great Western Society and is today preserved at Didcot Railway Centre (Brian Morrison).*

former GWR, the LMS, the LNER and the Southern were still at their posts, Bulleid had one more remarkable design to spring upon a world which was not yet ready for it. This was the 'Leader' Class.

The 'Leader's are one of the great might-have-beens. Five were ordered, three were completed, only one was ever steamed. This was built at Brighton but much of its brief working life was spent based at Eastleigh. Bulleid, in a lecture in 1948 to the British Association for the Advancement of Science, made it clear that the 'Leader's were intended to answer the challenge of electrification. As such it was the most advanced design of steam locomotive ever to take the rails in Britain. It has been described in detail elsewhere, suffice it to note here that it was a twelve-wheel tank engine, the wheels grouped into two bogies, the whole totally enclosed with a cab at each end and a separate fireman's compartment amidships. This latter contributed to the Leader's downfall for the heat soon became unbearable. Other unconventional features inevitably gave rise to problems when testing began, but this was only expected and they might have been overcome. What really brought the experiment to a premature end was the retirement of Bulleid in September 1949, at which time his first Leader, No 36001, had been running for only three months.

The emphasis in locomotive design in those early days of nationalization was on simplicity, robustness and ease of maintenance, qualities which the 'Leader's shunned, but which the 'Britannia's, and indeed all 999 BR Standard steam engines typified. With their creator gone and no longer able to protect and nurture them, the 'Leader's had no future.

Nevertheless tests went on with No 36001 for another year and in the spring of 1950 it was announced that she was being equipped at Eastleigh for trials with the former LNER dynamometer car, the same vehicle which had raced behind *Mallard* when the Gresley Pacific achieved the world speed record for steam, an event with which Bulleid, as Gresley's second in command, was closely associated. The firebox area of No 36001 had been much reduced with an extra row of bricks put in to try to cut down the heat reaching the fireman, but this meant the grate area was now barely sufficient to cope with the demand of the six sleeve-valve gear cylinders.

An impressive feature of the 'Leader' was her ability at starting. With all her wheels powered she quite outshone the Bulleid Pacifics in this department; as one eye witness commented, there was a 'complete absence of slipping or fuss on starting'.

There is no record of No 36001 ever being called on to haul revenue paying members of the public, although when looking through contemporary accounts I thought for one moment that I had dis-covered one; *The Railway Observer* for July 1950 records that during the previous month '36001 left Eastleigh behind the 5.5 pm Bournemouth West to Waterloo'. I took this to mean the 'Leader' had charge of it, but of course on re-reading it I realized it didn't. The report adds that the 'Leader', 'when observed near Shawford was going quite as well as the 'Lord Nelson', No 30852, on the regular train'. But then we are told that the return from Woking to Eastleigh was not until sometime between two and three next morning so goodness knows what went wrong to so delay the 49 mile trip. The 'Leader' gave indications of an ability to develop considerable power when on 2 November 1950 she maintained 50 mph up the bank from Eastleigh to Lichfield with fifteen carriages totalling 480 tons. But this was almost her last effort. Shortly afterwards she failed on the road and did not run again. After going into store with her four sisters, two of them incomplete, all five were broken up.

The disappearance of the Southern engines was not quite the end of the story, for on leaving Eastleigh Bulleid took over as CME of the Irish Railways, CIE, and there he produced a turf burning locomotive which bore a strong resemblance to the 'Leader's. Like them it was totally enclosed and ran on two powered six-wheel bogies, although it had a single cab rather than one at either end. Again, like the 'Leader's, dieselization did the Turf Burner to death; it ran less than 2,000 miles, none of them in revenue earning service. I saw it laid up at Inchicore Works in 1959, it was an impressive-looking machine, though less imposing than the 'Leader's which were tremendous looking beasts.

Nationalization found the entire 'Lord Nelson' Class employed on the Bournemouth line, from Bournemouth and Nine Elms sheds. Their last appearance as the flagships of the Southern was in the summer of 1948 when Nos 30856, 30861 and 30864 of Bournemouth Shed were repainted in an experimental apple green livery, virtually the old LNER one, and allocated to the 7.20 am up and the 1.30 pm down expresses. The carriages, mainly new Bulleids, were in plum and spilt milk, the first break from green since late LSW days. The locomotives and carriages worked together into the 1949 winter service, but after the transfer of Nos 30856 and 30861 to Nine Elms this no longer applied, by which time the colours had in any case not met with official approval. All corridor carriages were now officially supposed to wear blood and custard, although many Bulleid and Maunsell ones never did lose their green livery, and the 'Nelson's all acquired Swindon green.

The last six 'Merchant Navy's, in the short lived but very fine blue livery, entered service early in 1949. They took up residence at Bournemouth, displacing six 'Lord Nelson's, which went to Eastleigh.

They in turn took over work previously performed by 'King Arthurs's, Waterloo-Bournemouth and Ocean Liner expresses, and main line stoppers chiefly.

By the end of 1948 the oldest of the 'King Arthur's, the original Urie engines of 1918, had reached their thirtieth birthday. Thirty years tended to be the average life span of British main line steam locomotives, but it was difficult to think of the 'King Arthur's as old; for many they epitomized Southern steam. They were all repainted in GWR lined green and continued to be well looked after. Quite a few went into store in the winter months, usually a sign that a locomotive's days were numbered, but with the tremendous fluctuation in seasonal traffic on the Southern, and the fact that they were joined by several almost new Bulleid Pacifics, this did not necessarily signify. Two front rank duties which the 'Arthur's still performed were Ocean Liner expresses and the through Birkenhead to Bournemouth trains. I often used to see them at Oxford at this time, whence they worked on the latter service, and the long, parallel lines of their boilers and fire box, neat dome, relatively small chimney and windowless cab were in marked contrast to a GWR's 4-6-0's sil-houette. They had disappeared from regular weekday duties on Waterloo to Bournemouth expresses, but still found work west of Bournemouth and would often reach the 80s on the racing stretch between Dorchester and Wareham.

However all good things come to an end. The Bournemouth line expresses, with their plethora of Bulleid Pacifics and 'Lord Nelson's, had no need of BR designed 'Britannia's, but there was a niche for the smaller 4-6-0s and 2-6-0s on secondary duties. First to arrive was Class '4MT' 2-6-0 No 76005 which reached Eastleigh Shed on 2 January 1953 from Horwich Works where it had been built. It moved on, along with No 76006, to Bournemouth, and by July another thirteen, Nos 76007-76019 had been allocated to Eastleigh.

The new engines were generally popular, being easy to maintain, and they displaced Drummond's last 4-4-0s, the 'D15's, from the cross-country Portsmouth, Southampton and Eastleigh, and Salisbury trains, all being withdrawn by 1956. The ex Brighton 'N15X's also went, the LBSC war memorial engine No 32333 *Remembrance* in April 1956 and the last one, No 32331 *Beattie,* in July 1957, although not until it had had a final fling on a Waterloo to Bournemouth express, taking over from a failed 'Merchant Navy' on 3 November 1956.

At around the same time Standard Class 4 4-6-0s were allocated to Exmouth Junction, but were soon to be seen on the Bournemouth line, whilst their bigger brothers, the Class 5s, went to Nine Elms and proved themselves capable of substituting for Pacifics when necessary. Thus came the end of the 'King Arthur's.

The Urie engines all ended their days on the Bournemouth line, at Nine Elms, Basingstoke, Eastleigh and Bournemouth sheds. First to go was No 30754 *The Green Knight* in January 1953, then a stay of execution for nearly three years before No 30746 *Pendragon* went in November 1956, after which they were withdrawn thick and fast as Standard 4-6-0s multiplied on the Bournemouth line until only one, No 30738 *King Pellinore* saw out 1957, and he was taken out of service in March 1958. The issue of *Trains Illustrated* which recorded his end, merely noting it amongst other withdrawals, is of especial interest for it made a much greater fuss of the last run by a Brighton Atlantic, the return journey being behind King Arthur No 30976 *Sir Dodinas le Savage*, whilst featured most prominently of all was the inaugural press run of English Electric 1 Co-Co 1 No D200, the first of BR's fleet of production main line diesel-electrics, between Liverpool Street and Norwich.

But diesels had already begun regular work on the Bournemouth line. The pioneer LMS locomotives, Nos 10000 and 10001 and the SR ones, Nos 10201-10203, had all been tried out on both the Waterloo to Exeter and Weymouth routes, but the first diesels to go into regular passenger service—and they are still at it to-day—were diesel-electric multiple units which were introduced in 1957.

On 16 September hourly semi-fast services began to operate between Portsmouth and Salisbury via Eastleigh, hourly stopping trains began work between Portsmouth and Southampton Central, and hourly stopping ones between Winchester and Southampton Terminus. On 4 November 1957 the Winchester trains were extended over the Watercress line to Alton, and a further service of hourly stopping trains between Portsmouth and the old Midland and South Western route as far as Andover Junction began. This revolution was ruthlessly pursued by eighteen two-car units. They not only covered 6,058 unit train miles each weekday, compared to a puny 2,587 steam passenger train miles, but put out of work twenty steam locomotives and 42 of the ancient carriages of which the *Southern Evening Echo* had complained.

The travelling public loved the new trains, to the extent that passenger journeys went up by nearly 48 per cent in the first full month of the new services, whilst revenue increased even more, by nearly 56 per cent. So popular were the new diesel units that a third coach had to be added to each one and the English Electric engines uprated to 600 horsepower. Later, when further units were constructed at Eastleigh, their operations were extended to Basingstoke and Reading, from Basingstoke to Salisbury, and from Salisbury deep into Great Western territory to Westbury and Bristol.

Above left *A BR Standard Class '4MT' 2-6-0 pulls out of Southampton Central with a westbound goods, January 1967. Towering over the famous gantry is the* Queen Mary *in the Western Docks.*

Right *One of the 1957 Eastleigh-built Hampshire diesel-electric multiple units, No 1126, emerging from Southampton Tunnel on a Portsmouth-Salisbury working, June 1979.*

Chapter 23
The 1950s

We are now embarked on the very last phase of steam working on the Waterloo to Weymouth line — although there is an epilogue. The DEMUs which arrived in 1957 to work many stopping and semi-fast services in the Southampton area heralded the beginning of a new era; but although on many parts of BR diesel locomotives were ousting steam from express work too, on the Southern's Weymouth main line it still had ten good years left.

One of the first routes to experience wholesale dieselization was the former GW West of England main line and consequently the 'Warship' diesel-hydraulic locomotives numbered in the D800 series began to be seen on the Western Region line to Weymouth, although more common were DMUs. On 6

April 1959 the entire Bristol to Westbury and Weymouth line was dieselized, most of the services being provided by cross-country DMUs. These had the great merit, from the passengers' point of view, compared to a Southern Region DEMU, of a splendid view fore and aft through the driver's cab windows — unless he had either absent-mindedly or malevolently left the blinds down. New vistas of delight opened up on what had always been a picturesque route, and as the Western DMUs were rather more luxuriously appointed than their Southern Region diesel-electric counterparts, they were greatly welcomed. They did not however generate any significant increase in traffic. Population, except in and around Yeovil, was if anything on the decline, and it had never amounted to much, particularly on the bare, windswept downs above Maiden Newton and Evershot. The Great Western had been generous

A Westbury to Weymouth DMU passing the closed Came Golf Club Halt, south of Dorchester, November 1981.

Above *The down Royal Wessex passing Shawford behind the original LMS main-line express diesel-electric locomotive No 10000 in the summer of 1954* (Colour Rail).

Below *The 'Royal' 'T9' 4-4-0 No 30119 in immaculate condition in the summer of 1948* (Colour Rail).

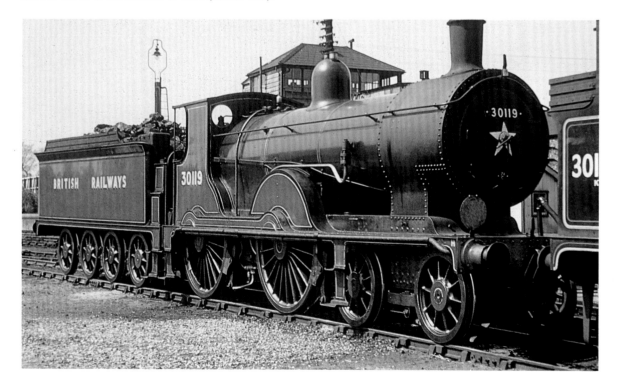

Above *The preserved 3SUB motor car No 1293 of 1925 in the National Railway Museum, York.*
Below *Urie 'King Arthur' No 30742* Camelot *in 1948 (Colour Rail).*

Right *'Merchant Navy' No 21c11* General Steam Navigation *about to leave Nine Elms depot to take out a Bournemouth express from Waterloo in the summer of 1947 (Colour Rail).*

Above *A Waterloo and City tube carriage newly repainted in Network South East livery on display at Waterloo, 22 November 1986.*

Below *Class '422' Waterloo-Weymouth EMU, due to enter service in 1988 (British Rail).*

with its stopping services, between Dorchester and Weymouth, a total of around twenty in each directions throughout the last forty years of its existence, but north of Dorchester this declined to no more than ten, sometimes less. The through expresses to Paddington, and also to Birmingham and Wolverhampton, were much the most important feature of the route, and until September 1958 one could travel to Weymouth by the 'Cornish Riviera'. This was made possible by that peculiarly Great Western institution, the slip carriage. Other companies may have employed a limited number of slip services, but the Great Western used them with more enthusiasm, and for longer, than anyone else. As late as 1958 three GW design carriages, built by British Railways in 1948, were converted for slip operation. As the 'Cornish Riviera' had now reverted to chocolate and cream livery, albeit composed of BR Mark 1 stock, the three slips were so painted, and thus for just one summer it was possible to turn back the clock ten years, board a genuine GWR designed carriage painted in more or less genuine GWR livery attached to the rear of the 10.30 am 'Cornish Riviera' departure from Paddington, be slipped at Heywood Road Junction, Westbury, and arrive at Weymouth in the charge of a GWR built 4-6-0.

The 'Cornish Riviera' slip ended in September and the last slip to Weymouth went the following January when the 3.30 pm out of Paddington ceased. This had got passengers into Weymouth in three hours, twenty-seven minutes, which beat the best the Southern Region could do from Waterloo by four minutes.

The takeover of the GW line to Weymouth in 1950 by the Southern Region had posed a long term threat to the future of through trains from Paddington, and in 1959, on 26 September, the threat materialized. On that day No 7010 *Avondale Castle* hauled the last boat train for Paddington out of Weymouth, and next year all through services between Weymouth and Paddington ceased. After 103 years of rivalry, of varying intensity, the South Western had won: the ghost of Charles Castleman must have smiled. Yet the Western wasn't quite finished and shortly after HSTs had taken over the Paddington to West of England services there was an afternoon train which in 1981 ran non-stop to Castle Cary in one hour, twenty-five minutes and after a wait of ten minutes one could pick up a Bristol to Weymouth train which enabled one to do the through journey in two hours, forty-five minutes. The last part of the journey was by stopping train, even so the overall time was roughly equal to that of the Waterloo to Weymouth through trains, and if the HST could have been persuaded to turn left at Castle Cary and run non-stop to Weymouth then the overall time from Paddington could probably

have been brought down to an even two hours. Fanciful stuff, but I nevertheless much enjoyed my only journey whilst the non-stop schedule to Castle Cary was in operation, taking afternoon tea as we sped down the Kennet Valley on my way from Paddington to Weymouth over Brunel's original route.

The Western Region route to Weymouth may have lost the battle with the Southern, but by a curious twist of fate at about the same time Southampton lost out to Weymouth over sailings to the Channel Islands. On 1 January 1959 the Shipping Manager at Weymouth had taken control of both ports and in June 1961 the British Transport Commission announced that all its sailings to and from Jersey and Guernsey would be from Weymouth.

Southampton protested vehemently. But the BTC was adamant. Overall the services were making a loss and by concentrating operations at Weymouth the number of boats could be cut from six to three, with a saving of £209,000 but no reduction in services. The popular day excursions could only continue if they were operated from Weymouth. New works to improve facilities at Weymouth Quay had been sanctioned in February 1960. The BTC might have added that the Channel Island services were absolutely vital to the future of the Dorset port, whilst Southampton, with its many ocean going routes, could survive the loss much more easily. That it didn't is probably due to the fact that there has always been an element amongst the population of Weymouth which considers a commercial port rather lowers the tone of the place and discourages the holidaymaker. When one contemplates the vast numbers of the latter which flock to Weymouth's golden sands each summer, the charm of the dockside pubs, cafes, and other buildings, the crowds who wander up and down the quays watching the fishing and other boats unloading, and the excitement when the Channel Island or Cherbourg ferry comes into sight around Portland Bill and approaches across the bay, then one may well think that element a loony one, but there it is.

The *St Patrick*, the last Great Western designed ship, had been transferred from the Irish Sea to the Channel Island run, being joined in 1960 by two new sisters, the *Caesarea* and the *Sarnia*.

There had always been overcrowding at times during the summer months, which was hardly surprising when one considers that 87 per cent of the traffic carried each year was handled between the beginning of May and the end of September. This wasn't much consolation to the families who were herded slowly up the gangways, of which there never seemed to be enough, on hot, sticky high summer Saturday middays, but nevertheless at the end of the

1961 season the three ships operating out of Wey-mouth had carried 11 per cent more passengers than the six ships which had worked from Weymouth and Southampton the previous year.

Trains still ran over the tramway to the Quay, and on Saturday afternoons there were no less than four departures within a space of 1½ hours, the 2.45, 3.00 and 4.00 to Waterloo, and the 4.15 which divided at Westbury, one section going to Birmingham Snow Hill, the other to Cardiff. GWR pannier tanks mono-polized the workings from the mid 1930s, in particu-lar the outside cylinder 1366 class especially built for dock work, but in April 1961 a Class '03' 204 hp diesel was transferred to Weymouth Shed and by the end of 1964 steam had gone.

A further economy saw boat trains withdrawn during the winter season from November 1962, Southern National providing a bus for the passengers and a van for their luggage between the Quay and Town stations. In 1963 the winter fleet was reduced to two ships and the *St Patrick* went to Southampton to operate the Le Havre service, but this was losing money and it came to an end in May 1964. The *St Patrick* stayed at Southampton, however, for the St Malo run which she worked twice weekly through the summer; in between she worked day excursions including a fortnightly one from Weymouth to St Malo which was the first regular run from Weymouth to the Continent for over fifty years. The following summer, 1965, the *St Patrick* moved east again, this time to Dover and with her departure railway steamers ceased to run between Southampton and

France for the first time this century. When the *St Patrick* was broken up in 1971 she was the last former GWR designed ship still afloat. Other opera-tors were soon to fill the gap left at Southampton by Sealink, as the shipping division of BR had become, notably Townsend Thorensen and P&O for by the late 1970s running car ferries between Southampton and Cherbourg and other continental ports was big business.

Back on dry land much that had long been familiar was also disappearing. Even before Beeching, branch lines had been succumbing to road competitions, but with his advent as Chairman of British Railways the process greatly accelerated during the 1960s. There were many such lines which probably could never have justified their existence once the motor had established itself, but there were others which could, certainly on social grounds, which Dr Beeching nevertheless swept away. Both categories could be found feeding into the Waterloo to Weymouth line.

One has to travel 36 miles out of Waterloo before one comes to a station closure on the main line itself and even this, Bramshot Halt, three-quarters of a mile east of Fleet, was hardly a proper station, being exclusively for the use of the adjacent golf club — it went in 1946. The first closed branch to be en-countered is the Basingstoke to Alton one which as we have seen gave up the ghost long before the Beeching era, in the 1930s. At Alton it had connected with the main line to Farnham and Waterloo, electri-fied in 1937, and two branches. The Meon Valley line to Fareham, Gosport and Portsmouth was opened in

Far left *Castle Cary, junction for the Paddington to West of England and Weymouth lines. An HST stands at the down platform, June 1981.*

Left *A Southern Railway signal arm mounted on a GWR post at Weymouth.*

Right *The preserved Bulleid Pacific No 34016* Bodmin *at Alresford, Mid Hants Railway, 27 June 1981.*

1901 and closed in 1955. The Alton, Alresford and Winchester Railway opened in 1865, and although single track, had become a useful diversionary route, particularly on Sundays for Waterloo to Southampton, Bournemouth and Weymouth. Whilst not the most heavily used of lines it carried a fair number of local people, both to work, and for shopping and other trips, to Winchester and the south and to Alton and the north. Despite this and its undoubted strategic value it featured on the Beeching hit list in 1963. The fight to save it was a long and hard one, but although the line outlived the steam era British Rail ran its last train between Alton and Winchester shortly before midnight on 7 February 1973. Notwithstanding the opportunity this opened up for the preservationists — one they have seized with spectacular success as we shall later see — it is now generally agreed that pushing through closure was wrong-headed and short sighted and that British Rail should have electrified the line.

Another success of the preservation movement has been the Basingstoke Canal. At various places between Woking and Basingstoke glimpses of it can be had from the railway, but by the post Second World War years all sign of commercial activity had vanished. Although the railway had almost brought it to an end back in the first decade of the present century, the Harmsworth family, who had bought it in 1923, refused to let it die and were so successful that by 1935 31,577 tons was carried, against 1,295 in 1907. Even so it was only the lower reaches which were used commercially, chiefly coal and timber

from Woking and below to the London Docks. Barges were built and repared at Ash Vale and pleasure boats penetrated towards Basingstoke, although the wharf in the town was sold in 1936 and later became the bus station.

Mr A. J. Harmsworth died in 1947 and two years later the canal was sold for £6,000. Small pleasure boats continued to use it but in 1967 plans were put forward to fill in sections. All over the country canals were being similarly threatened and it would have been particularly sad if this, the only canal of any substance in Southern England south of the Thames had disappeared. Fortunately there were those prepared to do something to prevent this happening and in 1966 the Surrey and Hampshire Canal Society was formed.

Surrey and Hampshire County Councils were persuaded to buy their portions of the canal, the preservationists chipped in with their money but even more importantly they had time and energy, and restoration went ahead. The railway played its part for a 2 ft narrow gauge line was laid along the bank where access by road and water was impossible and it has since made a great contribution to the work. One of the first sections was known as 'BR Straight' because it ran alongside the Waterloo to Weymouth line and passing drivers would often give a friendly hoot as they sped past. The Manpower Services Commission has sponsored successive schemes and as I write it is hoped the entire 32 mile long canal will be fully open again in 1988.

Chapter 24

Closures

The long stretch from Basingstoke to Winchester is interrupted by just one station, Micheldever, or Andover Road as it was long ago before the LSW West of England line was constructed. For many years the sidings at Micheldever were a rich source of interest for enthusiasts on account of the old carriages which came to rest here, gently rotting and rusting away before being broken up, or, as happened to a lucky few in the late 1960s and 1970s, beginning a new career in preservation. Approaching Winchester the line passes the site of Winchester Junction, where the branch from Alton came in, the trackbed of which is still clearly visible. At almost the same point the Didcot, Newbury and Southampton line passed under the LSW route.

After its heyday during World War 2 the DN&S gently settled back into a rural byway despite what one might have thought on looking at a map and noting the direct link it made between Southampton, Oxford and the Midlands. The trouble was that the pattern of rail travel from the South to the Midlands and the North had long been set by way of the

A boundary marker, dated 1880, on the site of Winchester Chesil Station, June 1986.

important junctions of Basingstoke and Reading. It was main line all the way with excellent connections, it was possible to avoid reversing in Reading General by taking the west curve and a few through trains did this, so the Didcot, Newbury and Southampton simply couldn't compete. I often make the journey from Wareham to Didcot, which, if there is no convenient through train, can involve changing at Southampton, Basingstoke and Reading, and am sometimes commiserated with in terms of 'if only the old Newbury line was still open'. Well it would have been a pleasant enough journey meandering through the Hampshire and Berkshire Downs, but it wasn't one for those in a hurry. A catholic band of former GWR and LSW locomotives hauled the three coach trains, '2251' Class 0-6-0s and elderly 4-4-0s in the shape of 'Duke's' '9000's and 'T9's, and, best remembered of all *City of Truro*. This famous engine took up residence at Didcot depot in March 1957 after its first return to steam and regularly worked the 12.45 pm to Southampton Terminus and the 4.56 pm back. The celebrated 4-4-0 was transferred to Swindon depot in September 1958, by which time the closure of the DN&S was imminent. The Newbury-Winchester passenger services ended on 7 March 1960 and those between Newbury and Didcot on 10 September 1962; all goods traffic ceased in 1964. Parts of the track bed were used to improve the A34 trunk road, other bits are still clearly identifiable and have become footpaths, whilst Winchester Chesil station site is now a multi-storey carpark. The impressive brick viaduct which runs beside the Winchester by-pass—a particularly nasty piece of road— and which carried the line over the water meadows of the Itchen immediately before it joined the Waterloo to Weymouth line at Shawford Junction is still largely intact, although in a much neglected state. It must surely be demolished before long.

Curving in from the west immediately north of Eastleigh station is the line from Romsey and Salisbury. Despite the advent of the DEMUs stopping passenger services between Romsey and Eastleigh ended on 5 May 1969, when the one intermediate station, Chandlers Ford, closed. However through passenger trains still pass this way and it is a vital link for the heavy freight traffic which is carried between Eastleigh and Salisbury and beyond.

Up the line from Romsey the Andover line branched northwards. Like the Didcot and Winchester line its importance as a through route between Southampton and the Midlands had fallen away after 1945 and inevitably the entire route between Romsey and Cheltenham became a candidate for closure. First to go was the northern section, the old Midland and South Western Joint, which had always been steam operated, latterly chiefly by Swindon built 43XX 2-6-0s and Manor 4-6-0s. The last train departed from Andover for Swindon on 11 September 1961. A short section near Swindon remained in use for some years for goods traffic, and a preservation group is working on the reopening of part of the route between Swindon and Cricklade. As with the Chandlers Ford line DEMUs could not save the Andover to Romsey service, one of the reasons being that, although hourly, it ran between Andover Junction and Portsmouth rather than Southampton, the latter being much the more popular destination for both commuters and shoppers. In 1962 the DEMUs were indeed thus diverted but by then closure had been proposed, and it duly followed on 5 September 1964. Freight continued for another three years between Andover Town and Junction.

Southampton itself did not escape the closures of the 1960s. The most notable was that of what had

Steam returns to the Midland & South Western Joint Railway. GWR 4-6-0 No 4930 Hagley Hall *from the Severn Valley Railway at the former Andover Junction alongside a Salisbury to Basingstoke train consisting of a 4TC propelled by a Class '33', 22 March 1986.*

once been the town's principal station. Latterly the Terminus had been no more than the destination of stopping trains from Didcot and some DEMUs and thus with the former gone the logic of concentrating all services on Central station was inescapable. Nevertheless Tite's handsome structure, with its spacious glass covered concourse was vastly more impressive than any other railway artefact in Southampton and even in the not always enlightened 1960s it was unthinkable that it should be demolished. Central station, rebuilt in the mid-1930s with the concrete, curved glass and metal window frames which are so evocative of that era, plus a tall clock tower, was quite acceptable but nothing like as grand. As I write the station building itself is being completely restored, the concourse is a car park, the platform area is derelict, and on the other side of the back wall of South Western House which supports the iron framework of the concourse are various BBC television and radio offices. The tracks running alongside the station and over Canute Road into the Eastern Docks remained in use, both for goods and passenger traffic. The former was soon to cease, the link alongside Canute Road between the Western and Eastern Docks was removed, and the once vast rail network within the old docks withered away, until but one fragment survived. This is the single line from Northam, past the Terminus and over Canute Road into the docks beneath the grandiose South Western House. Nowadays it has but one function, to convey boat trains to and from the *Queen Elizabeth 2*.

Northam station, being served only by trains to and from the Terminus station, closed on the same day, 5 September 1966, and the curve linking Terminus and Central and forming the third side of the Northam triangle, was taken out. Central became

Above *A stopping train for Bournemouth via the old main line leaving Brockenhurst in 1956. The carriages are Ironclads, the engine a Drummond '700' Class 0-6-0* (Dr Ian C. Allen).

Left *The trackbed of the old main line via Ringwood in the New Forest west of Brockenhurst, June 1986.*

plain Southampton.

Westwards again, on from the city's principal station, and the three suburban ones around the edge of Southampton Water, Millbrook, Redbridge and Totton, are all still in business. The latter lost some of its trains on 14 February 1966 when British Rail handed a valentine to the citizens of Marchwood, Hythe and Fawley by taking away their passenger service. This probably did the proprietors of the Hythe ferry a good turn for the bus service to and from Southampton and the western shore of Southampton Water—one the LSW had pioneered back in Edwardian times—was inevitably circuitious and the bottleneck where the Fawley Road joins the main A35 certainly got no better when the passenger trains ceased to run. There have been various agitations to restore them but the locals have had no luck so far.

All the New Forest stations on the main line have survived and both the Town and Pier stations at Lymington at the end of the branch from Brockenhurst are still busy. However, but for the other route

'57' Class pannier tank No 4691 of Templecombe shed shunting milk tankers at Bailey Gate, onetime junction of the Wimborne and Broadstone lines, 1964 (Dr Ian C. Allen).

which branched off at Brockenhurst, the original main line to the west, Castleman's Corkscrew, the 1960s brought disaster.

The direct link between Salisbury and Bournemouth, which joined the old main line at West Moors, came to an end on 9 September 1963. No- one was very surprised at this, which had actually been proposed before Dr Beeching's wholesale closure plans, for the line carried very little traffic in its later years. Quite why this was so is difficult to determine for plenty of people have always wanted to travel between Bournemouth and Salisbury; perhaps they found the Wilts and Dorset bus service more convenient, particularly as it went by way of Ringwood, a town which generated plenty of traffic.

Ringwood was the busiest place on the railway line between Brockenhurst and Wimborne but it couldn't save it. In the opinion of the clerk to Dorset County Council, Arthur Templeman, and many others it should have done, and so should the great traffic potential of a decent commuter service from Wimborne through Broadstone and Creekmoor to Poole and Bouremouth. But British Rail was indifferent to any opinion and statistic which was contrary to their avowed intention of shutting the line and,

like too many others in the 1960s who ought to have known better, seemed more than half inciined to the notion that the time would shortly be on hand when the motor vehicle would render all railways redundant. One has only to observe the huge amount of traffic crawling in towards Poole and Bournemouth from the vastly expanded Wimborne, Corfe Mullen, Broadstone, Canford Heath and Creekmoor areas each morning around 8.30 and out again each evening, to realize what a loss has been suffered with the disappearance of the railway line. Okay so it's not on the scale of the London suburbs, of Reginald Perrin's exact prediction of his lateness into Waterloo each morning and where BR's excuse was never the same twice, ranging from points failure at Raynes Park to a suicide at Earlsfield, but it's big enough. The population of the Poole and Bournemouth conurbation is approaching the half-million and much of the expansion since the 1960s has taken place close to where the Wimborne line once ran. Closure date was 2 May 1964, although Wimborne remained open for freight into the 1970s. The last passenger to alight at Wimborne was Her Majesty the Queen, the Royal Train bringing her to Poole and Cranborne Manor in July 1969.

Linked with the fate of the Wimborne line was that of the Somerset and Dorset. 71 miles of meandering single track with passing loops it went through nowhere of much importance—if we define important as a large population and a fair bit of

Above *The last LMS Class '2P' 4-4-0 to be built, No 40700 of Bath shed (Somerset and Dorset), enters Parkstone with a Bath to Bournemouth train consisting of four Maunsell corridors in 1957 (Dr Ian C. Allen).*

Left *A BR Standard '9F' 2-10-0, No 92245, at Poole with a summer Saturday Somerset and Dorset line Bournemouth West to Manchester London Road express, August 1962 (Colin Caddy collection).*

Below *Rebuilt 'West Country' Pacific No 34004* Yeovil *about to leave Swanage with a Saturdays only Waterloo express, August 1963 (Tony Trood).*

industry—and was the archetypical candidate for closure. Many who had never travelled over it, ie virtually the entire population, even of Somerset and Dorset let alone the rest of Britain, nevertheless had grown to love it, chiefly through the masterly photographs of Ivo Peters of the Royal Crescent, Bath. Derby-built 4-4-0s piloting Eastleigh designed Bullied Pacifics, ubiquitous Midland 0-6-0s and Stanier '5's, unique Deeley 2-8-0s seemingly equally at home on long freights and summer Saturday rakes of Stanier corridors, ancient Johnson 0-4-4Ts, all were shown most evocatively at work in what was fondly seen as the very epitome of rural England. Titfield Thunderbolt territory.

Unfortunately such a railway is a natural born financial disaster, which the peak summertime 'Pines Express' from Bradford to Bournemouth could do little to obviate (the mind boggles at what a citizen of Bradford would have made of his surroundings in the unlikely event of his sleeping through the entire journey and being tipped out into Durley Chine, or indeed of a Bournemouthite similarly finding himself in Forster Square.) An awful lot of dithering took place before the final decisions were made, and even then the agony was prolonged when the bus service which should have been ready to take over on Monday 3 January 1966 wasn't. Of course one had in the first place to be naive, insensitive and a dedicated car owner to imagine that a rural bus service was any sort of substitute for the railway, but eventually the

A clay train on the surviving section of the Swanage branch approaches Furzebrook in May 1981. The wooden bodied, four-wheel open wagons, many of pre-Nationalization origin, are hauled by a Class '33' diesel-electric.

traffic commissioners, unlike practically everyone else, pronounced themselves satisfied, the Bulleid Pacifics and '9F' 2-10-0s which had lately come to the line, including *Evening Star*, the very last steam engine built for BR, made their final runs, and on 6 March 1966 the Somerset and Dorset died. Freight continued to come out of Blandford until January 1969, the last bit of track was then removed and all that now remains are sections of trackbed and a few bridges and buildings, plus a surprisingly large number of engines. Bath Green Park station has been quite superbly restored, the station approaches have become a supermarket and a nearby road named after Ivo Peters, surely the only photographer of railway trains so honoured.

The Somerset and Dorset was one of the last all-steam worked lines on British Rail. Even at this late stage some locomotives off the Somerset and Dorset were transferred elsewhere rather than withdrawn. By 1966 the preservation movement was getting under way, and thus GWR 0-6-0 No 3205 (a number of Swindon built locomotives appeared on the S&D in its last years), two of the '7F' 2-8-0s, *Evening Star*, and several '4F's, Class '4' and '5MT' 4-6-0s, and 'West Country' and 'Battle of Britain' Pacifics which at some stage of their careers were Somerset and Dorset engines, have all been preserved.

Although goods trains still ran down the Hamworthy branch now that the line to Broadstone was gone Hamworthy Junction station lost its suffix; it did not, however, lose the arch which carried the old line through the trees clear of the harbour and that still survives.

The next branch to get chopped off was that to Swanage. It did a roaring trade in summer and for the

rest of the year was a vital link for the local community but this did not generate sufficient revenue
for the accountants at Waterloo, Westminster,
Brussels or wherever. DEMUs were introduced in
September 1966 and Class '33' diesel locomotives
took over the through workings to Waterloo. Freight
disappeared, except for clay workings from
Furzebrook, Swanage was reduced to a single track
layout with the rails in the goods yard uprooted and
the signal box demolished but these rationalizations
could not save the branch and it closed on New
Year's Day 1972. The daily clay train continued
over the two miles between Worgret Junction and the
English China Clay works at Furzebrook, many of the
wooden wagons in which the clay was carried to the
Potteries being of pre-nationalization origin. It was
thus still possible to see wagons with the old familiar
GWR, LMS, LNER and SR initials embossed on their
axleboxes trundling through Dorset in the 1970s.

A new traffic which originated in the 1960s and

which is still a source of much controversy was the
nuclear waste which regularly travels from the
Atomic Energy Research Plant erected on Winfrith
Heath—Thomas Hardy's Egdon Heath—west of
Wool, to Sellafield in Cumbria. The flask containing
the waste matter is carried on a special wagon,
hauled by a Class '33' and brought up in the rear by
a goods brake van. It can often be seen standing on
its siding within the plant from a passing passenger
trains. Understandably many railwaymen are wary of
this potentially lethal traffic and an inspector I once
travelled with said whenever he was on nuclear duty
he always carried a geiger counter for his own peace
of mind. There are strict instructions regulating the
minimum distance from a mess hut the train can
stand if it is brought to a halt by signals or some other
cause.

There were two halts on the Waterloo to Weymouth specifically for the use of golfers. One, as we
have seen, was Bramshott near Fleet; the other was

Monkton and Came, south of Dorchester across the valley from Maiden Castle. It, like Bramshott, closed soon after World War 2. Through Bincombe Tunnel and on the other side of the downs the next station, another halt, Upwey Wishing Well, closed in January 1957. Upwey Junction, once the goods spur to Upwey, the last bit of the old Abbotsbury branch, became Upwey and Broadwey and survives as an unstaffed halt. Not many trains call there but with the building of a very large estate close by its service is improving. Radipole, the penultimate station between Waterloo and Weymouth, is the most recent station to close. Another halt, it had the distinction of being the last but two on BR to possess the famous GWR corrugated iron pagoda shelters. These were replaced by two less distinctive but more salubrious structures in 1975. In 1984 it was discovered that several thousands of pounds were needed to repair the platforms, BR therefore applied for closure and this was eventually granted. Although just round the bend from Weymouth station, it was handy for Radipole village and for my sister when she owned the greengrocer's overlooking the railway. It had a small, but select band of regular customers, who are now bereft.

The final closure we should note is that of the Portland branch. Passenger traffic had long gone, except for occasional specials, and the complete end came after the last enthusiast excursion and the final goods run on 27 March 1965.

Left *A Waterloo to Weymouth train passing the Atomic Energy Research Station at Winfrith, January 1986.*

Right *Standard '4MT' 2-6-0 No 76057 of Weymouth shed near Sandsfoot Castle on the Portland branch, 29 September 1963 (Colin Caddy collection).*

Below *The trackbed of the Portland branch in February 1986. The naval base and Portland Bill are in the background.*

Chapter 25
The last steam main line

The last years of steam on the Waterloo to Weymouth line came to be dominated by one type of locomotive, the Bulleid Pacific. Many of them, all the 'Merchant Navy's and around half of the Light Pacifics, ended their careers in a very different form to that in which they had begun them. Despite their virtues their vices were such that within a short time of the last 'Battle of Britain' entering service in May 1950 the decision was made that rebuilding of both types with an orthodox front end was necessary.

Naturally the appearance of the first rebuilt engine was eagerly anticipated, not least because it was known its streamline casing would be gone, although more important was the replacement of Bulleid's oil enclosed front end with three sets of orthodox Walschaerts' valve gear. 'Merchant Navy' No 35018 *British India Line* was the chosen prototype and it emerged from Eastleigh in February 1956. Both rebuilt and unrebuilt examples have been preserved and are at work so it is hardly necessary to describe the differences in detail. There was, not surprisingly, a suggestion of a 'Britannia' about the rebuild. Not perhaps as elegant but certainly with an air of purposefulness. The remainder of the class was similarly dealt with in the following three and a half years, the last being No 35006 *Peninsular SN Co* and No 35028 *Clan Line* in October 1959.

Next came the turn of the Light Pacifics and in June 1957 No 34005 *Barnstaple* emerged in rebuilt form. Although the great majority of the 'West Country' and 'Battle of Britain's had been built at Brighton all rebuilding work was carried out at Eastleigh. Almost exactly half the class, 56 out of 110, was dealt with; the rebuilding of No 34108 *Wincanton* in May 1961 brought the programme to an end. By this date electrification of the Kent Coast lines was under way and plans for the Bournemouth electrification were afoot; the 'King Arthur's were mostly all withdrawn, the 'Lord Nelson's and 'Schools' were going, more and more Bulleid Pacifics were being sent to the Western Section, and the expense of rebuilding engines which were not going to be needed beyond the 1960s could not be justified.

Whether the Pacifics were better in their original or rebuilt form is difficult to say. It was partly a question of priorities. If reliability was all important then the rebuilds had the edge, although some enginemen contended that there was nothing wrong with the original engines if handled properly. No 34092 *City of Wells* has behaved impeccably on the main line in preservation days, although this hardly compares with everyday conditions in the 1950s and 60s. Throughout their careers there was no doubting the speed propensities of all the Bulleid Pacifics, but they were prone to slip, though once again an example from the present preservation era belies this for two days ago I watched *Clan Line* back on home territory in Dorset pull away from Gillingham with eight carriages without the trace of a slip. Nevertheless both types of Bulleid 4-6-2s were notorious for losing their feet and for this reason their true haulage powers could never be properly exploited over the hills of the Somerset and Dorset line. The '9F's were better engines here, but a carefully handled rebuilt 'Merchant Navy' was the master of any train, both in terms of weight and speed, on the Waterloo to Weymouth line.

With dieselization of the Hastings line and then the Kent electrification, those greyhounds of the 1930s, the 'Schools' Class, returned to the Bournemouth line, although not to Bournemouth shed, in the late 1950s. On 22 June 1957 No 30907 *Dulwich* took out the 11.22 am Bournemouth to Waterloo and No 30904 *Lancing* had charge of the 12.35 pm but this was exceptional for their role now was a secondary one. They had to content themselves with Waterloo to Basingstoke, Salisbury and Bournemouth semi-fasts; they also took over Lymington boat trains from the 'D15's and some Salisbury to Southampton and Portsmouth trains from the 'T9s'. But with the virtual abolition of steam on the Eastern and Central Sections there were more than enough Pacifics available on the Western Section, along with the Standard 4-6-0s and 2-6-0s, for every type of duty from the 'Bournemouth Belle' to pick-up freights.

The last Drummond 4-4-0, 'T9' No 30120, was withdrawn and sent to Eastleigh, though not for breaking up, in June 1961; soon it was the turn of the most modern 4-4-0s on British Railways and all the 'Schools' were out of service by the end of 1962. The

Right *The first rebuilt Bulleid Pacific, 'Merchant Navy' No 35018 British India Line, has just arrived at Bournemouth West with the 'Bournemouth Belle', whilst across the platform is rebuilt 'West Country' No 34021 Dartmoor (Dr Ian C. Allen).*

Right *The 'Schools' Class returns to the Bournemouth line. On 6 June 1961, six months before withdrawal and eighteen months before the end of the class, No 30913 Christ's Hospital ambles through Earlsfield with the 6.22 am Bournemouth to Waterloo made up of seven Bulleid corridors and two vans.*

Below *One of the BR Standard '5MT' Class 4-6-0s which bore the names of Urie 'King Arthur's, No 73116 Iseult passing Worgret Junction with a Waterloo to Weymouth express, August 1965 (Tony Trood).*

Top *'M7' No 30107 passing Furzebrook with a Swanage to Wareham train in 1962. The push-pull unit is one of those converted in British Rail days from Maunsell main line stock. An open third identical to the first carriage has been preserved by the Swanage Railway and is once again in passenger service back in its old haunts (Tony Trood).*

Above *Standard '5MT' 4-6-0 No 73037 of Eastleigh shed approaching Branksome, having just come off the viaduct with a Bournemouth Central to Weymouth train, passes LMS-designed Class '2MT' 2-6-2T No 41295 of Branksome shed which has just left home to collect empty stock in Bournemouth West station, July 1964 (Dr Ian C. Allen).*

last 'King Arthur', No 30770 *Sir Prianius*, went at the same time. By 1959 all sixteen 'Lord Nelson's were allocated to Eastleigh shed, although they were not all regularly in steam. The first to go was No 30865 *Sir John Hawkins* in May 1961, and in little over a year none were left at work, No 30861 *Lord Anson* and No 30862 *Lord Collingwood* being the last survivors; they were withdrawn in October 1962.

And so as 1963 opened the three classes which had been the mainstay of Southern express services for so long were all gone, leaving the Bulleid Pacifics with a virtual monopoly of the principal, and much of the secondary, passenger services on the Waterloo to Weymouth line. True there were the Standard Class

'5' 4-6-0s, including twenty, Nos 73080-73089 and 73110-73119 which bore the names, although not the actual nameplates of withdrawn 'King Arthur's, but one could stand at Vauxhall on a summer Saturday and engine after engine backing down to Nine Elms would be a Bulleid Pacific, just as train after train bound either for the West of England or the Weymouth line would have one of these locomotives in charge. By 1962-63 they were often neglected-looking and filthy dirty and although still capable of excellent work the view of your average Waterloo to Weymouth express was not an inspiring one.

On empty stock working the 'M7's had disappeared, as they had from the Swanage and Lymington branches, being replaced by LMS type and BR Standard 2-6-2s and Standard 2-6-4Ts.

In 1963 the withdrawal of Pacifics began, unrebuilt 'West Country' and 'Battle of Britain's first, but soon rebuilt examples, and then the first 'Merchant Navy's went in February 1964.

Production main line diesels had already appeared on the Bournemouth route, following the LMS and SR designed prototypes, first in the form of the Derby/Sulzer Type 2s, later known as the 24s, and then subsequent to their introduction on the Kent Coast services in 1960, the Birmingham/Sulzer Type 3s numbered in the D6500 series. These quickly acquired the nickname 'Cromptons', on account of their Crompton Parkinson traction motors, and despite their later official designation as Class '33's it is one which has stuck.

'M7' in its declining years. No 30107 stands in Parkstone station with a Brockenhurst-Ringwood-Broadstone-Bournemouth train in the summer of 1962, composed of one of the long-lived Maunsell four-wheel passenger vans (many of which still exist in departmental service), an Ironclad two coach unit, and a BR standard Mark 1 corridor. By this date the remaining Bournemouth-based 'M7's were often unfit to take up their duties and rebuilt Bulleid Pacifics might be seen substituting for them (Dr Ian C. Allen).

Neither the most powerful nor the most impressive looking of the vast army of diesels which poured on to British Rail in the 1960s, the '33's have nevertheless proved one of its best investments. They have performed sterling service all over the Southern Region for 25 years and have become as familiar a feature of the Waterloo to Weymouth line and written as significant a chapter in its story as Beattie's distinctive 2-4-0s, Adams's and Drummond's elegant 4-4-0s, Urie's and Maunsell's handsome 4-6-0s or Bulleid's unique Pacifics.

Other diesels had by now also appeared at Waterloo, Western Region 'Warships' with hydraulic transmissions taking over West of England services in August 1964, and thus hammering another nail in the coffin of the Bulleid Pacifics. The old LSWR main line beyond Salisbury was reduced to a secondary route; from now on if you wanted to take an express to the West of England you had no choice but to make for Paddington. No doubt the ghosts of Brunel and Daniel Gooch smiled, as did other more tangible spirits as the age-old rivalry reasserted itself again. Much of the LSWR route was singled and to no-one's surprise, except BR's publicity department, delays became commonplace.

'Warship' diesels could be seen at Weymouth, having worked down the Western Region route, although they also sometimes came through on summer weekends via Basingstoke and Bournemouth

Left *Western Class '52' diesel-hydraulic No D1073* Western Bulwark *running through the pine-covered cutting of Meyrick Park with an inter-regional express, 16 May 1964 (Colin Caddy collection).*

Below *A rebuilt Bulleid Pacific approaching Poole with a down express in 1964. Poole Park lake is to the right of the tracks, Poole Harbour to the left (Dr Ian C. Allen).*

Bottom *The same location twenty years later, looking in the opposite direction, with a Class '33' propelling a Weymouth to Waterloo train composed of two 4TC units at the foot of Branksome Bank.*

Right *A Waterloo to Weymouth express composed of two 4TC units and a 4REP in the rear overtaking a DEMU on Portsmouth to Salisbury working beside the River Itchen south of St Denys, March 1980.*

with trains from the London Midland and Eastern Regions, as did the Brush Class '47's, a type of diesel which was to become almost as familiar between Eastleigh and Wareham as the '33'. Neither must we forget the Class '52' 'Western's, a diesel-hydraulic design which evoked the sort of adulation amongst the enthusiast fraternity—although not in BR accounting circles—which a dumbstruck older steam-orientated generation found hard to accept. These too came to Weymouth, often on lightweight stopping trains from Bristol with which they played over the banks where steam had previously laboured.

But dieselization was not to be the ultimate fate of the Waterloo to Bournemouth line. The Southern Region had never made any bones of its intention to electrify all its main lines and everyone knew it was only a question of when the third rail would be extended south of Woking to the Hampshire coast, and whether the trains would be locomotive hauled or, as elsewhere on the region, multiple units.

The announcement came in September 1964. 'London to Bournemouth—100 minutes' proclaimed the *Bournemouth Echo* in big black headlines on the 29th of that month, and the story filled the front page as well as several inside ones. The SR's Regional Manager, David McKenna, was quoted: 'We estimate that the Bournemouth scheme will bring an improvement in passenger revenue of £1.1 million in a ten year period...the majority of the increase in revenue should come from breaking the steam barrier and giving a better service, of which 20 minutes off the fast run to Bournemouth is a dramatic

example'. There was expected to be an increase in commuter traffic between the Southampton and Bournemouth areas, although it is difficult to see how they proposed closure of Boscombe station would contribute towards this. Under a picture of No 35021 *New Zealand Line* was the caption 'Steam on the Way Out'. Also in that issue of the *Bournemouth Echo* was an advert for a concert at the Winter Gardens featuring Nina and Frederick plus Bill Haley and his Comets, both supporting the principal attraction, Manfred Mann. That's the trouble with looking through old newspapers, it's impossible not to get side-tracked.

Multiple units were to be the order of the day, not a surprising decision given that this had been Southern main line practice since the Brighton electrification of 1933, although given the drastic deterioration in the units riding qualities over the years, not everyone welcomed the decision. Still the '4CIG's and the '4BIG's then replacing the original Brighton units seemed to be behaving themselves so everyone hoped for the best. It was not considered economic to extend the electrification beyond Bournemouth to Weymouth and this gave rise to perhaps the most interesting feature of the scheme, the adoption of a push-pull system.

Eleven four-car units of no less than 3,200 hp would be assembled and each of these would be capable of working with two further, non-powered four-car units. The power units ('4REP's) would consist of two open seconds, each with a driving cab, a corridor brake first, and a motor buffet car, whilst the trailer units ('4TC's) would have two similar driving open seconds, a side-corridor first, and a side-corridor brake second. Twelve car trains would be the norm for the Waterloo to Bournemouth expresses; at Bournemouth (the Central suffix would go as the West station was to close) a specially fitted Class '33' diesel-electric locomotive would couple on to the front trailer unit (at busy times both '4TC's) and off it would go to Weymouth. The '4REP' would then take up a return working to Waterloo after coupling up with the '4TC's which had been propelled by a Class '33' from Weymouth. Thus the powered '4REP' would be at the back pushing out of Waterloo and at the front pulling on the up journey.

The hourly expresses would stop only at Southampton, which would be reached in 70 minutes from Waterloo, and the overall journey time Waterloo to Bournemouth would be 1 hour 38 minutes. For much of their journey the new trains would run at 90 mph.

Actually to call them new was not strictly speaking accurate. In typical Southern, one might say South Western, good-housekeeping, penny-pinching traditions the great majority of the 128 'new carriages' were secondhand conversions from steam stock, only the 24 '4REP' driving trailer seconds being brand new. Admittedly the interior refurbishments of the other 124 carriages were so extensive that it was not obvious that the carriages had been around for some time, not that is until one stepped outside and realized that they were Mark 1s: Mark 2s had been in production for other regions for some considerable time.

The '4REP'/two '4TC' combination was also to work the hourly Waterloo to Bournemouth semi-fasts. These called at Clapham Junction, Woking, Basingstoke, Winchester, Eastleigh, Southampton Airport, Southampton, Brockenhurst and New Milton and completed the journey in 2 hours 5 minutes.

Finally, stopping services, calling at all stations between Surbiton and Bournemouth, would run every hour and would take 8 minutes short of 3 hours. These would be handled by new—and they actually were new—four coach units, the '4VEP's, which were in effect up-dated versions of the '4LAV's which the Southern Railway had provided for Brighton line stopping and semi-fast services. They were to seat 232 second class and 24 first class passengers in what could not be described as excessive comfort, particularly as there were to be only two lavatories per set.

Electrification was certainly to be welcomed, but the whole scheme had something of a second division air about it. The Pullmans of the 'Bourne-mouth Belle' would vanish, as would any hint of named trains or the suggestion that any particular service was in any way special. It would all be egalitarian, uniform, hopefully quite efficient, and rather dull.

As if to hammer home the notion that the Bourne-mouth line was henceforth to be little more than an extension of the suburban network the first of the new units to enter service, the '4TC' trailers, were painted not in the Inter-City blue and grey then being adopted outside the Southern Region, but in the miserable-looking all-over blue reserved for stopping and semi-fast services.

Before electrification became a reality steam on the Waterloo to Weymouth line enjoyed an Indian summer. Although more Class '33's and even four Class '47's were drafted in to Nine Elms and Eastleigh as stop gaps, the lined green paintwork on the Pacifics which remained on top link work reappeared from beneath layers of grime and this was reflected in their performances as they rediscovered that sparkle which had once made them amongst the most exciting performers on British Railways.

The 4VEP Class '423' EMUs have monopolized the stopping services on the Waterloo to Bournemouth and Portsmouth lines for twenty years. No 7771, newly repainted in Network South East livery, leaves Portsmouth Harbour on the 08:05 to Waterloo, 7 September 1986.

Chapter 26
Electrification

The end for steam came on 9 July 1967. For several months diesel and electric traction had powered most of the workings on the Weymouth line. A number of the '4VEP' EMUs were working on the stopping services and the first three '4REP' express units had gone into regular service, together with a number of the '4TC' trailer units, at Easter time. The 'Bournemouth Belle' occasionally still saw a 'Merchant Navy' at its head, and on 8 May for example it had Standard '5' 4-6-0 No 73043, but the usual motive power for the Pullman train in its last months was a Brush Type 4 diesel-electric (Class '47'). There were, of course, many steam specials in the last months and weeks, and one Pacific in especial demand was the last unrebuilt 'West Country', No 34102, which was still active during the last week. The end itself was not especially dramatic with no final commemorative runs or ceremonies.

On the last Saturday there were only two steam-hauled departures from Waterloo, the 7.15 to Basingstoke and Salisbury which went out behind Standard Class '3' 2-6-2T No 82029, which was most unexpected, and the 8.30 to Weymouth which had

A Brush Type 4 (Class '47') diesel-electric approaching Vauxhall with the down 'Bournemouth Belle', January 1967.

'Merchant Navy' No 35023 in charge. Like all the Bulleid Pacifics which lasted into 1967 it had lost its nameplates, partly to prevent them being stolen by so-called enthusiasts, and partly so that BR could sell or otherwise dispose of them. On the Sunday three steam-hauled trains arrived at Waterloo, one empty stock from Fratton behind Standard Class '5' No 73029, another an ocean liner express from Southampton behind Light Pacific No 34021, and the third the 14.11 from Weymouth which came in, appropriately, behind the last 'Merchant Navy' to be built, No 35030. The very last steam train to pull out of Waterloo was the 18.20 Ocean Liner express for Southampton Docks in the charge of rebuilt 'West Country' No 34037.

Melancholy rows of lifeless engines congregated at Salisbury and Weymouth sheds. The latter had become one of the last strongholds of steam on the Southern Region with 'Merchant Navy's being allocated for the first time in 1964 and in January 1967 it could claim the distinction of being the home of the ten most powerful passenger steam engines still at work on BR, all ten surviving '8P' 'Merchant Navy's being shedded there. The very last steam engines to leave Weymouth for the scrapyard were Nos 34093, 34095 and 73092 which were towed away in January 1968. The shed lasted as a signing on point until October 1970 and was then demolished. Today a

Left *BR Standard Class '3MT' 2-6-2T of Nine Elms shed approaching Clapham Junction with an empty stock train of four early Bulleid corridors in January 1967.*

Left *The Hythe Pier tramway, June 1986.*

Right *A Class '73' electro-diesel with the empty stock of a* Queen Elizabeth 2 *boat train races a Class '33' diesel-electric north of Northiam, May 1986.*

housing estate stands on the site, practically the only reminders of the last steam depot on the Waterloo to Weymouth line being Great Western Terrace, the road which used to lead to it, and some iron fencing following the angle of the line which used to give access to it off the main line. Nine Elms was razed to the ground and London's famous vegetable and fruit market moved out from Covent Garden to take over the site. Bournemouth shed became a car park, East-leigh was rebuilt to serve diesels and electrics, and Basingstoke shed was demolished.

There was one group of citizens in the Southampton area to whom travel by electric train was no novelty. These were the good folk of Hythe. As long ago as 1870 there had been plans to build a railway along the village's pier from which ferry boats plied across the Solent to Southampton. This railway, or tramway, was eventually built in 1922 and antici-pated the main line electrification which was to come 45 years later in that it operated on the third rail principal. Three narrow gauge battery locomotives built during World War 1 for the Avonmouth Mustard Gas Factory were bought and converted to pick up power at 200, later 240, volts. Three Drewry unsprung bogie carriages were purchased to run with them. One of the locomotives was subsequently scrapped to provide spare parts for its more fortunate companions, but otherwise little has changed since the line was opened. The trains, recently repainted in a jolly two tone blue and cream livery, still trundle up and down the pier, 65 years after their inauguration, delightful antiques perhaps but performing a much valued service. The 15 minute

ferry trip and the three minute ride down the pier remains the fastest, and far away the most pleasurable means of getting from Hythe to Southampton, and there is often the bonus of sailing alongside the QE2 berthed at her terminal or beneath the towering decks of a container ship heading for one of the berths at the far end of the new docks on the River Test.

Meanwhile, what of the new all-electric mainline services inaugurated on 10 July 1967, the day after the last steam train departed from Waterloo? Well in the first place they weren't yet all electric for not all the '4REP's and '4VEP's had been delivered from York Works. That might not have mattered too much for there were the Class '33' diesels and six of the powerful Brush Class '47's, although the Southern had asked for more of these, but the region had also introduced new timetables right across all three sections, Eastern, Central and Western, and the result in the words of the *Railway World* for September 1967, was 'probably the worst weeks of chaos that the Southern has ever known'. The principal reason for this sad state of affairs had nothing to do with the demise of steam but was 'largely because staff were unfamiliar with new work-ings which allowed little margin for delay in such matters as coupling and dividing branch portions of through trains and in speedier terminal turn-rounds'. So much of the smooth working of a railway and a sense of efficiency and concern depends ultimately not on the planner of timetables but on the railway-man who has to make it all work, and if he is neither adequately trained nor informed, and gives the

impression to the hapless passenger that this bothers him not one iota, then the railway is in trouble. Chris Green, the Sector Director of Network SouthEast, of which the Waterloo to Weymouth line is today a part, realized this from the start and said shortly after his appointment in January 1986 that one of his two central aims was 'to improve customer care by way of improved staff morale'. Unfortunately neither management nor the ordinary railwaymen had got their act anything like as well together twenty years earlier and hence the misfortunes of the first weeks of the new timetables in the summer of 1967.

One reason for the shortage of motive power on the Waterloo to Weymouth line at this time was the non-appearance of the Class '74' electro-diesels. The electro-diesel is an ingenious animal, being essentially an electric locomotive which is also able to operate at reduced power on non-electrified lines. The Southern had 49 of these, the highly efficient Class '73's, introduced in 1962, and it was planned to supplement them with ten Class '74's, electro-diesel rebuilds of the Class '71' straight electrics dating from 1958. Not only can an electro-diesel work in multiple with others of its type but also with electric or diesel-electric multiple units, including the '4TC' trailer sets, and, of course, it can haul ordinary carriages, vans and wagons. Thus such machines were of immense use on the Bournemouth line, particularly when there was a shortage of multiple units, and it was a pity the '74's were not ready until some six months after the new timetable had been in operation. As it happened, whilst the '73's have performed admirably the '74's proved unreliable and they, and the '71's, were all withdrawn by 1981.

Gradually things were sorted out. The late deliveries arrived, the last of the Bulleid coaches, still in green livery, were withdrawn, although at least one ended its days with BR in maroon livery on the

Scottish Region, and the express units, and then the stopping ones, were repainted blue and grey so that at least the colours were up to date even if the Mark 1 ancestry of the Bournemouth line stock seemed more and more antiquated against the later Mark 2s and then the Mark 3s taking over in increasing numbers elsewhere on the BR network. The contrast is most noticeable whenever a through train of London Midland, Scottish, Eastern or Western Region stock reaches Southern metals at Basingstoke. Not only is the outline of the later carriages more in keeping with the 1980s, but most importantly the seats are more comfortable, some of the stock is air-conditioned and above all else it rides much better.

In making a journey through the New Forest between Christchurch and Totton first in a '4REP' and then in an inter-regional locomotive-hauled train you would, to quote a railwayman 'think you were riding a different line'. The fears that some of us had when it was decided to use multiple units for the Bournemouth electrification have sadly been realized for their riding when they have been out of works for some time can be nothing short of diabolical. Some stretches of line are worse than others, and I certainly wouldn't advise anyone to attempt a hot drink whilst lurching through Brockenhurst for example. Some regular travellers claim that the motion is marginally easier with the '4REP' at the front, ie pulling in the direction of Waterloo, but marginal is certainly the word. West of Bournemouth whether being pushed or pulled by a '33' the '4TC's behave perfectly respectably. It is to be hoped the new units, under construction as I write, can equal the superb riding qualities of the HSTs which are both pushed and pulled simultaneously.

Mention of inter-regional trains brings us to a pleasing development of the 1970s and 80s. With the

Left *Bournemouth depot, built on the approach to the former West station, in August 1986 with No 47 379 from a Newcastle to Poole express and 4REP No 3008.*

Right *The 14:38 Poole to Manchester Piccadilly, hauled by a Class '47', sets out on its journey and is about to cross Poole High Street in the teeth of a snowstorm, January 1986.*

closure of the Somerset and Dorset line in 1966 its most famous train, the 'Pines Express', was transferred to run via Southampton and Basingstoke. But BR seemed to see little future in such services. Motorways and improved trunk roads had greatly speeded up travel for the motorist between the South and South-West and the Midlands and the North, and with faster than ever rail services on the main lines to and from London it was anticipated that the demand for long-distance trains between the Weymouth and Bournemouth line and the Midlands and the North would virtually disappear.

It didn't happen. There were still a great many travellers who didn't mind if the journey was not quite as quick as was technically possible if they could ensconce themselves in a comfortable window seat at Bournemouth, Southampton or Winchester, close to the buffet car, relax and enjoy the ride until they arrived at their destination at Birmingham, Manchester, Newcastle or wherever and avoid both the traumas of struggling across London with their luggage and the hazards of traffic jams on the Winchester by-pass, lane closures on the M1 and pile-ups at the end of the bridge over the Manchester Ship Canal. To give credit where it's due, by the mid 1970s British Rail sensed this reversal of a trend and decided to cater for it. New, or rather cascaded, coaching stock was introduced, released by the introduction of HSTs, but still very up-to-date, catering was improved, and more trains serving a variety of destinations were put into service.

There are some fascinatingly obscure and faraway stations one can reach to-day from Poole and Bournemouth without changing; Sandwell and Dudley, Kircaldy and Blackpool North to name but three. Two summers back it was possible on a Saturday to travel from my local station, Wareham,

which serves a population of all of 5,000, without changing to all three mainland capitals, London, Cardiff and Edinburgh. The latter destination became obtainable when the daily Glasgow and Edinburgh train was extended on a Friday night through to Weymouth, returning next morning. It has since gone back to terminating at Poole but as compensation it has been named the 'Wessex Scot' and the Edinburgh portion now goes right up the east coast of Scotland to Dundee. One leaves Tayside at 07:55 and 11 hours 45 minutes and some 528 miles later one arrives by the shores of Poole Harbour.

British Rail admits that the cross country line by way of Crewe, Birmingham, Oxford, Reading and Basingstoke is not a good timekeeper, and I've sometimes cursed when I've been up to an hour late getting into Bournemouth. But I've also known a train make up 25 minutes between Wolverhampton and Winchester and arrive dead on time at Bouremouth, and when I was in charge of 41 ten year olds travelling between Crewe and Wareham and we were able to deposit them in the arms of their waiting parents four minutes early my gratitude to British Rail was boundless. I've never travelled the entire 528 miles all in one go—I suppose someone must have done—but it's an epic journey by any standards and when one considers the vast number of connections which have to be made and the scope for delays, to get within even an hour of right time is quite an achievement. To be served in the buffet with a Dundee pork pie by a still cheerful Glaswegian as the train passes the TVS studios beside the River Itchen and slows for the curve on the approach to the tunnel which takes the line under the heart of Southampton is the very essence of all that makes rail travel unique and, at its best, the most civilised method of getting about yet devised.

Chapter 27
New horizons

Waterloo was always one of the cleanest of the London termini, at least since its rebuilding, probably because a large proportion of its trains were electrically propelled, and today it is one of the most attractive. The news cinema may have gone but the cultural content of the immediate vicinity of the station is practically 100 per cent, although whether this includes the former Great Train Robber who for many years after his release from prison had a stall under one of the arches I cannot say! There is the Royal Festival Hall, the Queen Elizabeth Hall, the National Theatre, the Old Vic, the Hayward Gallery and the National Film Theatre all within a hundred yards or so of one or other of the station entrances, and in the Swinging Sixties Waterloo achieved the rare distinction of entering the hit parade when that enduring group The Kinks recorded *Waterloo Sunset*. The station was famous for its bright, jolly piped music, long before muzak was thought of and totally overdid it (I write this fresh from the bizarre experience of taking off from Faro airport, Portugal on a scorching hot August noon to the strains of Mario Lanza belting out *Overhead the Moon is beaming* through our Boeing 757). Which reminds me that one of the delights of the modern Waterloo is palm trees on the concourse, a foretaste of the promenade at Weymouth I suppose.

Waterloo took the lead in finally laying to rest the old railway sandwich chestnut, if you will excuse the mixed metaphor. When Casey Jones's fast food restaurant and take away opposite platforms 10 and 11 was proposed ten years ago a number of senior BR types threw up their hands in horror, apparently at the possible lowering of tone. I ask you, lowering the tone of BR catering, or at least its image? Anyhow the public loved it and Casey Jones's success changed BR's attitude nationwide to food and drink both on stations and trains. It's called giving the public what it wants.

Not all the services in and out of Waterloo are EMU operated. There are some diesels, they were introduced into regular service here later than at another main line London terminus. Today four classes are commonplace. There are the '08' and '09' shunters (the latter with an uprated maximum speed of

25 mph are unique to the Southern), the '33's and the '50's; there are also the Class '73' electro-diesels. The '50's are based on the Western Region and work the Exeter and West of England trains.

The LSW was, to quote Adrian Vaughan 'the pioneer in Britain of low-pressure pneumatic signalling', in other words power assisted signalling, and in 1904 the 23 miles between Woking and Basingstoke were re-equipped with pneumatic power boxes in between sections of semaphores working automatically. Since then the Waterloo to Bournemouth line has continually been upgraded and an extensive resignalling scheme is presently under way at Waterloo. Colour light signalling came into use between Hampton Court Junction and Waterloo in 1936, when the present concrete power box on the Richmond side of Waterloo station overlooking Westminster Bridge Road was opened, and other new boxes came into use at Wimbledon in 1948 and a panel one at Surbiton in 1970. Gradually the semaphore signals down the line have been replaced by colour lights, although many still remained at the time of electrification, and now, since the Southampton resignalling with its panel box at Eastleigh in 1980-81, there are no semaphores until Hamworthy, 115 miles from Waterloo.

Between Waterloo and Vauxhall the line curves its way past the Houses of Parliament, office blocks, a faded slogan urging travellers to 'use a theatre every time', tenements, markets, the Bennie Lift factory, the back of the gasometer which overlooks the Oval, the art deco Battersea Power Station, the equally famous Dogs' Home ('So you come from Battersea, do you know the dog's home?' 'I didn't know he'd been out.' Boom, boom), and the imaginatively repainted Vauxhall Bridge, perhaps inspired by the adjacent Tate Gallery. Beyond Vauxhall station the line follows the original 1838 course and therefore straightens out. Past Stewarts Lane depot, Queens Road station, under the Eastern and Central Section routes out of Victoria, past unprepossessing-looking flats puts by the LCC, predecessor of the late, lamented GLC, and a Victorian pub, the Duke of Cornwall, beside which 'S15's used to simmer waiting the road into Nine Elms depot whilst their drivers

Above *Palm trees grace the Waterloo concourse, 1986.*

Right *Waterloo in June 1982. 4TC No 423 is the leading unit of a twelve coach Weymouth express, on the right is a Class '50' with an Exeter train, in the sidings to the left beyond the Windsor station are Class '415' (4EPB) and '416' (2EPB) Bulleid-designed EMUs.*

Right *The mural beneath Waterloo signalbox.*

Class '73/1' No 73125 Stewarts Lane 1860-1985 about to take out the 17:35 Waterloo to Weymouth on 6 January 1986, the 4REP scheduled to power it having failed. Unfortunately the '73' itself failed at Clapham Junction.

licked their lips expectantly. On the opposite side, in the narrowing space between the South Western and Brighton lines, are various small industrial concerns including one which does something to old cars and which years ago used to do something similar to old Rolls-Royces. So to the busiest station in the world. 2,300 trains pass through or stop at Clapham Junction, which is actually in Battersea, every 24 hours, Monday to Friday. Much modernized in the 1980s it is still a vast, rambling affair, covering over 11,000 hectares, and even though the Bournemouth electrification robbed it of many of the empty stock movements which kept a fleet of 'M7's and later Standard 2-6-2Ts and 2-6-4Ts busy day and night, it remains a place of fascination for anyone interested in seeing a railway at work.

A line which has seen a revival in its fortunes of late is the West London Extension by which a number of trains work through Kensington Olympia to and from the Western and London Midland regions each day. The last steam suburban services in London worked between Clapham Junction and Kensington, a curious distinction when one considers how early the South Western and Brighton

were in the field of electrification. Class '33's and '4TC's now operate the morning and late afternoon trains which are chiefly for the benefit of post office workers, although there's nothing to stop anyone else sampling a trip past Battersea back gardens and over the Thames at Chelsea into bed-sit territory. Great Western type semaphores survived on the line within sight of Clapham Junction station until 1983.

South of Clapham Junction the Brighton and South Western lines diverge as both cut through Wandsworth Common. Hereabouts you can pick up a turn of the century three bedroom semi-detached in a not particularly good state of repair for £95,000; or could as I write in August 1986, probably doubled by the time this appears in print. For that price you could get four villas in the Algarve, each with a much better view of the sea and sunshine record superior to anywhere in Wandsworth, although admittedly the train service isn't so good. I mention that chiefly because I happen to be writing this in the Algarve, having had my first view of a '4REP' from around 30,000 feet as we flew out over Bournemouth yesterday morning. However back to Wandsworth.

If it wasn't for the cutting one could see Wandsworth Gaol which seems to get used nine times out of ten whenever film-makers require an exterior view of a typical prison; I suppose it's popularity is chiefly due to its accessibility.

On past Earlsfield cemetery and station and the

River Wandle from which Wandsworth gets its name. When I was a trainee reporter on the *Croydon Advertiser* I once attended an enquiry at which an elderly resident recalled catching trout in the Wandle. That would have been back in the 1870s for little but industrial and human waste has flourished since then in the Wandle which rises in the North Downs and flows into the Thames opposite the Chelsea houseboats.

Beyond Earlsfield station there is a complex of carriage sidings and maintenance depots on the up side, with a blue painted Bulleid corridor in departmental service, and over 100 carriage cleaners, some of whom make use of Wimbledon Staff Halt. A reinforced concrete flyover which the Southern Railway erected in the 1930s carries the up local line over the fast lines; south of here the fast lines are between the local ones. Keep a lookout as you flash through Wimbledon station and past the District Line

Below *Class '455' EMUs at Clapham Junction, May 1986.*

Bottom *District Line Underground trains at Wimbledon, 19 September 1980.*

Mural at Surbiton station, 1986.

Underground trains for, amongst the 60,000 passengers who use it every weekday, you may see a Womble or John McEnroe throwing a tantrum. From here on suburbia gets steadily posher, once beyond the downside engineers yard where there are usually some old Southern Railway, and sometimes Great Western and London Midland and Scottish vans in residence. Raynes Park with its staggered platforms for the suburban lines only, where the first and the last trolleybuses in London used to swish by down below, is where the Epsom and Chessington South lines diverge. The row upon row of blooms which Carters Tested Seeds used to tend so carefully have been replaced by a barracks-line development of flats. I suppose there was more profit in selling the land than the seeds but the narrow slits, they can hardly be called windows, of the flats which face the railway are a miserable contrast to the generous gardens of the Victorian and Edwardian villas and inter-war semi-detacheds elsewhere hereabouts in which there's always the possibility of a glimpse of domestic drama being played out.

Dull, faceless tower blocks are a feature of New Malden, followed by the rustic sounding Berrylands which is chiefly distinguished by never having had a goods yard on account of being a late developer; it was built by the Southern Railway in 1933.

Surbiton was rebuilt around the same time, 1936-39, in the not unpleasing concrete and glass style then in vogue to the designs of the same J. R. Scott who was responsible for the floridly Edwardian Victory Arch at Waterloo. He must have undergone a traumatic conversion in the intervening fifteen years for the styles could hardly be more dissimilar. The large goods yard at Surbiton is now a car park. We have not yet passed a single goods yard still used for its original purpose, nor will we within the sub-urban area. The daily pick-up goods which depended for much of its business on domestic coal disappeared around the time steam was being phased out and the yards have become either car parks for commuters who once walked or rode by bus, trolley, or cycle to their local station, or they have been sold for redevelopment.

The Hampton Court line branches off beyond Sur-biton, we cross the Kingston by-pass, another 1930s development, and now we are into the ribbon development of the inter-war years which slithered out along the arterial roads and beside the railway and makes the demarcation line between town and country almost impossible to define. Sandown Park Racecourse, then Esher, Hersham, Walton-on-Thames and Weybridge, the line cuts straight through the Thames Valley until the river turns northwards to Staines, Runnymede, Windsor and Great Western territory. Byfleet and New Haw is another station built by the Southern Railway, in 1927, but the location is chiefly notable for the junc-tion by which goods trains from the great mar-shalling yards at Feltham used to gain the main line. The reduction in rail freight and the revolution in that which remained with the concentration on con-tainerization and bulk loads rendered Feltham redundant and it had closed by 1970. The junction, which with the Weybridge-Addlestone Junction line forms a triangle, is still used by freight and passenger trains and leads to a useful diversionary electrified route to Waterloo by way of Staines and Richmond.

West Byfleet, which celebrates its centenary in 1987, is the last station before Woking, the extent of third rail penetration from 1937 to 1967.

Two famous buildings stand side by side on the down side immediately before Woking station. The most remarkable in appearance is the Shah Jehan Mosque. Mosques are no longer particularly unusual in Britain but that at Woking was the very first. It was built in 1889 on a site once owned by the Necropolis Company and formerly occupied by the Royal Dramatic College. Prince Albert laid the foundation stone of this, a home for 'decaying actors and actresses' in June 1860. Money was raised by grand fêtes at the Crystal Palace and various West End theatres and amongst the trustees were Dickens, Thackeray and Charles Keen. Unfortunately, despite numbering Queen Victoria and Prince Albert amongst its patrons, it had to close in 1877 and in 1884 one Dr Gottlieb Wilhelm Leitner bought the land on which it stood. Dr Leitner, a naturalized Hungarian, had travelled extensively in the East and he built an Oriental Institute on the land, where the culture of India could be studied and where Muslims and Hindus could live according to their own customs. The architect of the mosque, the funds for which came chiefly from the Princess of Popal, was W. I. Chambers. It was built in Bath and Bargate stone. For a while the Institute flourished, there were many Indians in the district serving with the British Army, and some of those who had died here and had been buried at Brookwood were reinterred in the grounds of the Institute. However, after Leitner's death in 1899 it fell into disuse. After some thirteen years the Shah Jehan Mosque once again became a place of worship when the first Muslim missionary to Europe, Khwaja Kamal Ud Din, arrived, and so it continues down to the present day.

I learned much of the foregoing from Mr M. A. Jalal, the caretaker, who was living beside the mosque, although he was hoping to be rehoused by Woking Council, and who showed me round. I also met the Iman, Qari Bashoff, who drove up in a rather ancient Hillman Minx, but who nevertheless looked absolutely the part. His attire and the cool, tiled, carpeted interior took me instantly back to the many mosques I had visited in the Middle East and Pakistan. It was momentarily disorienting to step back into the shade of oak and ash trees planted in the grounds and walk back past the 1920s semi-detached villas which line the road linking the mosque with Woking station.

Next door to Woking's famous mosque is a building with an equally notable history, and one which like it reflects changing social and moral attitudes.

The Woking Homes began in 1885 as a refuge for orphaned girls in Jeffreys Road, Clapham. They were founded by the Vicar of All Saints', Lambeth, Canon Allen Edwards, MA, who took a great interest in the many railway families in his parish, which included Nine Elms, and from the start LSW railwaymen contributed financially to the upkeep of the orphanage. Such was the demand that much larger, purpose built premises soon became necessary and so in 1909 Woking Grange, a new building on land beside the railway, was opened. It had room for 150 children and its aim was that no child of a dead or disabled LSW railwayman would be turned from its doors. In 1923 it became the Southern Railwaymen's Home for Children and extended its care to all dependants of all the SR's constituents. By 1935 a hospital block, gymnasium and further residential accommodation had been added. One method of raising money for the Orphanage, which older readers will remember with affection, was the dog with a collecting box strapped to his back. Called London Jack, he collected £4,000 between 1923 and 1931. Death did not bring his good works to an end for after he died he was stuffed and put on display on platform one at Southampton Central until 1968. Like other railway artefacts London Jack was eventually preserved and by 1976 was at Sheffield Park on the Bluebell Railway. In 1969 there was some correspondence about London Jack in the *Southern Daily Echo* and one reader claimed that London Jack had collected 'over £450 and was originally stuffed and used at Waterloo and then Southampton Terminus before coming to Central'. The truth seems to be that there were several dogs who went under the collective title of London Jack. This particular one was replaced by a working model of a car ferry which a British Rail spokesmen said, apparently without a hint of embarrassment, was 'much more in keeping with modern times'. Another reader wrote that he had known London Jack's trainer, Walter Wiggins, during 1916-18 when he was a young apprentice at Nine Elms locomotive depot. Apparently whenever a child deposited a penny in Jack's collecting box Wiggins always sent it on its way with the advice 'never indulge in excess beer, baccy, women or horses'. I like the 'excess'.

Changing times, and the emergence of the Welfare State under the guiding hand of Clement Attlee's post-war Labour Government, gradually reduced the need for permanent full-time accommodation for boys and girls, but other demands were growing and in 1946 a nursery for under-fives was opened and a year later the first retired railway employees came to live at Woking Grange. Over the years the Homes have developed a flexible response to the needs of railwaymen and their families. For instance a boy in a school in which I taught some years ago got into serious, but uncharacteristic, trouble with the police. His father was a signalman and understanding magistrates agreed that the boy should go to the Woking Homes and be allowed to spend weekends with his parents. He went to the local school there, enjoyed his time at Woking, and at sixteen got a job as a trainee chef at a big London hotel. Another railwayman, a sleeping car attendant, whose marriage had broken up, arranged for his daughter to live at Woking when he was away on duty, and she came home whenever he had several non-working days or was on leave.

By 1976 the number of elderly people at the Homes exceeded that of the children and by 1984 there were only fifteen of the latter. As Mr G. A. Warr, the Principal, told me, the present buildings are totally unsuitable for the needs of today and are pretty much incapable of further adaption and as the centenary of this fine establishment was being celebrated in 1985 various plans were under consideration to enable it to continue its work into the 21st century. Incidentally one of the centenary commemorative events was the naming of a Class '73' locomotive after the Woking Homes.

Right *Woking station, September 1985.*

Below *The grounds of the Railwaymen's Homes and the Shah Jehan Mosque, Woking.*

Chapter 28
Today

Straight and level, the 23 miles of quadruple track from Woking to Basingstoke take us from Surrey into Hampshire through sandy heathland and pine woods, past Pirbright Junction where the Alton line diverges and over the Guildford to Reading line, a long westward-penetrating tentacle of the SECR which enabled it to link up with the GWR and thus produce the spectacle which lasted into the 1950s of Swindon built engines hauling sets of Wainwright birdcage carriages. Later Western diesel-hydraulics worked over the line with stone trains for Merstham when the M23 was being built. If ever the Channel tunnel becomes a reality then its importance will grow enormously.

There are five stations between Woking and Basingstoke, Brookwood, beside the cemetery, Farnborough, Fleet, Winchfield and Hook. I still associate them with leisurely journeys around 1960 on Basingstoke and Salisbury slows when one could be certain of getting a run behind one of Maunsell's triumvirate of express classes, a 'Nelson', a 'Schools' or an 'Arthur', although mixed traffic 'H15's and

Basingstoke station, February 1986.

'S15's also took their turn. Between Winchfield and Hook a deep cutting takes the line under the M3 and a bit further on motorway and railway run parallel, separated by a field.

On the southern horizon is the hump of the Hog's Back, with the tower of one of our twentieth century cathedrals, Guildford, just beyond the easternmost slope. The stations between Woking and Basingstoke are built of wood, brick and iron, neat and well cared for.

Basingstoke is a rather better station viewed from the town than from the platform. It has had some recent additions which blend very well with the original red brick and has been tidied up so that as you approach either from the pedestrian underpass or swing round by road the overall effect is neat and pleasing. Originally it was planned that Hook would become a London overspill town after the Second World War but the inhabitants objected violently; not that that always makes any difference. However they got their way and instead the choice fell on Basingstoke. Not that the people here particularly welcomed the idea but London was determined it must have an overspill settlement somewhere in this

part of Hampshire, and the first new arrivals moved in, not without apprehension on both sides, in 1952. Since then the town has grown enormously, from 17,000 in 1952 to 75,000 in 1981 (129,600 in Greater Basingstoke). The station has been carefully incorporated into the new developments so that it is within a couple of minutes walk, along Station Mall past a series of reliefs of Drummond 4-4-0 No 716, of the central shopping precinct and the car park above it.

Basingstoke is a grand place for connoisseurs of office blocks. The older ones are as dull as those further up the line, but the most recent are infinitely better; bold and imaginative, great expanses of shimmering glass, with a myriad of reflections, splendid crystal palaces. The best of them to date is the Wiggins Teape building which must surely put the Hanging Gardens of Babylon to shame, having become almost engulfed, by design, by the foliage and greenery of Amazonian lushness which grows around and from within it.

On the opposite side of the station, beyond the Reading platform, are reminders of times past, the Great Western pub and next door the Livery and Bait stables. Next door to that, and patronized for all I know by the same clientele, is the BR Staff Association building.

The intermediate stations on the Basingstoke to Reading line, Bramley and Mortimer, betray their Brunellian origins although the line is Southern Region property. Not much of the Great Western is evident at Basingstoke itself today. The two road shed which was home to three Pannier tanks at nationalization, although 61XX 2-6-2Ts were regular visitors, closed in November 1950 and was demolished. After that Western Region engines

repaired to the Southern Shed. Reading trains terminating at Basingstoke still occupy the site of the GW station, a terminal platform reached through a hole in the wall of the up Waterloo fast line platform.

The growth of the town has ensured that Basingstoke is one of the busiest stations on the Southern Region, with the many passenger and freight trains off the Reading line merging with the stopping trains from Waterloo which terminate here and the Salisbury, Southampton and Portsmouth line services. Westwards are sidings, many of them occupied by derelict stock awaiting scrapping and sometimes new stock awaiting entry into service. Factories and warehouses occupy the land to the north, the oldest being of a stylish pale cream art deco design of the type found on the Great West Road at Hounslow, then comes a cottage with a magnificent crop of old railway signs in its garden, and after this Worting Junction. Here the Salisbury and Southampton lines diverge and generations of photographers have taken up their stance to record trains diving under, curving round and passing loftily over.

Now comes 19 miles through the woods and downs of some of the richest part of the Hampshire countryside, interrupted only by Micheldever station which comes immediately after Litchfield, Popham No 1 and Popham No 2 tunnels. The sidings where life-expired carriages awaited their end have been taken up but Micheldever retains other sidings serving two important terminals. There is the Elf distribution centre, which is not where garden gnomes come from but where oil is brought in trains of 102 tonne tankers from Ripple Lane, Barking, each brought up in the rear by an old Southern Railway bogie brake van. The first of these were rebuilds of the power units used by the LSBC for their overhead

Left *Class '73' Electro-diesel No E6029 heading a Waterloo-Southampton van train past withdrawn Portsmouth line 4COR motor-cars at Micheldever, March 1972.*

Right *Winchester station, April 1986.*

suburban electrification and made redundant when the SR standardization on the LSW system. Micheldever is also the gathering station for the oil exploration being carried out at the nearby Lark-whistle Farm oilfield, and ten wagonloads are taken out each week.

Approaching Winchester the earthworks of the branch from Alton can be seen to the east and shortly afterwards the line crosses the dual carriageway A34 which makes use of the trackbed of the Winchester to Newbury hereabouts and elsewhere. Although the preservationists never did achieve their original object of reopening the entire line from Alton to Winchester steam trains are running once again between Alresford and Alton and doing tremendous business. The Watercress Line has had some fierce internal squabbles but it has never lacked energy and enthusiasm, and has done a marvellous job of recreating an astonishingly complete tableau of the Waterloo to Weymouth line of around 1960, complete with rebuilt and unrebuilt Bulleid Pacifics, Maunsell and BR Standard 2-6-0s, and the celebrated Drummond 'T9' 4-4-0 No 30120 on loan from the National Railway Museum, all in the livery of that period, hauling rakes of BR Mark 1 carriages in green, carmine and cream, maroon and chocolate and cream. The only serious omission is a rake of Bulleid coaches and a few Maunsells such as the Bluebell Railway possesses, but the Watercress Mid Hants Line came into business much later in the day, by which time the only such vehicles still around were in departmental use, and although it has acquired some they require much restoration if they are ever to be put back into passenger carrying service.

Winchester station is a rather claustrophobic old place in yellow-grey brick and wood, the two tracks stretching seemingly endlessly away to the north and south, inviting a quick getaway, which is easy enough for Winchester is well served as is only right and proper for King Alfred's capital. There are Waterloo to Bournemouth slows and semi-fasts, extra rush-hour trains, at least one non-stop to Waterloo, inter-regional expresses and DEMUs to Reading and Portsmouth. A quick view of the cathedral tower is just possible on the down side half a mile south of the station before the erstwhile Shawford Junction where the connection used to be made with the Didcot, Newbury and Southampton Railway. A down slow line appears at Shawford station and an up slow immediately afterwards. The scenery hereabouts is very pretty, gulls wheeling over the willows and water meadows along the banks of the winding River Itchen.

Next station is Eastleigh and anyone who labours under the illusion that freight is no more than a hobby on the Southern will take a very different view after an hour spent here. One Thursday morning for example more freight trains passed me between 9.30 am and 10.30 am than passenger. These ranged from a military special for Wool, through oil trains from Fawley, a Speedlink from Severn Tunnel Junction, empty car flats and a parcels from Southampton, to the star turn, a mighty Class '59' on the 07:00 stone train from Merehead Quarry to Botley Aggregate sidings. The four General Motors Class '59's arrived at Southampton Docks from the USA on 21 January 1986 and have since proved themselves far and away the most powerful locomotives ever to run in Britain, No 59002 developing a sustained tractive effort of 110,000 lb on test. The four '59's have replaced no less than nine Class '56's and two Class '37's.

Top *Yeoman-owned General Motors No 59002 arriving at Eastleigh with the Merehead-Botley stone train, 24 July 1986.*

Above *Eastleigh, 24 July 1986. A Class '73' on a parcels train, a DEMU arriving from Portsmouth, and a 4REP at the head of a Bournemouth-Waterloo semi-fast.*

Left *Normandy, the 'B4' Dock 0-4-0T, built in November 1893 for service in Southampton Docks, at work on the Bluebell Railway, 7 September 1986, with Adams cutaway cab and Drummond chimney.*

Eastleigh has a complex of yards and in addition to the traffic mentioned also handles Ford Transit vans which are built at the works beside Eastleigh Airport and shipped by rail all over the country. Then there is the traction maintenance depot and, of course, the Works. This was under some threat early in 1986 but although BREL announced some redundancies these were less than many had feared and the future seems fairly secure, although the eventual withdrawal of the '33's lays a question mark over further cutbacks. Probably a greater variety of motive power is seen at Eastleigh than anywhere else on the Southern Region. Apart from the many EMUs and DEMUs there are the Class '59's, '56's, '50's, '47's, '33's, '73's, '09's and '08's, whilst other classes such as '37's and '45's turn up from time to time.

Traffic through Southampton Parkway, formerly Airport, station is increasing. The station has been rebuilt and a car park for 330 vehicles was opened in the summer of 1986. It has the advantage of being alongside the terminal buildings and could become a mini-Gatwick should the airport itself develop.

Entire books could be, and have been, written about railway developments at Eastleigh and Southampton. Inevitably they are in some respects out of date before they appear in print for things are always changing, so the reader will, I hope, understand if we are neither too detailed nor specific, but nevertheless, hopefully accurate.

Swaythling is closely followed by St Denys, a name I always associate with Paris, which is a typical late Victorian suburban station, rather grand for its humble purpose with four platforms for the Portsmouth and Winchester lines which come together immediately to the south of the station. The Portsmouth line does a U turn beyond St Denys so that one can sometimes see trains apparently heading back the way they have come on the opposite bank of the Itchen which curves right up to the tracks. There's a neat little cabin cruiser with a rakish funnel moored off the west bank which I swear has never upped anchor in all the years I've been passing it. Freight installations follow thick and fast, the two reception roads and eight sidings of Bevois Yard on the up side, Tunnel Cement and MAT transport sidings opposite with curious looking cement wagons with a dent in their middles as though Miss Piggy had just done a karate chop on them. Very likely there will be one or two more of the SR bogie brakes here, opposite Northiam Junction where the main line swings wheel-screechingly to the right, although the curve was eased a couple of years back.

The line to the Eastern Docks and past the disused Terminus station continues straight ahead, now singled, past the Aviation Hall, an excellent new museum whose chief exhibit is a Sandringham, no not a Gresley 4-6-0 but a flying boat which started out life in 1943 as a Sunderland and is, to date, the last flying boat to land on Southampton Water where its kind were once so familiar. A weed enveloped but still busy siding winds down to the water's edge at Dibbles Wharf where coal is discharged. A little further along Townsend Thornsen and P&O cross-Channel boats used to leave for Cherbourg and Le Havre but sadly they departed for good after a dock strike in 1984 and it is now no longer possible to sail from Southampton to France as it was for over 100 years. However not all is totally lost for when the QE2 does her regular transatlantic run in summer one may sail in her to Cherbourg.

Southampton's great rival for the Cherbourg and Channel Islands business, Weymouth, continued to operate these services until the end of summer 1986. Following the privatization of Sealink in 1984 their future has become very uncertain. Sealink opened up a Portsmouth to the Channel Islands route in 1978—Portsmouth has become a major ferry port in the 1970s and 80s, to the detriment of Southampton. It has the best road connections with London of all the four Hampshire and Dorset ferry ports, better than Southampton, Poole and Weymouth, and has been eager to expand its services, but it came a cropper in 1985 when Sealink introduced an up-market 'Bateau de Luxe' daily operation to Cherbourg and a similar 'Starliner' night one to the Channel Islands. The two ships involved, the *Earl William* and the *Earl Granville*, were refitted in Denmark at an estimated cost of £5 million and quite honestly to anyone who had experience of operating conditions and requirements on the Channel Islands route it seemed a perfect way of throwing good money after bad. The market for the luxurious, expensive service the new owners of Sealink were offering did not seem to be there; anyone spending the sort of money demanded would surely fly. So it proved. A drastic revision of services before the season was out proved necessary but could not avoid a thumping loss.

Meanwhile the Weymouth services had altered too. The popular night mailings were abandoned and instead the two ships operating out of Weymouth, the *Earl Godwin*, which had been on the route for many years, and the *Earl Harold*, renamed from the *Ailsa Princess* which was formerly a Stranraer to Larne ship although she had done the Weymouth to Cherbourg run for several seasons, worked a daylight service. They left Guernsey and Jersey at 07:15 and 07:30 respectively, arrived at Weymouth mid-afternoon and got back to the Channel Islands in the evening.

Both Sealink routes had to compete with the new

Channel Island Ferries which began operations out of Portsmouth in the spring of 1985. For most of the year their fares were cheaper than Sealink's and by the end of the season they claimed to have captured 80 per cent of the Portsmouth traffic.

Sealink had to do a great deal of rethinking before the 1986 season began. One boat operated all the Channel Islands to Weymouth services that summer and as I write receipts were reported to have improved over 1985. At the end of the season Sealink suddenly closed the service down and said that in future it would only operate during the peak summer months. For all its poor road connections Weymouth still provides the only quayside rail service and also has the advantage of a much shorter sea crossing than any of its rivals so hopefully its traditional links with the Channel Islands may survive. If they don't the loss to the town will be considerable.

From the junction with the line to the Eastern Docks the main Weymouth line goes right under Southampton, through the tunnel which every so often needs major surgery. The last time was in 1983 and the operation took two years. A narrow gauge line was laid inside, first one and then the other of the standard gauge tracks was taken up so the work could proceed around the clock without stopping. The multi-million pound business was carried out most efficiently with the minimum delay to trains and completed ahead of schedule.

Immediately beyond the tunnel is the main station with the cranes of the Western Docks on the left. The

Above left *Townsend Thorensen and P&O cross-Channel ferries in the Eastern Docks, Southampton, October 1979, with the P&O liner* Canberra *behind alongside the Ocean Terminal.*

Left *A sad end to nearly two centuries of regular, all-year-round sailings from Weymouth to the Channel Islands and France. Three Sealink British Ferries, headed by the* Earl William, *laid up at Weymouth in 1985 after the abrupt end of regular sailings in September.*

Above right *The OCL container ship* Liverpool Bay *arriving at Southampton from the Far East, September 1978, seen from the Hythe Ferry.*

Right *The* Queen Elizabeth 2 *prepares to leave Southampton for New York, July 1986.*

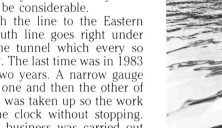

The turntable which once served the Western Docks, Southampton, is now at Didcot Railway Centre. The Great Western Society's first locomotive, 0-4-2T No 1446, stands on it on New Year's Day 1986.

The Ocean Freightliner Terminal, Southampton, May 1986. No 47376 is in charge of a train from Ripple Lane, Barking.

The world's longest liner, the Norway *(formerly the* France*) in the Western Docks, Southampton, in the summer of 1984. A Class '33' stands at the head of the Waterloo-bound boat train.*

view here still looks a little empty without the vast bulk of the Burmah Endeavour, the world's eleventh largest ship of 457,841 tons deadweight which was laid up at Berths 101 and 102 for some four years until July 1986 and almost became part of the landscape.

The docks have been through rough times. The switch to containerization and bulk handling and the great falling away in liner traffic put many dock workers on the dole. Nor surprisingly there were industrial disputes and strikes and inevitably shipowners took their business elsewhere, although some have come back. But the decline has been less than is generally supposed. Everyone notices the absence of the liners, although they have far from vanished, and if there are fewer shipping movements one of the chief reasons is that more big ships than ever call regularly at Southampton, bulk cargoes are swiftly loaded and unloaded and thus fewer ships are needed to deal with what is still an enormous volume of business. In 1980 the tonnage of container cargo was four times greater than the cargo handled in an average year immediately before containerization. 300,000 container units are handled annually, in 1984 more grain was exported from Southampton than from any other UK port, large numbers of cars are both imported and exported and the official figures for those working in port-related activities in the Southampton area is 30,000.

One famous feature which has gone is the Ocean Terminal. In one disastrous year, 1974, five of the six liners regularly using it went out of service, leaving only the *QE2* and in 1981 she moved up river to a new terminal at berths Nos 38 and 39. Used briefly for exhibitions, the onetime pride of Southampton had become a white elephant and in 1984 it was demolished. Scrap metal is now loaded from the site, just about as great a fall from grace as could be imagined.

Southampton, which was granted city status by the Queen in February 1964, is a fascinating place. Laurie Lee described it thus in 1934 in his sequel to *Cider with Rose*, *As I walked out One Midsummer Morning*: 'Southampton town...came up to all expectations, proving to be shifty and salty in turns, like some ship-jumping sailor who'd turned his back on the sea in a desperate attempt to make good on land. The streets near the water appeared to be jammed with shops designed more for entertainment than profit including tatooists, ear-piercing, bump-readers, fortune-tellers, whelk stalls and pudding boilers. There were also shops selling kites and Chinese paper dragons, coloured sands and traps and birds; and lots of little step-down taverns panelled with rum-soaked timbers and reeking of pickled eggs and onions'. If the dock area is less colourful today there are still the medieval walls, the old houses and some superb museums and an art gallery which puts in the shade anything that prosperous town down the line, Bournemouth, has to offer.

Excavations have revealed much of Saxon Southampton and there are plans for a vast Timebase Centre, a heritage complex telling the history of the city from its earliest days, incorporating an exhibition similar to that at the Jorvik Centre in York and a transport museum, all linked to the present museum by trams and a Gatwick or Birmingham Airport type overhead transport system running from the Timebase Centre to the railway station and car parks. One artefact which has been removed from Southampton and put to good use is the turntable installed in the Western Docks in the 1930s. This was bought by the Great Western Society, restored at Didcot Railway Centre, and has been used to turn many famous locomotives, *Evening Star*, *Sir Nigel Gresley*, *King George V* and *Blue Peter* to name but four, as well as all the regular residents, although curiously no former Southern Railway locomotive has yet renewed acquaintance with it.

The exit to the west from Southampton takes us past both freightliner terminals. On the up side is Millbrook, opened on the site of a former goods depot in 1968, and a little further along, on the down side, Maritime, opened in 1972. They are the only freightliner terminals on the Southern Region and handle 10 per cent of all Freightliner business. Within the docks is the Port Office parcels terminal which is served by rail, but the regular twice daily trains ceased running when BR most unfortunately lost the parcels contract to road competition in the summer of 1986. Boat trains still run into the Western Docks for the various cruise liners which call. An event which brought back memories—and the rare sight today of two boat trains on the same morning—was the visit on 26 July 1984 of the *Norway*, which as the *France* had regularly sailed between Le Havre, Southampton and New York. The longest liner in the world, she now normally cruises in the Carribean, but comes occasionally to Europe. She looked quite superb in her blue and white livery, and by a happy coincidence was in port at the same time as her old rival, *Queen Elizabeth 2*.

The line curves past Redbridge station with its engineers depot, and round the edge of Southampton Water with a view past the container berths and right down the length of the Western Docks. The Romsey and Salisbury line heads northwards and at Totton the single track Fawley branch heads south-east to the vast refineries on the edge of the Solent.

Chapter 29
Through the New Forest

There now follows what some consider the most attractive section of the route, through the New Forest. For 20 miles the line curves through the heart of the forest, across heathland and through woods, and at almost any point along those 20 miles it offers a better chance, indeed the certainty, of seeing some of the hundreds of ponies and perhaps deer which live here than do the roads. An excellent barometer of the seasons is the Forestry Commission camp site alongside the line between Lyndhurst Road and Beaulieu Road (for Lord Montagu's National Motor Museum) stations. From the middle of May to mid-September it is full to capacity, as are all other sites in the forest. I once saw a handsome black and pink sow strolling amongst the caravans and tents, and sheep and the occasional pony sometimes lets its curiosity conquer its shyness.

Just before Brockenhurst station, on the down side, is a delightful neo-Gothic castellated lodge, opposite the Sixth Form College playing fields. Brockenhurst is a busy station, the junction for the Lymington branch, but it is not as important as it was in the days when the old main line, Castleman's Corckscrew, diverged here, and when later it was the terminus of the Motorail trains from Stirling.

Out beyond the heathland, west of Brockenhurst, there is a view of the hills of the Isle of Wight above the Needles. I have often wondered if it is possible to see the spire of Salisbury Cathedral which is some 20 miles to the north-west—it is after all the tallest in the country—but I think Salisbury itself is too low-lying.

There are three more New Forest stations, Sway, New Milton and Hinton Admiral, each an oasis of suburbia between sea and forest. New Milton serves Barton-on-Sea which might more accurately call itself Barton-in-Sea, for the cliffs are being eaten away at a ferocious rate and there are instances of cliff-top residents opening their back doors after a night of wind and rain, and finding most of their garden lying on the beach below.

About here the buffet usually closes, its engraved glass mural featuring such long vanished wayside attractions as a Class '71' at Eastleigh Works, and the Museum of Transport at Clapham disappearing from

view. The line passes in and out of Dorset more than once before it leaves Hampshire for good as it crosses over the River Mude within sight of Christchurch and its ancient priory and the even more ancient Hengistbury Head, a rich source of pre-historic finds. If it is clear we may see right across the bay to the Purbeck Hills and the Old Harry Rocks, twin of the Needles some fifteen miles away. Until the local government boundary changes in the early 1970s the border wasn't reached until Poole and for many it still seems strange that Bournemouth should be in Dorset rather than Hampshire.

Two more rivers swiftly follow, the Avon and its water meadows and fishermen, then Christchurch station and the Stour. From here on the line is built up on either side, except for parks and gardens, until we are clear of Poole. We are still travelling at around 60 mph as we sweep past a row of 1920s bay-windowed semi-detacheds overlooking a recreation ground with behind them what looks for all the world like the upperworks of a red brick, Italianate, Victorian church tower but is actually a water tower. Through Pokesdown with its wide open spaces where there was, until electrification, quadruple track, then the abandoned Boscombe station, although the coal yard still functions, served by road. We're slowing now, squeezing through one of the bores under the wide road bridge with perhaps a yellow No 25 on top, which if it had a couple of poles sticking up from its roof could pass as one of the trolleybuses which served Bournemouth with distinction for over thirty years. We curve round and come to a halt within the high, red brick walls of the listed structure which was for most of its life known as Bournemouth Central, and which still bears an ornamental inscription to that effect, picked out in stones at the London end of the down platform.

How many holidaymakers have alighted here and found the mild climate, the wooded chines, the view across the bay to the Isle of Wight and the Purbeck Hills, and the all pervading air of affluent gentility so greatly to their liking that they have returned year after year, finally to settle? In the words of John Betjeman Bournemouth 'wears a large and wealthy coat of precious firs. Beneath it we may glimpse the flaming colours of her dress, the winding lengths of crimson rhododendron, the delicate embroidery of her flower beds...her voice is the twang of the tennis racket...the lap and roar of waves upon her sand and shingle, the strains of stringed instruments from the concert hall of her famous pavilion'. Betjeman wrote the above in 1949 when blue painted 'Merchant Navy's were in charge of the 'Bournemouth Belle' and there were still malachite green 'King Arthur's and 'Lord Nelson's at Bournemouth shed. Although he did not ignore 'the jazzy blocks of flats and hotels' which were beautiful neither then nor now, but now are vastly more numerous, the self-satisfied essence of the town which he captured remains; 'a noble lady with ample bosom'.

The perfect way to arrive at Bournemouth was in its famous all-Pullman express but with the end of steam in the summer of 1967 such a train was seen as an anachronism and it was withdrawn, and with the steady decline of such luxury travel throughout the BR network it seemed only a matter of time

Far left *Through the New Forest.*

Left *A Liverpool to Poole express, hauled by a Class '33', passes the junction where the Lymington branch diverges, and where the Ringwood line once did, in September 1980. At this time a new connection from Brockenhurst station was being put in to keep Lymington trains clear of the main line, hence the somewhat curious condition of the track on the right of the picture.*

Right *The Waterloo to Weymouth line becomes part of Network South East, Bournemouth station, August 1986.*

before the very name Pullman would exist only in history and in museums. By 1980 the only Pullmans still operated by BR were a rake of very modern ones between Euston and Manchester—not a route traditionally associated with such travel—whilst the Steam Locomotive Operators Association was gathering together a set of all-metal Pullman cars dating from the 1960s. But with the ban on steam traction throughout the Southern Region there seemed little chance that Pullman would ever again be seen on the Bournemouth line. But nostalgia is a powerful force and if cleverly and forcefully marketed there is money to be made out of it. Thus at a price of £11 million James B. Sherwood's 'Venice-Simplon Orient Express' of restored Pullmans came into existence.

Normally the eight restored Pullmans run between Victoria and Dover or Folkestone but since the train's introduction in 1982 they have ventured on occasions down the Bournemouth line. Then in early 1985 it was announced that the 'Bournemouth Belle' would be restored. Each Saturday from May until September the Pullmans, four of which had in their pre-preservation days regularly worked on the Waterloo to Southampton and Bournemouth line, left Waterloo at 10:35 and after stopping at Southampton at noon and Brockenhurst at 12:19, reached their destination at 12:41. The return journey started from Bournemouth at 3.45 pm. The cost, which included something called 'brunch' and afternoon tea and champagne, was a cool £80. Although passenger loadings from observation were, not surprisingly, light, the 'Belle' ran again throughout the 1986 summer season.

At present, as since 1967, the through Weymouth trains cease to be electric at Bournemouth, shed their

'4REP's and perhaps one of the '4TC's, the lights dim for a short while until the waiting '33' backs down, the driver revs up as though not quite able to shake off the motor-cycling days of his youth, and what has of late been dubbed the Dorsetway journey to Weymouth resumes.

In the early spring of 1986 the decision for which many local people had long campaigned, to electrify the line right through to Weymouth, was announced. It finally lifted any threats to its future and meant that the time expired '4REP's and '4TC's could finally be laid to rest and replaced by a brand new fleet of 24 five coach trains—although being the Southern the term brand new has to be qualified for the power equipment of the REPs was to be re-used in the new units. Still the proposed air- conditioning, power-operated doors, public address system and hopefully above all else, much better riding was greatly to be welcomed.

The third rail already extended to Branksome, the station beyond Bournemouth, across the handsome viaduct spanning the Bournemouth Valley, although you have to look hard to see the trickle of water which gave the town its name. This viaduct is one of a pair, the other giving direct access from Bournemouth Central to Bournemouth West. When the West station was closed the servicing and stabling depot for the new electrics was set up in its yard, but with the penny-pinching perversity which characterized the Bournemouth electrification scheme, the track on the viaduct leading from the main line to the depot was taken up so that all trains entering the depot have to reverse in and out of Branksome station.

Above left *The Venice-Simplon Orient Express Pullmans winding their way down Weymouth Harbour Tramway, May 1985.*

Left *£80-a-go-passengers alight from the 'Bournemouth Belle' at its destination, August 1986.*

Above right *Crowded conditions on a four-coach Waterloo to Weymouth train (it should have been eight) between Hamworthy and Wareham, March 1986.*

Right *Electrification reaches Wareham. Insulator pots stacked ready for installation on the down platform, May 1986.*

Chapter 30
The final stretch

From Bournemouth to Branksome the line is surrounded by the pine trees which gave the Somerset and Dorst's principal express its name, then it's down the bank past gardens and tennis courts. Through Parkstone station and a view straight ahead of Poole Harbour and the Purbeck Hills. Then round the curve and out over the causeway with Poole Park and its lake and, sometimes, some fine model yachts on the up side, and on the down the harbour with hundreds of full size yachts and at frequent intervals a slab-sided grey and yellow Truckline ferry gingerly making its way between them and Brownsea Island. Truckline, which sails several times a day between Poole and Cherbourg originally with just lorries but from 1986 with private cars too, has done much to revive the fortunes of the port of Poole and turn it into one of the busiest of Britain's smaller ports.

The railway cuts through the heart of Poole, over the pedestrianized High Street where dozens of shoppers stand waiting for the barriers to rise after our passing, although the more athletic take the ancient iron footbridge beside it. Poole station, rebuilt in the 1960s, has the merit of being close to the town centre, but in all other respects is woefully

inadequate. The circulating area by the booking office must have been designed with a depleted troup of midgets in mind, the bus shelter on the down platform is a disgrace and for most passengers their lot consists of waiting on the dreary, windswept platforms. Even when the train arrives their misery is not over for BR has amusingly arranged that one end of the station is on a sharp curve so that, for no extra cost, passengers can enjoy the thrill of leaping the gap between the platform edge and the train!

Past the sidings where the inter-regional trains pause before working back to Bournemouth depot, and what used to be Holes Bay Junction where the Somerset and Dorset trains headed north, then it's out across Poole Harbour again, dinghies and mud flats on the up side, yachts, one or two hulks and the tall chimneys of Hamworthy power station on the down. The first semaphore signals of our journey are at Hamworthy, controlled by a single storey wooden box on the down platform. The line to Hamworthy Quay and the long disued passenger station curves away and goes on curving until it turns back on itself to finish not much more than half a mile from Poole station on the opposite side of the Quay. A variety of

Left *A Class '33' in charge of a 4TC on a Waterloo-Weymouth train arriving at Poole, April 1983.*

Right *The Royal train with HM The Queen and HRH The Duke of Edinburgh aboard running alongside Poole Harbour near Rockley in March 1981. The train had spent the night on the Swanage branch, in the cutting just beyond Worgret Junction, and was heading for Poole. It would later take the Royal party back to London.*

freight keeps an '09' busy at Hamworthy, '47's power the trains in and out, including steel from Belgium which is conveyed on some of the oldest wagons in everyday use on BR, flats built by the GWR in the 1940s. Ironically they once brought steel out of South Wales, now they take it in.

For a third time the main line crosses Poole Harbour, past the caravans at Rockley Point, with the Arne Peninsula forming the opposite bank. This latter is a still undeveloped and remote part of Purbeck, despite its proximity to Poole. The Royal Society for the Protection of Birds has a large reserve here and such rare species as the Dartford Warbler live undisturbed on the heathland. The 'most dramatic ruin in all England' to quote more than one guidebook, Corfe Castle, stands guard over the harbour whilst the Saxon tower of Wareham's parish church can also be seen a mile up the Frome river which flows into Poole Harbour opposite Arne.

Poole Harbour, as any local will confidently tell you, is the second largest in the world, after Sydney. But I've also heard it stated that since reclamation around the shores of the latter Poole has gone to the top of the list. Then there are those who will tell you that there are several large natural harbours in South America which have never been accurately measured and which probably outstrip both Sydney and Poole. All I know for sure is that Poole Harbour is very large and although it can only be really thoroughly explored by boat much of it can nevertheless be seen at different points along the route of the railway from Parkstone to Wareham.

Holton Heath station, two bare platforms on the straight stretch of track from the harbour shores to Wareham, was built to serve the vast Royal Navy ord- nance and weapons research depot here, and there used to be extensive sidings into it; a few remain, hidden amongst the long grass immediately east of the station opposite the derelict signal box. A retired cousin of mine tells how when he was a youth and working in an office in Poole he heard a dull boom one morning which rattled the windows. Immediately he guessed there had been an explosion at Holton Heath; it was one which killed several workers. The Navy still maintains a presence but most of the site has been redeveloped as an industrial estate. There have been several tentative plans to link it by rail again but nothing has yet come of them.

Wareham used to be the junction for Swanage and may be again one day. The Swanage Railway preservationists and restorers, with the support, either active or passive, of the vast majority of the local people, and despite the opposition of an ill-informed and self-seeking small but vociferous minority, has done great things, bringing back steam trains to Swanage, relaying the track much of the way to Corfe Castle and obtaining the unanimous vote of the County Council to restore the line right through to BR metals at Furzebrook. The railway has some genuine pre-nationalization carriages which once worked on the Bournemouth and Weymouth lines, and which, unlike many on other preserved railways, can actually be ridden in, and if it has been slow in restoring its main line engines it has achieved a genuine coup in the repatriation of 'M7' No 53 from the USA for this was a locomotive which, like many of its sisters, worked on the Swanage branch. Many unemployed local youths have found at least temporary work on government funded schemes and have learned skills and seen their efforts benefit the

Left *Road and rail traffic at a stand-still at Wareham during the Arctic-like conditions of January 1978.*

Right *Swanage station, June 1986. The carriage on the right is Maunsell open third No 1381, built in 1930, and restored to passenger service at Swanage after nearly twenty years in departmental use by BR.*

Right *Dennis Howell's GWR designed 0-6-0PT No 9466, based at Quainton, visited Swanage in the summer of 1986 and is seen here on the turntable outside the engine shed. On the bank beyond is the body of LSW carriage No 0695, built as a six-wheel composite by the Birmingham Railway Carriage and Wagon Company (who also built the '33's) in 1885.*

Right *Les Hayward's beautifully restored Corfe Castle station, September 1986.*

Top *47187 prepares to leave the oil depot at Furzebrook with a train of ten 100-tonne tankers for the refinery at Llandarcy, 18 February 1985.*

Above *47187 crosses the River Piddle at Wareham on its way to pick up an oil train at Furzebrook, 18 February 1985.*

Left *A Waterloo to Weymouth train passing Worgret Junction, January 1986.*

community, although it is a pity that the rules of the game cannot be altered to make their enjoyment more permanent. Equally valuable both for the individual and for the community has been the new lease of life the railway has provided for retired people who have been able to put their many areas of long acquired expertise to good use.

Corfe Castle station, which is owned by the council, has been beautifully restored by Les Hayward who found the semi-derelict, listed building ideal headquarters for his electronics firm, Westpoint. It also happened that his grandfather was once the stationmaster and he had lived for a time as a boy in the station house, so he had a natural affection for it. The woodwork and awning have been repainted into Southern Railway green and yellow, and the Purbeck stone building with the mass of the castle towering above it is in one of the most picturesque settings imaginable. The picture will be complete when trains once again steam in and out of the platforms.

A few years ago it would have needed a great stretch of the imagination to see the Isle of Purbeck as Britain's largest onshore oil field. But that is what it has become. The threat that this poses to a unique environment has to be weighed against our overwhelming need for oil, and on the whole the damage has been kept to a careful minimum; certainly the oil men are accurate in their claim that the terminal at Furzebrook is less visible than the much older clay works on the opposite side of the tracks.

Although the narrow and standard gauge lines which once served the various clay pits in Purbeck have gone the Worgret Juction to Furzebrook section of the Swanage branch remains open and is kept busy with both oil and clay traffic. The latter virtually disappeared in the mid-1980s but in the summer of 1986 returned on a permanent basis. I have travelled the branch on both oil and clay trains, the latter in the days when a '33' came down each morning and took several sheeted, four wheel wagons to Poole and then to Eastleigh where they were remarshalled. Now one bogie hopper wagon is capable of handling the lot and as I write it is attached to the daily oil train. This is a Class '47' duty and the load is usually ten 100 tonne tankers. The steep and curved approach to Worgret Junction and the long bank up through Parkstone occasionally give problems, particularly if the rails are wet and greasy although when I travelled on 47157 on a damp January day the warning light denoting a slip never flickered. However since the addition of the loaded clay wagon there have been some anxious moments and BR considered substituting Class '56's: as I write the '47's are still in charge. Sometimes wagon loads of clay go abroad and English China Clays found that Speedlink

offered a quicker service to Czechoslovakia, for example, than anything road services could provide and thus exotic wagons from deepest mainland Europe have been spotted in Dorset.

Wareham is a handsome station, although not the town's first, having been put up in 1886 when the Swanage branch opened. Opposite is the Railway Hotel with a quite beautiful, and what must be valuable, picture of No 453 *King Arthur* done in tiles on the wall facing the railway, a most appropriate medium for an area where clay excavation and ceramic work go back beyond Roman times.

The final 22 miles to Weymouth is through the heart of some of the best scenery Dorset has to offer. The line cuts across Wareham Common, over the River Piddle (Queen Victoria when she visited the town was told it was the Trent), then curves away from Creech Barrow, the highest point in the Purbeck Hills, at Worgret Junction, and alongside the water meadows of the River Frome which flood extensively each winter and spring. The station buildings at Wool, except for the LSW signalbox, are modern and attractive, although not the equal of St Joseph's Roman Catholic church a little further along and beside the railway, which is one of the finest religious buildings erected in the South of England this century. The interior is unique and, if stark on first acquaintance, gradually absorbs one by its remarkable unity and lack of compromise. The parish has been blessed with successive priests of great sincerity and each with a highly individual sense of humour, whilst the present Church of England incumbent, John Goodman, is well known for his writings on the Great Western Railway. He once introduced me to a retired driver of the 'Cornish Riviera' living in the village so I retaliated by introducing him to another inhabitant who had spent his boyhood travelling to and from school on the Tralee and Dingle Railway. There are at least two old carriage bodies in use as homes in Wool which I suspect are of LSW origin, and recently another was demolished down at Lulworth which was said to have come from the Somerset and Dorset. More remarkable is the holiday home in a farmyard at Stoborough, a mile out of Wareham on the Swanage road which I am pretty sure was a Royal saloon built by the South Eastern Railway for Queen Victoria.

Wool goods yard remains open for traffic for the military camps at Bovington and Lulworth and many of the passengers are military personnel; a notice on the down platform gives them a phone number to ring to summon transport.

From Wool the line runs alongside the high perimeter fence of Winfrith Atomic Energy Research Station, built on land where Thomas Hardy and Gustav Holst walked together and which inspired the

latter to write *Egdon Heath*, the title which the former had bestowed on this expanse of gorse and heather. It is the home of many varieties of orchid and other wild flowers, of adders, grass snakes, lizards, deer and a whole host of birds. Half of Winfrith Heath is still untouched, although it will not remain so if plans for a second power station on it are passed. Seven-eighths of the heathland of Dorset has vanished in the last 150 years and it would be a tragedy if the precious remaining acres were squandered and lost.

The final station before Dorchester is Moreton. It is now unstaffed and most of its buildings removed. One of the many cinema and TV productions filmed in Dorset used the station yard at Moreton as its base a couple of years back. The action took place during World War 2 and a telephone box of the period was set up in a corner of the yard. The story goes that an elderly inhabitant of the village attempted to make a call from it and got quite irate when she pressed button B and failed to get her five new pence piece back.

From Moreton to Dorchester South the line is single, the singling taking place in 1985. As, apart from summer extras, there is only the basic hourly

service in each direction (no regular goods trains are found west of Wool) this is of no great consequence, but there have been threats to extend the single track as far as Wool or even Wareham, and this would be a rather different matter.

An agreement with their next door neighbours, the brewers Eldridge Pope, enabled BR to provide the new station at Dorchester South on which work began in the spring of 1986. The modern signal box east of the station houses the panel which controls the line between Moreton and the outskirts of Weymouth. It replaced the old GW box situated at the junction of the lines from the West and South stations. There was also a box at the north end of Dorchester West but this disappeared in 1972, and the first Great Western box encountered on the former Paddington to Weymouth main line today is at Maiden Newton. Both goods yards at Dorchester have gone, the former LSW one being the more recent casualty. It lasted until 1980 and part of the agreement with Eldridge Pope for the new station was that they could take over some of the yard.

Past the cemetery and the playing fields and the modern housing estate below the great grass-covered ramparts of Maiden Castle and then up the bank we go to Bincombe Tunnel. From its southern portal there are glorious views across Weymouth Bay to Portland, then down the final bank through Broadway and Upwey and the encroaching suburbs of Weymouth and so round the last curve, under a gantry of upper quadrant semaphore signals and so to rest, 168 miles, 63 chains from Waterloo at Weymouth's handsome new station. Planned in the 1930s, the once impressive but latterly ramshackle remains of Brunel's structure were finally replaced when the Mayor of Weymouth officially opened its successor in July 1986. Although modest compared to what Weymouth offered the rail traveller in the heyday of the rivalry between the Great Western and the London and South Western Railways, it reflects the sensitive thinking which has epitomized station rebuilding in the 1980s. Constructed of red brick,

glass and wood, ideally placed in the town centre next to the bus station and with space for a new bus and coach interchange in its forecourt, it shows what could have been done at Poole twenty years ago. Ready in plenty of time for its first electric train it was the first station out of Waterloo to display the Network South East slogan, although it has to be said that this is very much its most westerly outpost and Weymouth has always been considered part of the West Country. Never mind, it is a price well worth paying if it indicates the desire and intention to promote the railway as a vital part of the transport needs of Dorset and to ensure the story of a line which was completed twenty years after Queen Victoria came to the throne continues into the 21st century and beyond.

Top left *The last hand-worked level crossing on the Waterloo to Weymouth line, East Stoke, between Wareham and Wool. No 33109 is passing with the 10:35 Waterloo to Weymouth, 18 February 1985.*

Above left *Thomas Hardy country. A Weymouth to Waterloo train passing Wool Bridge Manor, where Tess of the D'Urbervilles stayed, February 1986.*

Above *Western Class '52' diesel-hydraulic No 1055 and 4TC No 413 at Weymouth on a cold, damp, misty February morning in 1975. The Western has charge of the 10:05 to Bristol, the 4TC is the front unit of the 09:35 to Waterloo. At this date Weymouth station was still lit by gas lamps.*

Right *The new Weymouth station, a few weeks after opening, August 1986.*

Appendix 1

Staff employed at stations between Waterloo and Weymouth, March 1986

Waterloo	860	Woking	78	Sway	2
Vauxhall	17	Brookwood	5	New Milton	1
Queenstown Road	4	Farnborough		Hinton Admiral	1
Clapham Junction	75	Fleet	199	Christchurch	3
Earlsfield	7	Winchfield		Pokesdown	2
Wimbledon	54	Basingstoke		Bournemouth	242
Raynes Park	12	Micheldever	2	Branksome	5
New Malden	10	Winchester	72	Parkstone	1
Berrylands	3	Shawford	1	Poole	20
Surbiton	29	Eastleigh	83	Hamworthy	2
Esher	4	Swaythling	2	Wareham	11
Hersham	5	St Denys	5	Wool	6
Walton on Thames	13	Southampton	83	Dorchester South	12
Weybridge	10	Redbridge	3	Weymouth	29
Byfleet & New Haw	3	Totton	2		
West Byfleet	7	Brockenhurst	12		

Appendix 2
Preserved Weymouth line rolling stock

The Southern being a fairly compact system its carriages and wagons tended to visit most parts, unless, as with the electric multiple units, they were built for specific routes, or, as with the Tunbridge Wells to Hastings line, there were particular restrictions. Locomotives were rather more selective about their haunts, and although some pre-grouping types were transferred away from their line of origin others stayed there or thereabouts all their working lives. Weight and size restrictions often prohibited the larger and more modern engines from certain parts of the system; the 'Lord Nelson' and 'Merchant Navy' Classes were most noticably affected in this respect.

Records of carriage allocations were far less comprehensive than those for locomotives, and therefore it is often not possible to state categorically which preserved Southern carriages regularly worked on the line. I have therefore tried to make intelligent guesses and given vehicles the benefit of the doubt if it seemed likely they would have known the line well. The homes and habits of locomotives are pretty well documented and one can be more definite. Of course just about every item of preserved Southern rolling stock probably visited some section of the Waterloo to Weymouth line during its working career, even, for example, the SECR 'P' Class 0-6-0Ts on the Bluebell Railway and the SECR designed continental third brake on the Keighley and Worth Valley Railway, but one has to draw the line somewhere. I have not included wagons for, with the exception of the few LSWR built examples which obviously would have frequently visited the line, just about any of the hundreds preserved up and down the country from the Dart Valley to Strathspey could have done. This also applies to the many BR Mark 1 carriages which understandably, but somewhat depressingly, form virtually the entire fleets of many preserved lines. The preserved Pullmans are certainly of interest and they are referred to at various points in the text but are not included here, chiefly because they too tended to wander. It can be assumed that most of those built before nationalisation which still survive worked at some time either on the 'Bournemouth Belle' or 'Ocean Liner' expresses to and from Southampton Docks.

Carriages

Number	Type	Date	Originating company	Location
1228	non-corridor third	1900	LSWR (rebuilt SR 1935)	Bluebell Railway
847	n/c tri-composite brake	1903	LSWR	NRM, York
11	invalid saloon	1906	LSWR	Kent & East Sussex Railway
70	dining car	1907	LSWR (rebuilt SR 1931)	Mid-Hants Railway
959	n/c first/third composite	1907	LSWR	Kent & East Sussex Railway
76	dining car	1908	LSWR (rebuilt SR 1931)	Mid-Hants Railway
1520	n/c third brake	1910	LSWR	Bluebell Railway
494	corridor third	1911	LSWR	Bluebell Railway
1282	corridor third brake	1921	LSWR	Knebworth House
7851	dining car	1923	SR (LSWR design)	Mid-Hants Railway
1353	corridor third brake	1923	SR (LWSR design)	Mid-Hants Railway
3204	corridor third brake	1925	SR (LSWR design)	West Somerset Railway
1365	dining car	1927	SR (rebuilt as open third 1949)	Bluebell Railway
6575	corridor composite brake	1929	SR	Bluebell Railway
6601	corridor composite brake	1930	SR	Mid-Hants Railway

1381	corridor open third	1930	SR	Swanage Railway
3719	corridor third brake	1930	SR	Mid-Hants Railway
2768	corridor third brake	1931	SR	Swanage Railway
6686	corridor third brake	1935	SR	Bluebell Railway
1309	corridor open third	1935	SR	Bluebell Railway
6699	corridor composite brake	1935	SR	Mid-Hants Railway
4958	Royal Mail van	1939	SR	Mid-Hants Railway
4365	corridor third brake	1947	SR	Swanage Railway
4366	corridor third brake	1947	SR	Swanage Railway
5761	corridor composite	1947	SR	Swanage Railway
4211	corridor third brake	1947	SR	Mid-Hants Railway
5768	corridor composite	1947	SR	Bluebell Railway
5761	corridor composite	1947	SR	Mid-Hants Railway
4279	corridor third brake	1949	BR (SR design)	Bluebell Railway
1481	corridor open third	1950	BR (SR design)	Bluebell Railway
1482	corridor open third	1950	BR (SR design)	Bluebell Railway
2515	corridor third brake	1951	BR (SR design)	Bluebell Railway

Locomotives

No	Class	Type	Date	Originating company	Location
314	'0298'	0-6-0WT	1874	LSWR	Quainton
W8	'Terrier'	0-6-0T	1877	LBSCR (sold to LSW 1903)	Isle of Wight Steam Railway
488	'0415'	4-4-2T	1885	LSWR	Bluebell Railway
209	'O2'	0-4-4T	1889	LSWR	Isle of Wight Steam Railway
563	'T3'	4-4-0	1892	LSWR	NRM York
96	'B4'	0-4-0T	1893	LSWR	Bluebell Railway
102	'B4'	0-4-0T	1893	LSWR	Bressingham
245	'M7'	0-4-4T	1897	LSWR	NRM York
53	'M7'	0-4-4T	1905	LSWR	USA (due to come to Swanage Railway)
120	'T9'	4-4-0	1899	LSWR	Mid-Hants Railway
499	'S15'	4-6-0	1920	LSWR	Mid-Hants Railway
506	'S15'	4-6-0	1920	LSWR	Mid-Hants Railway
777	'N15'	4-6-0	1925	SR	Hull
31874	'N'	2-6-0	1925	SR	Mid-Hants Railway
31806	'U'	2-6-0	1926	SR (rebuilt 1928)	Mid-Hants Railway
850	'Lord Nelson'	4-6-0	1926	SR	Carnforth
828	'S15'	4-6-0	1927	SR	Eastleigh
1618	'U'	2-6-0	1928	SR	Bluebell Railway
31625	'U'	2-6-0	1929	SR	Mid-Hants Railway
31638	'U'	2-6-0	1931	SR	Bluebell Railway
925	'V'	4-4-0	1934	SR	NRM York
926	'V'	4-4-0	1934	SR	USA
928	'V'	4-4-0	1934	SR	Bluebell Railway
841	'S15'	4-6-0	1936	SR	North Yorks Moors Railway
847	'S15'	4-6-0	1936	SR	Bluebell Railway
541	'Q'	0-6-0	1939	SR	Bluebell Railway
35005	'Merchant Navy'	4-6-2	1941	SR	Carnforth
33001	'Q1'	0-6-0	1942	SR	Bluebell Railway

35018	'Merchant Navy'	4-6-2	1945	SR	Mid-Hants Railway
34010	'West Country'	4-6-2	1945	SR	North Yorks Moors Railway
34016	'West Country'	4-6-2	1946	SR	Mid-Hants Railway
21C123	'West Country'	4-6-2	1946	SR	Bluebell Railway
34027	'West Country'	4-6-2	1946	SR	Severn Valley Railway
34039	'West Country'	4-6-2	1946	SR	Great Central Railway
34051	'Battle of Britain'	4-6-2	1946	SR	NRM York
34059	'Battle of Britain'	4-6-2	1947	SR	Bluebell Railway
35022	'Merchant Navy'	4-6-2	1948	BR (SR design)	Swanage Railway
34073	'Battle of Britain'	4-6-2	1948	BR (SR design)	Nene Valley Railway
35025	'Merchant Navy'	4-6-2	1948	BR (SR design)	
35027	'Merchant Navy'	4-6-2	1948	BR (SR design)	
35028	'Merchant Navy'	4-6-2	1948	BR (SR design)	Hereford
35029	'Merchant Navy'	4-6-2	1949	BR (SR design)	NRM York
34081	'Battle of Britain'	4-6-2	1949	BR (SR design)	Nene Valley Railway
34092	'West Country'	4-6-2	1949	BR (SR design)	Worth Valley Railway
34101	'West Country'	4-6-2	1950	BR (SR design)	Mid-Hants Railway
34105	'West Country'	4-6-2	1950	BR (SR design)	Mid-Hants Railway
76017	'4MT'	2-6-0	1953	BR	Mid-Hants Railway
75027	'4MT'	4-6-0	1954	BR	Bluebell Railway
75069	'4MT'	4-6-0	1955	BR	Severn Valley Railway
73082	'5MT'	4-6-0	1955	BR	Bluebell Railway
75078	'4MT'	4-6-0	1956	BR	Worth Valley Railway

Bibliography

Southern Daily Echo
Bournemouth Daily Echo
Dorset Evening Echo
Trains Illustrated
Railway Magazine
Parliamentary Papers 1907

Railway World
Modern Railways
Railway Observer
The Railway Times
The Echo, Great Western Society

Swanage Railway News
Bluebell News
Mid-Hants Railway News
The Builder
Illustrated London News

'Report on the Sanitary Conditions of the Labouring Class', 1842
Minutes of the Court of Directors, London and Southampton Railway
Minutes of the Court and Board of
Directors, LSWR
Locomotive Power Committee Minutes, LSWR
Electrification Papers, LSWR 1912-16
Southampton List and Shipping Guide, Southampton Shipping Bureau, 1889
Southampton Tourist Study 1979-80, Southampton City Council, 1980
Gateway to Britain, BTC 1956
Southampton Ocean Terminal, research project, D. J. Tapply, Kingston
Polytechnic Centre for Industrial Archaeology, 1981
Railway & Travel Monthly, January-June 1916 by Philip F. Groves
Town Planning in London, Donald J. Olsen, Hodder & Stoughton 1964
This is Waterloo, Colin J. Marsden, Ian Allan 1983
The Impact of Railways on Victorian Cities, John R. Kellett, Routledge & Kegan Paul, 1969
Introduction to Railway Architecture, Christian Barman, Allen & Unwin 1973
Railway Architecture, ed Binney & Pearce, Oxford Publishing Co 1979
Victorian Stations, Gordon Biddle, David & Charles 1973.
History of The Southern Railway, Dendy Marshall, Ian Allan 1963
War on the Line, Bernard Darwin, Southern Railway 1946
Bournemouth Railway History, Lawrence Popplewell, Dorset Publishing Co 1973
Main Line to Bournemouth 1885-88, J. A. Young, Bournemouth Local Studies Publications 1985
Great Western at Weymouth, John Lucking, David & Charles 1963
Dorset Railways, John Lucking, Blandford Press 1981
Branch Line to Swanage, Viv Mitchel and Keith Smith, Middleton Press 1986
Half a Century of Kingston History, F. Somner Merryweather, Kingston Gazette 1887
History of Brooklands Motor Course, William Boddy, Allen & Unwin 1957
Victorian Woking J. R. & S. E. Whiteman, Surrey Archaeological Society, 1937
Woking & District, A Dictionary of Local History, G. B. Greenwood 1938
Short History of Woking, Arthur Locke 1926
Within Living Memory, Diana Stanley, Hutchinson 1968
South Western Railway, Hamilton Ellis, Allen & Unwin 1957
Sir Herbert Walker's Southern Railway, C. F. Klapper, Ian Allan 1973
The Railway Navvy, David Brooke, David & Charles 1983
The Ways of Our Railways, Grinling, Ward Lock 1911
Branch Lines and Local Connections, Laurence Popplewell, Melledger Press 1985
LSWR Stock Book Peter Cooper, Kingfisher 1986
The Urie S15s. Peter Cooper, Urie 'S15' Preservation Group 1982
The Maunsell S15s by Peter Cooper, Kingfisher 1986

Greyhound 120, Peter Cooper, Urie 'S15' Preservation Group 1983
Stowe, the Bluebell Railway Preservation Society, 1982
Railways of the Southern Region, Geoffrey Body, Patrick Stephens 1984
Arthurs and Nelsons, S. C. Townroe, Ian Allan 1949
Bulleid's SR Steam Passenger Stock, David Gould, Oakwood Press 1980
Southern Steam, O. S. Nock, Pan Books 1972
The Bath to Weymouth Line, Colin Maggs, Oakwood Press 1982
Thames & Severn, Rex Christiansen, David and Charles 1981
Iron Bridge to Crystal Palace, Asa Briggs, Thames & Hudson 1979
Railway Carriages in the British Isles from 1830 to 1914, Hamilton Ellis, Allen & Unwin 1965
The Railway Age, Michael Robbins, Allen & Unwin 1967
Preserved Railway Coaches, Michael Harris, Ian Allen 1976

Index